LAWNS

Basic Factors, Construction and Maintenance of Fine Turf Areas

THIRD EDITION

Jonas Vengris
Professor Emeritus, Department of Plant and Soil Sciences
University of Massachusetts
Amherst, Massachusetts

and

William A. Torello
Assistant Professor, Department of Plant and Soil Sciences
University of Massachusetts
Amherst, Massachusetts

THOMSON PUBLICATIONS
P.O. Box 9335
Fresno, California 93791

ISBN Number 0-913702-19-6
Library of Congress Card Number
82-082822

Table of Contents

PREFACE TO THE SECOND EDITION

This is a completely rewritten, revised second edition of our book on turf. The main stimulus for revision was: (a) the success and wide use of the textbook and (b) the need to update its contents and to improve its organization.

It would be difficult to list here all the improvements in this edition over the first one. Actually, the book was rewritten, reorganized and adjusted to the present needs of all students taking introductory courses in turf sciences. A special survey was conducted to update the list of important turf weeds in the United States and Canada. My cordial thanks belong to all those participating in this survey. Morphological characteristics of major turf grasses were reviewed and are presented for identification purposes in the Summary of Chapter 3. In the course of this revision almost all of the recent extension literature concerning turf grass culture was assembled and freely used in updating the text.

Special thanks belong to Dr. D.T. Hawes, University of Maryland, who volunteered to review the first edition and provided valuable suggestions to improve this second one. Dr. E. O. Burt and Mr. DuVal Pucket at the Agricultural Research Center at Fort Lauderdale, Florida, were extremely helpful in preparing descriptions of the southern turf grasses. Turf grass seed descriptions were reviewed and partly prepared by Prof. C. H. Eiben, Seed Testing Laboratory, University of Massachusetts. My appreciation and thanks.

I am truly grateful to all turf specialists in the country who directly or indirectly are responsible for all improvements in this edition.

Jonas Vengris

PREFACE TO THE THIRD EDITION

Dr. W. A. Torello, Turf Management Specialist at the University of Massachusetts joined me in revising and updating our book on turf. In appreciation of his contribution, I am happy to include him as a co-author of this edition.

My gratitude and special thanks belong to Dr. James A. Spencer, Mississippi State University, State College, Mississippi, who not only reviewed but actually rewrote the whole chapter on lawn diseases.

Jonas Vengris
29 Valley Lane
Amherst, MA 01002

CHAPTER 1
INTRODUCTION

1.1 Definitions

Turf — a dense vegetative ground cover composed of close mown, stems and leaves of plants. A tightly knit plant community existing in intimate association with its environment. In other words, the upper stratum of the earth that is filled with the roots and shoots of grass along with other small plants, so as to form a sward or sod. The word turf is derived from the Sanskrit word *darbha* and means a tuft of grass. A grassy open area is also called a *green,* as in village green, town green or areas maintained for sports, like golf course greens.

Lawn — a turf maintained solely for ornamental value or for outdoor recreation. It is a ground cover comprised of fine grasses kept closely mown, especially near or around houses, schools, estates, or parks. The lawn is an important feature of the home landscape. It should provide the setting for all landscape elements — trees, shrubs, flowers, buildings — so that unity is apparent. A lawn may be imagined as the carpeted floor of an outdoor living room. It should be pleasing to the eye from early spring to late fall. A lawn is an area established with perennial grasses which are persistent when properly managed and mown at a 2-inch height of cut or lower, depending on the turf grass species established. The definition emphasizes three points: a) a lawn usually consists of perennial grasses, b) lawn perennial grasses persist under continuous close mowing and c) a lawn requires proper maintenance practices.

1. *The Turf grass Ecosystem* — A tightly knit community of turf-type plants existing in intimate association with its immediate environment. Environmental influences include *climate* (temperature, moisture, light, wind), *edaphic factors* (all characteristics of the soil), and *biotic factors* (animals, plants, and cultural practices including chemical applications). The interactions of all these factors determines the quality, extent, and manageability of a turf area.

Of course, besides lawns, turf areas are also established for golf courses, athletic fields, parks, cemeteries, airfields or roadsides. *Turf grass culture* — the science and practice of establishing and maintaining turf grasses for specialized purposes, such as cover for lawns, sports areas, roadsides, parks and similar locations.

1.2 Historical remarks

Ancient pleasure gardens of China, Assyria, Babylonia or Persia could be considered as prototypes of our lawns and turf (1, 8, 16). Areas covered with low growing plants were part of their gardens in biblical times. European contacts with those countries during the 11-13th century Crusades helped in developing interests, and gardens became a popular feature in Western Europe and England.

In the past a lawn was not the pure grass *sward* as we understand now but rather an imitation of a natural meadow. Classical as well as medieval gardens had areas carpeted with grass intermixed with other flowering plants. Tufted walks were also a feature of medieval gardens. Walks and lawns were made of short grass or chamomile (*Anthemis* sp). In England, chamomile as a lawn plant is still surviving in some old-fashioned parks. In the 18th century lawns became more appreciated and it became fashionable to keep close mown lawns around the homes. Original bowling lawns should be considered as a forerunner for our modern turf greens for various outdoor sports. Bowling games were, however, very popular in France and England during the 14th century.

Although 17th century manuals discussed establishment and maintenance of turf areas, turf management depended more upon the experience and knowledge passed on from one generation to another. Thus, like few other specialized agricultural practices, it was considered more an art than a science. Earlier lawns were mown with regular scythes or before that kept groomed, as in England, by allowing sheep to graze them. After mowings, raking and carrying away clippings was normally an accepted practice. Turf management was revolutionized by the invention of a lawn mower around 1830 by Edwin Budding in England. Therefore, England can be considered the cradle of turf culture. The first motor-driven lawn mower was developed in 1900.

The advancement of agricultural sciences in the areas of soils, fertility, breeding of agricultural plants, and mechanization, also brought about improvements in turf management. The first turf experiments were started in the United States by J. B. Olcott at Manchester, Connecticut in 1885. He investigated species of various grasses suited for turf production. According to his trials the best turf grasses were bent grasses (*Agrostis* spp.) and fescues (*Festuca* spp.). At the university level the first turf grass research was started at the Rhode Island College of Agriculture (now University of Rhode Island) around 1890. Other experimental stations around the United States followed Rhode Island's pattern and started turf grass research programs. Immediately after the First World War, research projects were initiated at California, Florida, Massachusetts, New Jersey, Kansas, Nebraska and other experiment stations. Although turf grass research at the USDA was started as early as 1900-1908, support by federal agencies and by experiment stations developed slowly. In 1920, the U.S. Golf Association (U.S.G.A.) established a "Green Section" whose main objective was to direct research of golf turf. Green Section and USDA cooperated in golf course turf studies at the Arlington, Virginia turf gardens. In 1942 USDA research plots were moved to Beltsville, Maryland. Shortly thereafter, interest and research in turf grass culture advanced in Great Britain, Canada, Australia, South Africa, New Zealand and many other civilized countries around the globe. Interest and support in the U.S. and abroad increased tremendously after the Second World War.

1.3 Turf in today's life

The objectives of turf grass management encompasses both the establishment and proper maintenance of high quality turf stands over the entire growing season. Major turf areas are: lawns, roadsides, parks, recreational areas, golf courses, athletic fields, airports, cemeteries and highway right-of-ways.

The importance of turf grass management increases steadily in the U.S.A. The following factors reflect the importance of turf to today's society.

1. Increased building construction with increases in population and emphasis on urbanization and suburban living. A high quality turf also elevates property value.

2. Emphasis on recreation, sports, and outdoor living.

3. New roads, turnpikes, landscaping and, most of all, emphasis on the need to beautify the country.

4. The understanding and appreciation of arts, aesthetic values, better taste, beauty and style of the average citizen.

5. The need to prevent erosion by establishing turf areas and thus protecting our natural resources.

There are big changes occurring in this country and, therefore, the future turf management, lawns and landscaping will be more and more in demand. Today turf grass industry encompasses the development, production, and management of specialized grasses for utility, beautification, and recreational facilities. It involves science, development, and the sale of turf grass products and services.

Summary

1. Turf is an area where the upper stratum of earth is filled with roots and shoots of grasses and other small plants, so as to form a sward or sod.

2. A turf grass ecosystem is a tightly knit community of turf-type plants existing in intimate association with its immediate environment. Environmental influences include *climate* (temperature, moisture, light, wind), *edaphic factors* (all characteristics of the soil), and *biotic factors* (animals, plants, and cultural practices including chemical applications). The interactions of all these factors determines the quality, extent and manageability of a turf area.

3. Lawn is ground covered with fine grass kept closely mown, especially around the house, school, on an estate, or in a park. Lawn is usually established with perennial grasses persistent with close continuous clipping.

4. The first turf grass experiments were conducted in the U.S.A. in Connecticut by J. B. Olcott in 1885 and at Rhode Island College of Agriculture (Univ. of R.I.) in 1890.

CHAPTER 2
FLORA OF TURF AREAS

A turf area is comprised of various "seeded" turf-type grasses upon establishment. After establishment, however, other unwanted plant species may encroach upon and thrive in the turf. A good lawn owner and turf grass manager should be able to identify most of these plants.

2.1 Classification of plants

Flowerless (Cryptogams) plants

    a. Algae
    b. Fungi (including bacteria), mildews, molds, mushrooms
    c. Mosses
    d. Horsetails (e.g. Equisetum spp.)
    e. Ferns (e.g. bracken fern, sensitive fern)

All the above mentioned plants are common invaders of turf grass areas.

Flowering (Phanerogams) plants

Seeded grasses as well as most common weeds of our turf areas are flowering plants. They may be monocotyledonous (monocots) or dicotyledonous (dicots) plants.

**Figure 2.1
Dicotyledonous
seedling.**

    a. *Dicotyledons* or so-called broad-leaved plants (dandelion, plantains, chickweeds, knotweed, etc.) have two cotyledons in the seed, i.e. two first leaves in the seed plant. Veins of leaves are usually branched and form a network. Each vein consists of a single vascular bundle with xylem and phloem. Vascular tissues in the stem form a single ring of vascular bundles. In woody plants a cylinder of xylem (wood) is separated from a ring of phloem (bast) by cambium. Flowers of dicotyledonous plants usually consist of parts (e.g. sepals, calyx, petals, corolla) in fours or fives or multiples of these numbers, rarely in threes.

Dicots have a terminal or apical type of growth with vital meristems located in the terminal position of stems and in the apex of roots. In the axils of leaves there are lateral growing points (buds). Growth in diameter is due to the cambium layer. In short, broad-leaved plants have growing points on tips of shoots and roots and in the axils of leaves.

Figure 2.2
Monocotyledonous
seedling

b. *Monocotyledons* (grasses, sedges, onions, etc.) have single cotyledons, i.e. only one first leaf in emerging seedlings. Veins of the leaves are usually parallel. The vascular bundles in the stem are scattered or arranged in more than one ring and there is no cambium. Flower parts are in threes or in multiples of threes. The actual growing (meristematic) regions in grasses are: (a) shoot and root apices, (b) axillary buds, and (c) intercalary (i.e. inserted) meristems located immediately above the nodes and in the leaf at the base of sheaths and at the base of blade. In grasses there is no cambium and no secondary thickening.

The major and most desirable plants of a turf grass community are the grasses. As such, the grasses will be discussed in great detail.

2.2 Botanical characteristics of grasses

Grasses are herbaceous plants, except bamboo which is a tropical or subtropical grass with a woody stem. A most interesting feature in grasses is that plants during the vegetative phase of development initiate leaves, axillary shoots (tillers, rhizomes and stolons) but have no internodal elongation. Grasses make vegetative growth with very little elongation of stems, thus vegetative parts of grasses consist mostly of leaves. The stems and the growing points (buds) are concentrated near ground level. This characteristic makes grasses ideal for mowing and grazing — the mower or animals leave stems and buds (growing points) undamaged, whereas in dicots cutting removes growing points and inhibits plant growth or even kills the plant. The vegetative growth of a turf grass is therefore initiated by *intercalary meristems*.

Roots

Grass roots are fibrous and form a very dense root system. Primary (seminal) grass roots originate from the radicle in the seed embryo and are effective for only a few weeks. In annual grasses they may function throughout the whole life of the plant. A few weeks after seed germination adventitious (secondary) grass roots appear. They originate from the basal portion of the stem at the soil surface (crowns). They may also develop from nodes or rhizomes, stolons, and tillers. The best initiation and growth of roots for northern cool-season grasses occurs usually during the cooler spring and fall periods. Deterioration and death of roots usually occurs during warm, dry summer periods. Optimum temperatures for root growth and development are somewhat lower than for shoot growth. Root growth may even occur in winter if temperatures are above freezing. Optimum temperatures for southern warm-season grasses are higher compared with cool-season grasses.

The life span of individual adventitious roots varies considerably depending on species and environmental conditions, (e.g. Kentucky bluegrass roots may last more than one growing season, whereas rough bluegrass or redtop roots are replaced each year (41)). Southern warm-season grasses usually have thicker and longer root systems than cool-season northern grasses. Roots of Bermuda grass under regular management practices reach 6 ft. or more. Zoysia also has a deep root system but, in general, it is shorter than that of Bermuda. Bent grasses and annual bluegrass are characterized by shallow root systems.

Well developed roots are needed to supply grasses with water and plant nutrients present in soil. This is especially important during moisture and heat stress in summer. Close continuous mowing, high temperatures, excessive nitrogen, and poor conditions for photosynthesis (shade) depress root growth and increase foliage (shoot-root ratio) considerably. It is important that shoot-root ratio be low. The root system should be three times larger than the shoot density (on a dry weight basis).

Stems

In the young grass seedling during the vegetative stage of growth, the stem apex or apical growing point is located near soil surface. Leaves extend above the stem apex by overlapping sheaths. Leaf primordias are formed above each other without apparent separation. At this stage basal nodes are pressed together at the ground level (crown). The crown at this stage of grass development includes stem apex with unelongated internodes. *Crown* is a region of a plant near the soil surface where tillers, lateral shoots, stolons, adventitious roots are initiated, conjoin. After injury by pests or environmental factors, grass survives if crown tissues remain viable. Later, in the axils of the leaf, primordia are formed and the activity of intercalary meristems cause the stem to elongate during the reproductive stage of growth. The culm (stem) elongates with the inflorescence at the top. Commencing first at the second internode, elongation of the shoot begins, attended by initiation of an intercalary meristem at the base of each internode. Pronounced elongation of successive internodes occurs during the reproductive phase of grass development. A leaf arises at a node and its sheath encircles the internode above. The stem of grasses is a cylindrical culm with nodes and hollow internodes. Some grasses even in the vegetative stage of growth, like Canada bluegrass or western wheat grass, have somewhat elevated growing point and apex can be removed by cutting (1). Of course, the use of these grasses for turf production is limited.

Tillering. At a certain grass maturity level when a certain number of leaves are developed, axillary buds are formed in the axils of the leaves. These buds develop to form shoots so that a dense rosette-like tuft of shoots with extremely short stems are gradually built up. This process is called tillering. Tillering is branching from unelongated stems. Tillers arise between the leaf sheath and main axis (intravaginally) from the axils of leaves. Species, plant physiological (plant hormones, auxins), as well as environmental factors play a role in tillering of turf grasses. The rate of tillering in northern cool-season grasses is high in spring and fall and slower during the dry warm summer period.

In the vegetative stage, apical growing point, internodes of stem and tillers remain compressed and short and leaves arising at the nodes form partially overlapping whorls enclosing the shoot apex which remain near the ground level. Due to this fact it is possible to mow or graze grasses frequently without destroying their ability to produce continuous new growth.

Rhizomes and *stolons*. Bunch type grasses, like ryegrasses, chewing red fescue or sheep fescue, spread by tillering only. They have tufted growth and spreading habit. Among perennial grasses there is a tendency towards the formation of rhizomes or stolons (Figure 2.4). Rhizomes (rootstocks) are underground stems identified by their nodes. Stolons are like rhizomes except that they are horizontally creeping and rooting above the

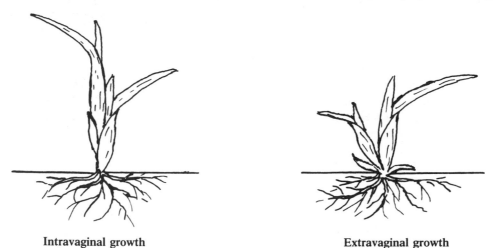

Intravaginal growth   **Extravaginal growth**

Figure 2.3 Intravaginal and extravaginal growth of grasses.

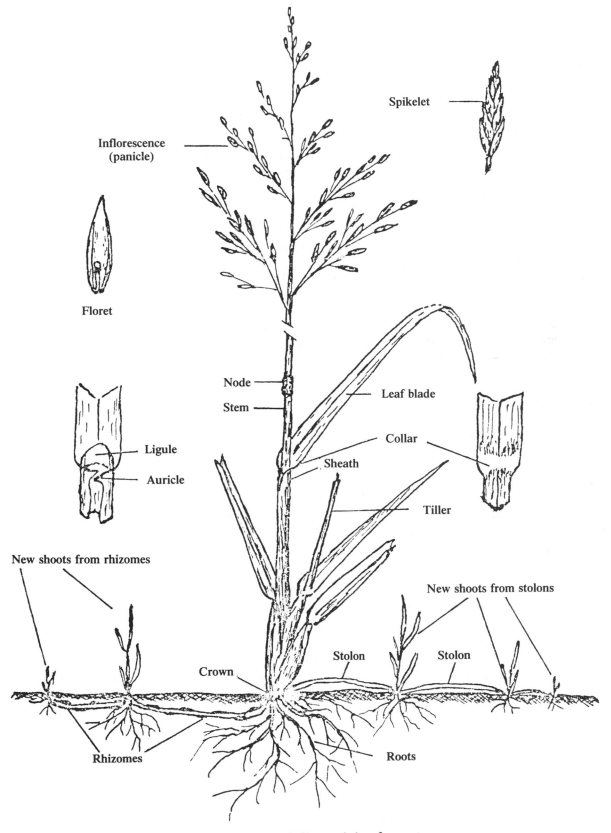

Figure 2.4 Botanical characteristics of grasses

ground stems. Secondary lateral shoots arising extravaginally, i.e. new shoot grows outside basal sheath by penetrating it (Fig. 2.3 and 2.4), with some grasses can elongate above ground (stolons) and with some grasses can elongate below ground (rhizomes). Rhizomes from roots are distinguished by the presence on the surface leaf scales at definite intervals, the nodes. New shoots (stems) develop from the buds at the nodes. If chopped, each piece which possesses a node may produce a shoot and roots. Rhizomes exposed to light form above ground shoots. Kentucky bluegrass and quack grass are examples. Stolons are like rhizomes except that they are horizontally creeping and rooting above ground stems. Creeping bents are a good example of stoloniferous grasses. Bermuda grass as well as zoysias have both rhizomes and stolons. Rhizomes and stolons develop from lower buds on plant axis or from buds on rhizomes and stolons, respectively. Rhizomes and stolons of turf grasses usually function as storage for carbohydrates. They possess intercalary meristems whose activity causes their elongation.

Leaves

Leaves of a grass consist of a leaf blade (lamina) and the lower part, the leaf sheath. In the seedling the youngest expanding grass leaf forms a hood over the stem apex. Later ligule and with some grasses auricles are developed at the apex of the sheath. Blade elongates from basal intercalary meristem located at the base of blade just above the ligule. The leaf sheath develops last and enlarges from intercalary meristems. The developing leaf blade is carried up through the tube formed by the leaf sheath of the next older leaf, and at this stage the bud-shoot may be folded or rolled. If folded, its outline is flattened oval; if rolled, the section will be round. Grasses with leaves folded in the young stage (i.e., bud-shoot) have flattened vegetative shoots, while those with rolled leaves have cylindrical shoots (Fig. 2.5). This distinction applies only to vegetative shoots. Flowering shoots in which the stem has elongated are circular in outline whether the leaf blade is folded or rolled.

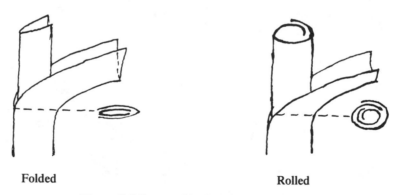

Folded   **Rolled**

Figure 2.5 Forms of bud-shoots in grasses

Blade. The blade is the upper, non-clasping part of the leaf above the collar and ligule (Fig. 2.12). It is usually flat when fresh but sometimes narrow leaves are tightly folded as to appear solid or bristle-like. Blades may be flat, v-shaped, rolled, or have both margins rolled inward. The width of the blades, although variable within a certain species or on a single plant, are of considerable value in identification of many grasses. Blades also vary in shape and size. The upper surface of the leaf blade may be smooth (flat) or corrugated (ridged), glabrous or hairy. The lower surface is usually flat but it may have a central keel. The shade of green color in the blade, glossy or of dull color, may also be helpful in identification of various grass species. The various forms of blades are shown below.

Sheath. The sheath is the tubular basal portion of the leaf which envelopes the stem or the young leaves. The veins of the sheath are normally inconspicuous, but can appear as ridges or distinct lines in some species. The midnerve of the blade may extend downward to centimeter or more, forming a keel at the back of the sheath. The sheath may be either closed or open. When closed it is united into a cylinder. Ruptured closed sheaths should be distinguished from naturally split ones. Frequently the edges of a split sheath overlap.

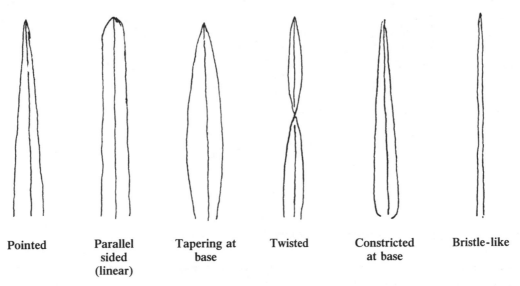

| Pointed | Parallel sided (linear) | Tapering at base | Twisted | Constricted at base | Bristle-like |

Figure 2.6 Leaf blade of grasses

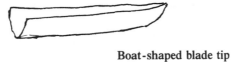

Boat-shaped blade tip

Figure 2.7 Boat-shaped blade tip of Kentucky bluegrass

The grass blade forms in cross-section are shown below.

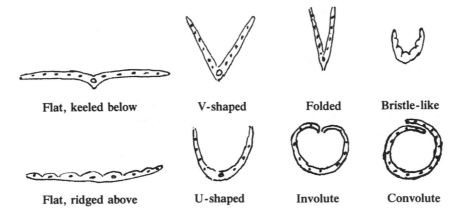

| Flat, keeled below | V-shaped | Folded | Bristle-like |
| Flat, ridged above | U-shaped | Involute | Convolute |

Figure 2.8 Grass blade forms in cross-sections

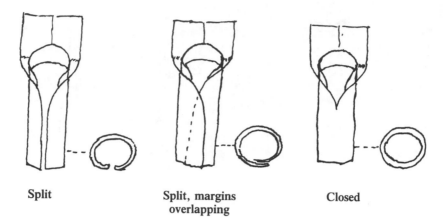

Split   Split, margins   Closed
                         overlapping

Figure 2.9 Characteristics of sheaths of grass leaves

The surface of the sheath may be rough to the touch or smooth, glabrous or hairy, pale green or tinted with purple or red at the base. Sheath margins are usually thin, hyaline, paper-like, or herbaceous. Some species have cilia or are fringed with hairs.

Collar

Collar — meristematic growth zone marking the division between the sheath and the blade. Cells of the collar provide orientation movements of the blade and decide its position — angle to the stem. Turf grass collar may be broad or narrow, continuous from one margin to the other, or divided by a midrib. The collar is usually lighter in color than the rest of the leaf. It is usually smooth but it may be hairy over the whole surface (quack grass) or have hairs or cilia on margins only. The various types of collars are presented below (Fig. 2.10).

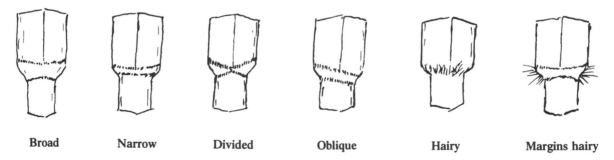

Broad   Narrow   Divided   Oblique   Hairy   Margins hairy

Figure 2.10 Characteristics of grass collars

Auricles. The base of the blade at its two margins often projects to form two small earlike portions called auricles. They may be absent. They differ in shape and thus help to identify various grasses in the vegetative stage·of growth. Among turf grasses auricles are prominent in ryegrass (*Lolium* spp.), tall fescue and quack grass.

Ligule

The ligule is the apparent projection or outgrowth from the top of the sheath. It is usually thinner, and more membraneous than the sheath. Ligule shape and size help to distinguish various grasses in vegetative stages of growth. As shown below, it may be simply a fringe of hairs, or absent. The length of the ligule may vary from minutes to more than 10mm.

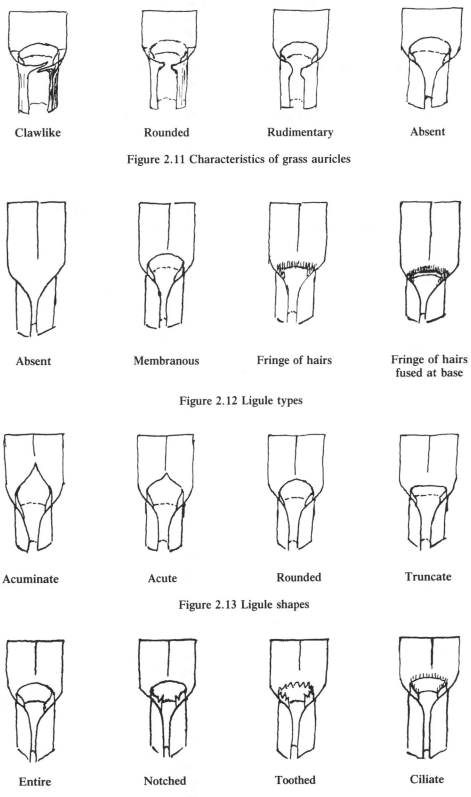

Clawlike   Rounded   Rudimentary   Absent

Figure 2.11 Characteristics of grass auricles

Absent   Membranous   Fringe of hairs   Fringe of hairs
                                                              fused at base

Figure 2.12 Ligule types

Acuminate   Acute   Rounded   Truncate

Figure 2.13 Ligule shapes

Entire   Notched   Toothed   Ciliate

Figure 2.14 Ligule margins

Flower

In grasses the external parts of the flower (perianth), sepals (calyx) and petals (corolla) are reduced to 2-3 minute, scale-like lodicules. Three stamens represent male organs. The female organs, pistils, consist of three united carpels of which only one is functional. A pistil is provided with 2-3 styles with feathery stigmas. The pistil contains a single ovule which develops into the seed. Actually grass "seed" is a fruit and usually includes lemma and palea. Lodicules do not provide protection to the flower. Protective functions are carried out by bracts. Each flower is subtended by a bract, the lemma, and bears on its axis a bracteole, the palea. The lemma usually encloses the edges of the palea, so the true flower is completely surrounded by lemma. Lemma, and palea with the true flower (lodicules, stamens and pistil) is constant in grasses and the whole of this structure is called a grass floret (Fig. 2.15). Lemma often has an awn or beard. Palea is never awned and is usually thin and two-keeled.

Florets form a spikelet. At its base bracts are known as glumes. The axis of a spikelet is called a rachilla. The spikelet consists of a pair of glumes, and a rachilla bearing a number of florets. The number of florets varies from one to about twenty. The spikelet is the basic unit of the whole inflorescence.

Inflorescence

Inflorescence is a flower-cluster of a plant, mode of flower-bearing. The most common types of inflorescence in grasses are the spike, raceme, panicle and spike-like panicle (Fig. 2.16). In a spike flowers are sessile or nearly so upon a more or less elongated common axis (ryegrass, goose grass, quack grass). Spikes are usually simple, but branched or clustered spikes are found in some grasses (Bermuda grass). In raceme flowers are pedicelled upon a common and elongated axis (St. Augustine grass, zoysias, crabgrass). The panicle is a compound inflorescence with branching pedicelled flowers (bluegrasses, bents). Foxtails and timothy are examples of spike-like panicles.

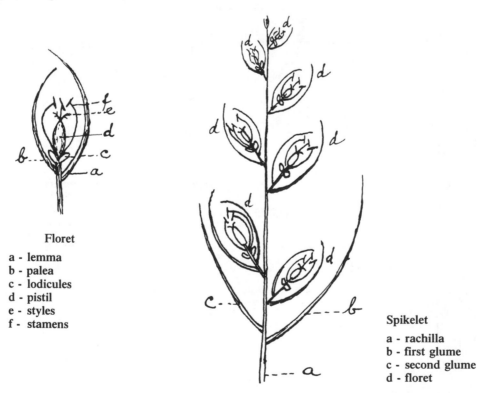

Floret

a - lemma
b - palea
c - lodicules
d - pistil
e - styles
f - stamens

Spikelet

a - rachilla
b - first glume
c - second glume
d - floret

Figure 2.15 Diagrams of floret and spikelet

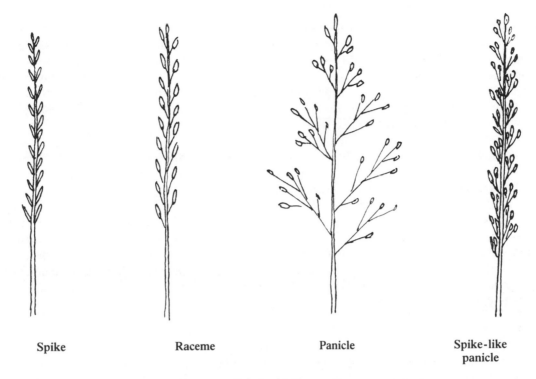

| Spike | Raceme | Panicle | Spike-like panicle |

Figure 2.16 Diagrams of various inflorescences common in grasses

2.3 Physiological remarks

Green parts of grass, leaves and stems contain chloroplasts with chlorophyll. Chlorophyll with the help of sun energy, water and carbon dioxide (0.03% in air) produce carbohydrates. In photosynthesis only about 1-2% of sun's incident energy is used. Carbohydrates are the end product in photosynthesis (a):

$$(a) \quad 6\ H_2O\ +\ 6\ CO_2 \xrightarrow[\text{light}]{\text{chlorophyll}} C_6H_{12}O_6 \quad +\ 6\ O_2$$

water   carbon   carbo-   oxygen
             dioxide   hydrate

Photosynthesis and carbohydrate production is affected by the amount of chlorophyll, water, carbon dioxide, environmental conditions and plant nutrients. Under optimum environmental conditions and balanced plant nutrient supply, carbohydrate production will be at its peak. For various turf grasses optimum environmental conditions may vary considerably: shading, too low or too high temperatures affect carbohydrate production detrimentally.

Carbohydrates are utilized by plants to assimilate other compounds needed to build cell tissues, protoplasm, proteins. For these physiological-biochemical processes energy is needed. In grass, like all living organisms, respiration is a continuing process. Respiration actually is reversed photosynthesis: carbohydrates are oxidized to carbon dioxide and water (b):

$$(b) \quad C_6H_{12}O_6 \quad +\ 6\ O_2 \longrightarrow 6\ CO_2 \quad +\ 6\ H_2O$$

carbo-   oxygen   carbon   water
hydrate   dioxide

Carbohydrates serve as source of energy for plant growth and development. Energy fixed in photosynthesis minus energy used in respiration equals energy available for grass to grow. In other words grass will grow and will accumulate carbohydrates if photosynthesis is greater than respiration. The rate of respiration varies according to environmental conditions. Higher temperatures activate physiological grass processes and thus respiration rate is increased. At too high temperatures photosynthesis decreases but respiration increases and plant carbohydrate reserves will decrease. Carbohydrate reserves in grass increase when their production (photosynthesis) is higher than their utilization (respiration).

Carbohydrates are stored mostly in stems, rhizomes and stolons. Storage in roots and leaves is of lesser importance. Stored carbohydrates are utilized during periods of intensive grass growth in the spring. In northern cool-season grasses carbohydrate reserves in summer usually remain low and maximum accumulation in these grasses occurs in the fall when top growth is slow. Southern warm-season grasses accumulate carbohydrate reserves at higher temperatures than do cool-season grasses but generally the best accumulation occurs at temperatures below optimum temperatures for top growth. In northern grasses root growth and carbohydrate accumulation occur at the same time in the fall when temperatures are below optimum temperatures for top growth. In warm-season grasses root, top growth and carbohydrate storage may coincide in summer (26) as long as temperatures are not above optimum. At low temperatures growth of roots and tops are low and carbohydrate reserves are used for respiration.

2.4 Grass-like plants

There are many common plants occurring occasionally in turf areas which might be easily confused with the true grasses (Gramineae) on account of similarities in vegetative structures. These are usually sedge (Cyperaceae) or rush (Juncaceae) family representatives. Some characteristic points presented in the following table will serve to separate these grass-like plants from grasses (Table 2.1).

Table 2.1 Differentiation of grass-like plants from grasses

	Grasses	Sedges	Rushes
Stem	Usually hollow, cylindrical or flattened	Filled with pith rarely hollow, usually three-sided	Filled with pith, cylindrical
Nodes	Conspicuous	Indistinct	Indistinct
Leaf arrangement	In 2 vertical rows or ranks	In 3 vertical rows or ranks	In 3 vertical rows or ranks
Ligules	Present, rarely absent	Absent or weakly developed	Absent or weakly developed

Summary

1. Fungi, mildews, mushrooms, algae, moss, horsetails, ferns are flowerless (cryptogams) turf grass plants.

    Monocotyledonous (grasses) and dicotyledonous (broad-leaved) turf grass plants are flowering (phanerogams) plants.

2. Monocotyledons (monocots) have a single cotyledon in emerging seedling. Veins of leaves are parallel. The vascular bundles in the stem are scattered or arranged in more than one ring. Flower parts (e.g., sepals, petals) are in threes or multiples of three.

    Dicotyledons (dicots) have two first leaves in the seed plant. Veins of leaves are branched. Vascular tissues in the stem form a single ring of vascular bundles. Flowers of dicots usually consist of parts in fours or fives or multiples of these numbers, rarely in threes.

3. Grasses make vegetative growth with very little elongation of stems. The stems and the buds (growing points) are concentrated near ground level. The lawn mower or grazing animals leave stems and meristematic tissue (buds) undamaged. This characteristic makes grasses ideal mowing plants. Growing regions (meristematic tissues) in grasses are: main apical growing point, axillary buds and intercalary meristems at the base of internodes and at the bases of leave sheaths and blades.

    Broad-leaved plants have growing regions on tips of shoots and in the axils of leaves.

4. Rhizomes are underground stems identified by their nodes. Stolons are above the ground creeping and rooting stems.

5. Grasses of turf areas are kept in the vegetative stage of growth by mowing. Therefore it is important to identify grasses in the vegetative stage of growth. In identification of various grasses in the vegetative stage of growth differences in leaf blades, leaf sheath, ligule, auricles, collar are helpful.

6. Grasses in photosynthesis produce carbohydrates which are utilized as energy source for plant growth and development. Carbohydrate reserves in grass increase when their production (photosynthesis) is higher than their utilization (respiration). Stored carbohydrates are mostly used during periods of intensive lush grass growth in the spring. In northern cool-season grasses carbohydrate maximum accumulation and root growth occurs in the fall when top growth is slow. In warm-season grasses root, top growth and carbohydrate storage may coincide in summer as long as temperatures are not above optimum.

7. Grasses usually have hollow, cylindrical stems divided by nodes into internodes. Leaves are 2-ranked. Stems of sedges are usually three-sided and filled with pith. Rushes have cylindrical stems filled with pith. Both sedges and rushes have no conspicuous nodes.

CHAPTER 3
TURF GRASSES

3.1 Introduction

Agrostology is the science of grasses. For our purpose we are interested only in those grasses which can be used in turf production. Botanists list over 1,200 species of various grasses in the United States. Only about 20-25 species can be used for turf production. Main characteristics of turf grasses are that (a) they should be perennial and (b) should persist under continuous close mowing i.e., their main apical growing point remains at the soil surface due to un-elongated internodes. They normally spread by stolons, rhizomes and basal tillers. Basal lateral tillers are initiated when main shoots are clipped by mowing.

Most turf grasses originated in Europe and Asia. Grazing on natural pasture-meadow areas by animals in ancient times contributed in developing the mentioned characteristics of turf grasses. Most of the commonly used turf grasses were developed by breeders as forage grasses. Only in the last two decades has emphasis been put on developing specific grass cultivars for use in turf culture.

In systematic botany (taxonomy) closely related plants are combined into groups called *families,* such as the grass family *(Gramineae)* or the mustard *(Cruciferae)* family. A family is subdivided into groups showing similar characteristics. Such groups are called *genera* (singular genus). For example, the grass family is divided into many genera, such as bluegrasses *(Poa)*, ryegrasses *(Lolium)*. The genus is further divided into groups which have many characteristics in common. These groups are called *species,* like Kentucky bluegrass *(Poa pratensis)*, annual bluegrass *(Poa annua)*, etc. Species are sub-divided further into various ''cultivars'' or ecotypes (e.g. ''Baron'' Kentucky bluegrass).

Some of our turf grasses are better adapted for northern cool regions and some are more suited for the warm southern part of the country. The approximate transition zone between northern and southern turf grasses can be drawn through the northern borderlines of North Carolina, Tennessee, Arkansas, Oklahoma then drops to upper Texas and to the middle of New Mexico and Arizona. It then goes through a part of Nevada and continues westward to the Pacific coast through the lower part of California (Fig. 4.1).

The northern species grow best during the cool weather conditions in the spring and again in the fall and undergo partial dormancy during the warm and dry summer months. Their optimum growth temperature is between 60 and 75°F. It is a different story with southern warm-season grasses. These species grow most vigorously during a hot summer period. They start to grow in the spring when the weather warms up and becomes dormant after the first frost in the fall. Some southern grasses can survive as far north as Canada but they are green only 2-3 months and they are dormant and brown the rest of the year. Warm climate grasses best grow at temperatures between 80-90°F. They are deeper rooted, more tolerant to close mowing and reproduce better vegetatively as compared to the northern species. These grasses originate from Southern Asia, East Africa and South America.

In this chapter the main turf grass species will be discussed and their important botanical and cultural characteristics presented. Experiment stations and seed industries are working toward developing improved cultivars adaptable to various climatical regions or management practices. For the most important species, there are many varieties (cultivars) on the seed market. For detailed information concerning the most adaptable varieties for any region in the country consult your country agricultural agent or agricultural experiment station in your state.

3.2 Glossary of selected terms for grass identification

Acute — sharp-pointed
Annual — of only one year's duration from seed to maturity
Anther — the pollen-bearing part of a stamen
Apex — tip, point, summit
Auricle — earlike appendages at the base of the blade
Blade — the expanded portion of the leaf above the sheath
Bristle — short, stiff hair
Bud-shoot — that part of the developing culm enclosed in and protected by the preceding leaf sheaths
Cilia — marginal hairs
Ciliate — fringed with hairs
cm. — centimeter, 0.4 inches
Collar — the area, often ring-like at the juncture of sheath and blade
Convolute — rolled longitudinally, one edge is inside and the other outside
Culm — the stem of grasses or sedges
Digitate — finger-like
Dioecious — unisexual, with staminate and piltillate flowers on different plants
Fascicled — clustered, bunched
Floret — each flower of a spikelet
Glabrous — without hairs of any sort
Hirsute — covered with stiff hairs
Hispid — with stiff, bristly hairs
Hyaline — thin and translucent
Inch — 2.54 cm
Internode — the portion of stem between two nodes
Involute — rolled inwardly
Jointed — having nodes and internodes
Keel — angle or ridge on back of sheath or blade usually formed by midrib
Lacerate — with irregular cuts; torn looking
Ligule — a thin appendage on the inside of leaf at the junction of sheath and blade
Linear — long, narrow, with parallel margins
Membranaceous — thin, soft, and somewhat translucent
mm. — milimeter, about $1/25$ of an inch
Node — a joint, place where leaves are attached on the stem
Obtuse — blunt, rounded at the end
Peduncle — stem of solitary flower or of a flower-cluster
Perennial — lasting year after year, living more than two years
Petiole — the stalk of a leaf
Pilose — pubescent with soft, fairly long, straight hairs
Pubescent — covered with short soft hairs
Rhizome — an underground stem
Scabrous — rough to the touch, often referring to toothed margins
Sheath — the lower part of the leaf which envelopes the stem
Stolon — a creeping above ground stem, which roots and sends new shoots, where the nodes touch the soil
Truncate — ending abruptly as though chopped off

COOL-SEASON GRASSES

3.3 Bluegrasses (*Poa* spp.)

1. Kentucky bluegrass (*Poa pratensis* L.)
2. Rough bluegrass (*Poa trivialis* L.)
3. Canada bluegrass (*Poa compressa* L.)
4. Annual bluegrass (*Poa annua* L.)

The first two bluegrasses are widely used turf grasses in the northern cool region of the United States. Use of Canada bluegrass for turf is very limited. Annual bluegrass is common and a most troublesome annual weedy grass in turf. All these bluegrasses can be readily distinguished from other turf grasses and identified due to a transparent line on each side of the midrib (Fig. 3.1). The upper surface of the leaf blades is smooth, parallel-sided or slightly tapering to boat shape.

Fig. 3.1
a-midrib of bluegrasses

1. Kentucky bluegrass

Kentucky bluegrass is a perennial grass believed to have been introduced to the United States from Europe and Asia. Common K. bluegrass seed originates from natural stands in the United States. ⅓ of the seed is produced in the Midwestern states, ⅓ in the Northwestern states and ⅓ of the seed labelled common K. bluegrass is imported from Europe.

Description — In the vegetative stage of growth (bud-shoot-vernation) leaves are folded. *Blades* — keeled below, are 2-5mm wide, lower surface glossy, upper surface not ridged but has a characteristic midrib with a distinct light line on each side. Blades are parallel-sided (linear) with boat shaped tip. These translucent strips on either side of the midrib result from the large transparent bulliform cells flanking the midrib. *Sheath* — split, is somewhat compressed, smooth. *Ligule* — membranous is 0.4-1mm long, truncate. *Auricles* — are absent. *Collar* — divided by midrib, is glabrous, medium broad, may be *ciliate* on margins. *Inflorescence* is an open, pyramidal panicle with lower branches usually in whorls of five.

It is a perennial sod-forming grass that spreads by heavy rhizomes and seeds. K. bluegrass produces seed both sexually and by the *apomictic process,* i.e., seeds may be formed from mother cells without sexual fertilization. Thus seed formed by apomictic reproduction are genetically identical to the mother plant. 98% of bluegrass plant seed is produced by apomixis.

Adaptation and use — K. bluegrass is widely distributed throughout the United States except in arid regions and in the Gulf States. K. bluegrass is the most important and most widely used of the turf grasses in northern cool humid regions for lawns, cemeteries, parks, airfields and sport fields. Due to the vigorous rhizomes, recuperative potential is good and it is used in athletic fields and for sod production. K. bluegrass is also a pasture grass in the United States and Europe.

K. bluegrass, within regions of adaptation, grows well in areas having between 20 and 50 inches of precipitation and temperatures between 30 and 105°F. During dry, warm summer months it goes into dormancy. Root growth stops when soil temperatures

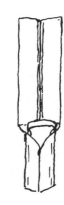

Fig. 3.2
Kentucky bluegrass
x 3

exceed 85-90°F. Trials indicate that some root growth may occur throughout the winter if fertility is adequate and if the ground remains unfrozen.

In the north, K. bluegrass prefers full sun; in the southern regions of adaptation it withstands shading better. For good growth K. bluegrass needs a good supply of water and does not tolerate poor drainage or high soil acidity. Well-drained heavier soils of good fertility that are nearly neutral in reaction are the best (pH 5.8-7.5).

Culture — K. bluegrass germinates (6-12 days) and establishes very slowly. Therefore a good clean seedbed is of prime importance. Because it becomes established slowly, K. bluegrass is often planted with a fast growing grass that will provide cover and prevent weed invasion while the bluegrass is becoming established. For lawns in the northeastern regions, K. bluegrass usually is used in mixtures with red fescue and perennial ryegrass. K. bluegrass withstands traffic moderately well and should be the basic component of most lawn mixtures which are to be maintained at a high to medium fertility level. For pure stands K. bluegrass seeding rate is 1-2 lbs. of seed per 1,000 sq. ft.

K. bluegrass responds best to fall and spring fertilization. On the other hand excessive late fall fertilization with high nitrogen analysis fertilizers prevents plants from physiologically hardening before winter and resistance to diseases and desiccation is thus decreased. Late spring fertilization combined with mowing too close and too infrequently is the most common reason K. bluegrass lawns do not survive hot summer weather. Late spring fertilization drastically lowers stored food reserves by stimulating top growth at the expense of the root system. Drought usually does not kill it, if fertilizers are not applied in late spring or early summer. K. bluegrass lawns need 2-6 lb. nitrogen per 1,000 sq. ft. per year.

K. bluegrass is susceptible to close mowing. It can be injured if mown closer than 1.0 inches. This weakens the grass and makes it more susceptible to diseases and weed encroachment. K. bluegrass in lawns should be mown 1.5 to 2 inches in height. K. bluegrass is susceptible to leafspot caused by various species of the fungus, *Helminthosporium*. It causes severe thinning and browning in the early summer. Powdery mildew (*Erysiphe graminis*) frequently infects K. bluegrass growing in shady locations with reduced air circulation. Fusarium blight, dollar spot and brown patch diseases are also common on K. bluegrass turf.

Varieties (cultivars) — Numerous different varieties of K. bluegrass have been developed and are currently available for public use. The new-improved varieties differ widely in characteristics such as disease resistance, color (shade of green), texture, density, and environmental tolerances. It is recommended that a "blend" of two or more of these improved varieties be used when establishing a lawn. This will reduce the chances of a lawn being totally wiped out by a disease or insect damage. Table 3.1 lists some of the available K. bluegrass varieties along with their major characteristics.

Table 3.1 Kentucky Bluegrass Varieties and Their Major Characteristics

Variety[a]	Resistance to				Thatching tendency	Spring greenup
	Leaf spot	Stripe smut	Fusarium blight	Dollar spot		
Kenblue[b]	P	E	F	G	L	G
Park[b]	P	P	F	E	L	E
A-20	E	E	G	E	M	G
A-34	G	E	G	E	M	G
Adelphi	E	E	G	E	M	E
Baron	G	G	G	E	M	F
Bonnieblue	E	E	G	E	L	G
Fylking	E	G	P	G	M	F
Glade.	G	E	G	F	H	G
Majestic	E	E	G	E	M	E
Merion	E	P	F	G	M	G
Monopoly	E	E	G	E	L	E
Nugget	E	E	F	P	H	P
Parade.	E	G	G	F	L	E
Plush.	G	E	P	E	M	G
Rugby	E	G	F	F	M	G
Sydsport	E	E	G	E	M	F
Touchdown.	E	E	G	E	H	G
Vantage.	F	E	G	E	L	G
Victa	E	E	G	E	M	F
Windsor	F	P	G	E	M	G

[a]Improved Kentucky bluegrass varieties are maintained at 4 pounds of nitrogen per 1,000 square feet per year and are mowed 2 or 3 times per week at a height of 1.5 inches. The turf is irrigated as needed to prevent wilt. Varietal performance may vary significantly under a more or less intensive management program.

[b]Common type Kentucky bluegrass varieties are maintained at 2 pounds of nitrogen per 1,000 square feet per year.

E = Excellent.   G = Good.   F = Fair.   P = Poor.   H = High.   M = Medium.   L = Low.

2. Rough bluegrass (roughstalked meadow grass)

A perennial grass native of Europe resembling Kentucky bluegrass. Found naturally in Canada and in the northern part of the United States down to North Carolina and the Pacific Coast. *Poa trivialis* has not received much attention in terms of research. Seeds are usually imported.

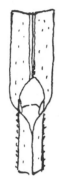

Fig. 3.3
Rough bluegrass x 3

Description — Leaves are folded in the bud-shoot. *Blades* — are 2 to 5mm wide, slightly tapering to boat-shaped tips with the lower surface glossy. The upper surface of the blades are not ridged but have a characteristic median midrib. *Sheaths* — are somewhat flattened, rough to the touch (retrorsely scabrous) on well developed older plants, and split partway. *Ligule* — is membranous, 2 to 5mm long, acute. *Auricles* — are absent. *Collar* — is distinct, broad, divided and glabrous. *Inflorescence* — is an oblong, open panicle. Rough bluegrass is lighter green than K. bluegrass. It spreads by seed and short above-ground stolons. Stems are erect to somewhat decumbent at the base.

Adaptation, culture — Because of the shallow root system, rough bluegrass does not tolerate hot dry conditions and does not withstand heavy wear. It is best adapted to cool, moist and shaded areas with rather rich soils. It tolerates low temperatures but tolerance to heat and drought is poor. As a shade tolerant grass, it is used in mixtures with K. bluegrass and red fescue on poorly drained (pH 5.8-7.2) soils. Due to the lighter colored turf of such mixtures, it is somewhat patchy. Regardless, in shady, moist areas rough bluegrass can be used in lawn mixtures (up to 20-30 percent). In warm humid regions it can be used for overseeding of dormant southern warm-season grasses. For maintenance nitrogen requirements are similar to K. bluegrass, 2-4 lb. N per 1,000 sq. ft. a year. Mowing height is normally adjusted to the main turf grasses in mixture but withstands cutting below 1 inch well. For pure stands seeding rate of rough bluegrass is 1-2 lb. per 1,000 sq. ft. No improved varieties are available on the market at present.

3. Canada bluegrass

Canada bluegrass is a perennial grass native of Europe. This bluegrass is seldom used in lawn mixtures and as a turf grass it can be useful in the upper part of the northern region only.

Figure 3.4
Canada bluegrass x 3

Description — In the vegetative stage (bud-shoot) the leaves are folded. *Blades* — are boat-shaped but not glossy, of bluish green color, the upper surface is not ridged but has a characteristic bluegrass midrib. Leaf blades are rather short. *Sheaths* — are compressed and split. *Ligule* — is rounded to truncate, 0.6-2.0mm long. *Auricles* — are absent. *Collar* — is narrow, divided, glabrous. *Inflorescence* — has a short, contracted panicle. Herbage — is blue-green. *Stems* — are not round but strongly compressed and it is an important feature in identifying the grass in its advanced stage of development. Canada bluegrass is an apomictic grass spreading by wiry rhizomes and seeds. Seed is produced abundantly and is easily harvested.

Adaptation, culture — Canada bluegrass is adaptable to open, rather poor and dry soils. It will grow in sandy or gravely soils of low fertility. It withstands shade better than K. bluegrass. It will not grow well in soils having high acidity or poor drainage. It is a tough grass and resists wear well. Due to basal internode elongation leaves removed by mowing result in a stemmy turf of poor density. Recovery after mowing is rather poor and it should be mown higher than 2 inches. Canada bluegrass can be used on less productive soils for conservation purposes, on roadsides and for poorly maintained lawns. Although Canada bluegrass withstands low fertility soils well, it responds to fertilization well and 2-3 lb. nitrogen per 1,000 sq. ft. per year can be used. Seeding rate for pure stands are 1-2 lb. per 1,000 sq. ft.

Leafier and low temperature hardy 'Canon' Canada bluegrass variety was developed at Guelph University, Canada and released in 1965. A large quantity of Canada bluegrass seed is produced in Haldimand County, Ontario (42).

4. Annual bluegrass

In cool humid regions annual bluegrass is a common annual weed in turf grass. It is sometimes used to overseed warm-season turf during the winter months, thus in the southern regions this grass is a winter annual plant. Some strains of this weedy grass produce creeping, rooting stems and act like perennial persistant plants. Annual bluegrass is adaptable to moist, cool and shaded, compacted (walks) areas. It withstands very close continuous mowing and it is a most troublesome weed on golf courses.

Poa annua could be distinguished by non-glossy, pale short, somewhat tapering to sub-acute leaf tips. Ligule is rather long (up to 3mm), round to acute. For more detailed description see Chapter 14, p. 133.

3.4 Fescues (Festuca spp.)

1. Red fescue (*Festuca rubra* L.)
2. Chewing fescue (*Festuca rubra* var. *commutata* Gaud.)*
3. Sheep fescue (*Festuca ovina* L.)
4. Tall fescue (*Festuca arundinacea* Schreb.)
5. Meadow fescue (*Festuca elatior* L. or *F. pratensis* Huds.)

Red, chewing and sheep fescues are fine textured grasses. The first two are most widely used in mixtures with Kentucky bluegrass. Sheep fescue is drought resistant and succeeds better than most grasses on eroded soils low in fertility and can be grown in most northern areas. Meadow and tall fescues are forage grasses. Tall fescue is also used in the United States as turf grass.

1. Red (creeping) and chewing fescues

Both these fine fescues were introduced from Europe. Besides K. bluegrass both are the most important lawn grasses of the northern cool humid regions.

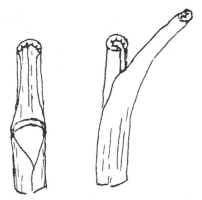

Fig. 3.5
Red fescue x 3

Description — Leaves are folded in the bud-shoot. *Blades* — broader blades (about 3mm) can be found on elongated shoots only; in turf, blades are rolled, narrow bristle-like 1-2mm wide and distinctly ridged, glossy below. *Sheaths* — are thin whitish, reddish tinted below, split partway. *Ligule* — is membranous and 0.3-0.5mm long, truncate. *Auricles* — are absent but usually with apparent enlargement and tapering toward bristle-like blade (Fig. 3.5). *Collar* — is narrow and indistinct. *Inflorescence* — is narrow and contracted panicle. In the vegetative stage of growth red fescue and chewing fescues are alike. Only the former one has short rhizomes, i.e., creeping type whereas chewings is a bunch-type grass, i.e., has neither stolons nor rhizomes. Although creeping red fescue possesses rhizomes, they are not aggressive as established plants. When seeded heavily both are able to form a dense sod that resists wear and mix well with K. bluegrass. Chewing fescue has intravaginal while creeping has extravaginal tillering and therefore the former forms a less dense, less uniform sod. They are superior to K. bluegrass in establishment, vigor, and in grass mixtures serve as valuable companion grasses.

---

* *Festuca rubra* var. *fallax* Hack or *Festuca fallax* Thuill.

Adaptation — Both have fine textured leaves. These fescues are adapted to northern humid regions. They grow well in shaded areas with poor, droughty and slightly acid soils. After injury they recuperate slowly and are not appreciated as sport or sod turf. As winter overseeding grasses, they provide good cover especially during the spring and fall transition periods in warm-season grass (bermuda grass) turf. Red fescues are widely used in lawn mixtures with K. bluegrass. After establishment red fescue retains dominance in shaded areas and K. bluegrass becomes dominant in sunny areas.

Culture — Red fescue should be fertilized moderately, 2-3 lb. N per 1,000 sq. ft. per year. Under liberal fertilization in mixtures, K. bluegrass will dominate. A red fescue lawn is tougher to mow than a K. bluegrass lawn. A sharp mower is required. A dull mower will shred the leaf tips so that they turn brown and unsightly. All commercially available varieties of red fescue are moderately susceptible to leafspot disease which often causes patchy, dead areas in turf during mid-summer. Red fescue is generally more susceptible to turf diseases when used in southern regions of its adaption.

Normal cutting height for red fescue is 1.0-2.0 inches. The seeding rate for pure stands is 3-4 lb. per 1,000 sq. ft.

Improved varieties of creeping red fescue include 'Pennlawn', 'Ranier', 'Banner', 'Highlight', 'Jamestown' and 'Illahee'. 'Pennlawn' is somewhat less susceptible to leafspot and performs better than other varieties. Pennlawn was developed in Pennsylvania and Ranier and Illahee in Oregon. Breeders are trying to develop varieties with more aggressive rhizomes and higher tolerance towards temperature extremes.

2. Sheep fescue

Used chiefly for establishing a durable turf on sandy soils and for bank stabilization along irrigation canals. In appearance it is very similar to red fescue only the leaves are somewhat narrower and bluish-gray in color.

Description — The leaves are folded in the bud-shoot. *Blades* — are 1-1.5mm wide and bristle-like, deeply ridged. *Sheaths* — are split. *Ligule* — is obtuse, rounded and 0.2 to 0.4mm long. *Auricles* — are absent. *Collar* — is divided, indistinct and medium broad. *Inflorescence* — is narrow panicle. A bunch grass.

Adaptation, culture — Sheep fescue is adapted to dry and poorly fertilized acid soils. Even heavily seeded sheep fescue forms a bunchy, uneven turf. It has a heavy fibrous root system which makes it suitable for loose sandy soil and steep banks. Sheep fescue is used in the arid northern plains east of the Cascades for soil stabilization and as a ground cover. It should be mown only occasionally at heights of not less than 2-3 inches. The seeding rate is 3-4 lb. per 1,000 sq. ft.

Fig. 3.6
Sheep fescue x 3

3. Hard fescue (*Festuca ovina* var. *duriuscula* (L.) Koch)

A fine textured, cool-season, perennial bunch grass. Similar to sheep fescue except that blades are wider and tougher and less drought tolerant than sheep fescue. Used for erosion control in low maintenance areas.

4. Tall fescue

A tall-growing, coarse perennial bunch grass that has dense basal leaves and a strong, fibrous root system. Tall fescue resists heavy wear and high temperatures. As a heavy duty turf grass it can be used from Canada to Florida.

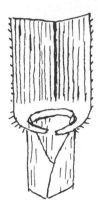

Fig. 3.7
Tall fescue x 3

Description — Leaves are rolled in the bud-shoot. *Blades* are 5-9mm wide, prominently ridged above, glossy below, margins are rough and hyaline. *Sheath* — is split, often reddish to purple at the base. *Ligule* — is membranous, greenish, 0.5-1.0mm long, truncate to obtuse. *Auricles* — are 0.2-1.5mm long and hairy. *Collar* — is broad, conspicuous, divided, and somewhat hairy on margins. *Inflorescence* — has an erect or nodding panicle.

Adaptation — Tall fescue is well adapted in transition zone turf areas. There is a long-lived perennial turf grass forming a good utility (road banks, playgrounds) or athletic turf. It is acceptable as a lawn grass (21) under proper management. In cooler and warmer climates than the transition zone, tall fescue usually deteriorates by invasion of bermuda grass in the south or K. bluegrass in the north and becomes a weed. Although tall fescue is a vigorous plant during cool weather, it has limited frost tolerance and winter kills in the north. Tall fescue tolerates heat well and is a widely used grass up to mid-Georgia and Arkansas. It withstands moderate shade and will grow in wet or dry, acid or alkaline soils but grows best in well-drained fertile soils. It has a good root system, tolerant to rough treatment and survives in places where other grasses fail. In arid regions it can be used under irrigation only.

Culture — Due to its coarseness tall fescue does not mix well with other turf grasses in adaptable regions and it should be a dominant grass when used in mixtures. In mixtures with K. bluegrass or with bermuda grass or bahia grass for athletic fields in southern areas it should be at least 70 percent of the mixture. Tall fescue should be mown at a height of over 1.5 inches. If mown continuously closer it will thin out. On average, it needs 3-4 lb. N per 1,000 sq. ft. per year. Over fertilization with nitrogen may weaken resistance to winterkill in northern regions. Tall fescue is somewhat susceptible to snow mold and brown patch. The seed rate is 5-8 lb. per 1,000 sq. ft.

There are few popular cultivars of tall fescue. Most popular are two improved strains of tall fescue: 'Alta' — selected at Oregon Experiment Station in 1940 and 'Kentucky 31', which was found growing on a Kentucky farm. 'Kentucky 31' is somewhat more heat tolerant than 'Alta' (23). Both are alike. Other varieties are: 'Fawn', 'Goa', 'Kenmont', 'Clemfine', and 'Rebel'. 'Clemfine' and 'Rebel' are new cultivars (1981) showing much finer leaf texture and better mowing quality.

4. Meadow fescue

This grass is very much like tall fescue but less coarse, and the auricles are not hairy. Leaf margins are scabrous. It is known and widely used as a forage grass and seldom used in the United States as turf grass. It is susceptible to crown rust, and leafspot.

Fig. 3.8
Meadow fescue x 3

3.5 Bents and Redtop (*Agrostis* spp.)

1. Colonial bent grass (*Agrostis tenuis* Sibth.)
2. Creeping bent grass (*Agrostis palustris* Huds.)
3. Velvet bent grass (*Agrostis canina* L.)
4. Redtop (*Agrostis alba* L.)

All three bents are fine-textured grasses most widely used for golf course putting greens, tees and fairways. Colonial bent grasses were used in lawn mixtures. However, disease susceptibility, including dollarspot, and thatch tendency have relegated bents to golf courses and special care lawns. In bluegrass turf, bent grass is a weed. Colonial bent grass may be used in high-quality lawns in cool moist regions. All bents are moisture loving plants. They are moderately shade tolerant with high requirements for fertility and maintenance. They stand slightly acidic soils (pH 5.6-7.0). In hot, humid weather they are more prone to disease.

Redtop is a short-lived perennial. It is sometimes used in lawn seed mixtures in the northern regions to provide quick cover while more permanent grasses, e.g., Kentucky bluegrass is developing. Recently, the use of this grass as turf grass has decreased.

Generally it is not too difficult to recognize bent grass but is rather difficult to identify different species of bent.

1. Colonial bent grass

Introduced from Europe. Known also as brown top or common bent grass, Colonial bent grass is used chiefly in high-quality lawns, tees and fairways.

**Fig. 3.9
Colonial bent grass
x 3**

Description — Leaves are rolled in the bud-shoot. *Blades* — are not glossy, sharp pointed, ridged on the upper surface, 2-4mm wide. *Sheath* — is split. *Ligule* — is membranous, truncate, 0.4-1.2mm long. *Auricles* — are absent. *Collar* — is distinct, narrow and oblique. *Inflorescence* — is open delicate panicle. Roots are shallow, fibrous. Colonial bent grass forms few short stolons and rhizomes and forms dense turf when heavily seeded and closely mown. Normally propagated by seed, which are badly contaminated with creeping types.

Adaptation — Well adapted to cool and humid regions. Fertile, fine textured, moist and slightly acid to neutral soils (pH 5.6-7.0) are best. It does not stand dry, hot soil conditions. It must be irrigated during dry periods. It is more expensive to maintain than ordinary lawn grasses. It is popular and used for lawn turf in New England along the Atlantic shores and in Washington and Oregon west of the Cascade Mountains. It also can be used as a component in general lawn mixtures in northern states. It is rather aggressive in mixtures with K. bluegrass.

Culture — Colonial bent grass lawns should be mown 0.5 to 1.0 inches high; watered and sprayed with fungicides regularly. Mown above 0.75-1.0 inches it becomes fluffy and forms undesirable spongy mats. Its ability to withstand close clipping adapts it for use on fairways where this type of maintenance is demanded. It is susceptible to most turf diseases, especially brown patch, snow mold and dollar spot. It needs 3-5 lb. N per 1,000 sq. ft., and the seed rate is 0.5-1 lb. per 1,000 sq. ft.

Most popular varieties are 'Astoria' and 'Highland'. They were developed in Oregon and released in the middle thirties. 'Highland' is more bluish-green and is the hardiest variety and competes well with bermuda grass in transition zones. 'Exeter' was released by Rhode Island in the early sixties and it is similar to Astoria but superior in color and suitable for lawns in the northeastern states. Some New Zealand and German varieties are suitable for lawn turf.

2. Creeping bent grass

Introduced from Europe, it is a fine-textured, stoloniferous, perennial grass.

Description — Leaves are rolled in bud-shoot. *Blades* — are sharp pointed, ridged on the upper surface, not glossy and 2-4mm wide. *Sheath* — is split and round. *Ligule* — is rounded and may be toothed, 1-3mm long. *Auricles* — are absent. *Collar* — is distinct, usually oblique. *Inflorescence* — has narrow, dense, pale or purple panicle. Creeping bent grass has long, fine stolons that produce roots at every node, and it develops a dense sod.

Adaptation — It is well adapted to cool, humid regions and widely utilized for golf course putting greens. It is used in the transition zone and for winter overseedings of southern turf grass. Some cultivars of this grass also are well adapted for use on fairways and tees under intensive systems of management. Sunny areas with soils having high fertility, low acidity (pH 5.6-7.0), good drainage, and high water holding capacity are the best. Its feeding and moisture requirements are high. Tolerates low temperatures but discolors early in the fall and greens up late in spring. High maintenance requirements restrict its use for lawns.

Culture — Because of its dense foliage and profuse creeping stems it requires close (0.2 to 0.5 inch) cutting, frequent brushing, and periodic top dressing to prevent formation of an undesirable mat or thatch. From 4 to 6 lb. N needed per 1,000 sq. ft. during the growing season. Higher cut turf needs less and closer cut needs more fertilization. Watering, fertilization and fungicidal preventive treatments are needed to insure good quality turf. Leafspot, brown patch and dollar spot are common diseases.

**Fig. 3.10
Creeping bent grass
x 3**

Two types of creeping bent grass are available commercially: (a) propagated vegetatively by planting stolons and (b) propagated by seed. The seeded bents are less expensive to establish. Besides, seeded turf is easier and cheaper to renovate. On the other hand seeds are usually not uniform genetically making a turf somewhat patchy. 'Seaside' and 'Penncross' varieties are propagated by seed. 'Seaside' is less aggressive than 'Penncross' but also less able to form thatch. It is susceptable to most diseases especially brown patch and snow mold. 'Penncross' was developed at the Pennsylvania Experiment Station. It produces excellent density, has good recovery from injury, and is rather resistant to diseases. The turf is soft, spongy and readily develops a thatch layer. It needs to be mown at 0.25 inches or lower and regularly thinned by vertical mowing. The seed rate for pure stands is 0.5-1.0 lb. per 1,000 sq. ft.

The most widely used vegetatively propagated varieties are: 'Arlington', 'Cohansey', 'Toronto', 'Congressional', 'Washington', 'Old Orchard', 'Pennlu', and 'Evansville'.

Mechanical mixtures of stolons of several varieties of the same color and growth habit often produce better turf than a single variety.

3. Velvet bent grass

Introduced from Europe, velvet bent grass is the finest textured of the bents and is used mainly for putting greens in New England and the Pacific Northwest states.

Description — Leaves are rolled in the bud-shoot. *Blades* — are sharp pointed, ridged, not glossy, 1.0-1.5mm wide. *Sheath* — is split. *Ligule* — is membranous 1 to 3mm long, rounded to acute. *Auricles* — are absent. *Collar* — is medium broad. *Inflorescence* — has loose, spreading panicle. It is a very fine-textured grass and produces extremely dense turf from creeping stolons. It has light green foliage and upright growth. Velvet bent can establish itself by seed or vegetatively by stolons.

Adaptation — Velvet bent grass is best adapted to the northern part of the cool, humid region, especially to coastal areas in New England and the Northwest Pacific. It does not tolerate prolonged high temperatures. It is adapted to a wide range of soil conditions but produces the best turf where fertility is maintained at a high level in low acidity and well drained soils. Velvet bent grass is tolerant to shade and moist, acid soils but does poorly on dry soils. It is not as aggressive as creeping bent grass but more aggressive than colonial bent grass.

**Fig. 3.11
Velvet bent grass
x 3**

Culture — Velvet bent grass establishes slowly and it is slow in recovery from all types of injury. It requires close mowing (0.2-0.5 inch), regular brushing and periodic topdressing. Because it is a succulent and fine textured grass, it does not require and will not withstand frequent dressings used for creeping bent grass. A regular program of fertilizing, watering, and disease control is necessary to maintain high quality turf. Nitrogen need is 3-5 lb. per 1,000 sq. ft. per year. Generally, velvet bent grass is susceptible to wilt.

Velvet bent grass can be established by seed or by vegetative propagation. 'Kingston', developed by Rhode Island Experiment Station in 1963, is aggressive, less susceptible to disease and also may be propagated by seed. Seed rate is 0.5-1 lb. per 1,000 sq. ft.

4. Redtop

Redtop, like ryegrass, is used as a companion plant to provide quick, temporary cover while more permanent slow developing grasses are established. Its use as a turf grass has decreased drastically.

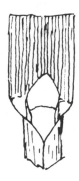

Description — Leaves are rolled in the bud-shoot. *Blades* — are sharp pointed, ridged on the upper surface, not glossy, 4-7mm wide. *Sheath* — is split. *Ligule* — is 1.5-5mm long, membranous, rounded to acute. *Auricles* — are absent. *Collar* — is prominent and divided. *Inflorescence* — reddish, spreading panicle. The redtop species consist usually of many individual types, ranging from definitely rhizomatous forms to plants that are noncreeping bunchy type. It is coarser than all bents. In commercial seed a bunchy type is normally dominant.

Adaptation — Redtop tolerates a wide range of soil and climatic conditions. It resists drought and has a low fertility requirement. It is well adapted to poor acid soils with poor drainage. It grows best in neutral and fertile soils. It does not tolerate high temperatures or shade.

**Fig. 3.12
Redtop x 3**

Culture — Redtop is a short-lived, perennial grass. It seldom lives more than 2-3 seasons when mown regularly at heights below 1.5-2 inches. When mown constantly at normal putting green heights, it seldom lasts more than a single growing season. It is sometimes seeded along in temporary lawns and on roadsides, waterways to prevent erosion. Its use as a companion grass in turf seedings has decreased considerably. It is used for winter overseedings of southern grasses but can't compete with other grasses such as red fescues or ryegrasses. Seeds are small and in mixtures for cover purposes more than 5% of redtop seed is not recommended.

3.6 Ryegrasses (*Lolium* spp.)

1. Annual or Italian ryegrass (*Lolium multiflorum* Lam.)
2. Perennial ryegrass (*Lolium perenne* L.)

Both were introduced from Europe. Annual ryegrass originates from the Mediterranean region. They are fast growing, temporary bunch grasses and are used in lawn mixtures for cover purposes and on sloping areas to prevent soil erosion.

Description — The vegetative growth of *annual ryegrass* is very similar to that of meadow fescue or tall fescue. It is distinguished by its smooth leaf margins, narrow, longer not hairy auricles. *Leaves* — are rolled in bud-shoot. *Blades* — 3-7mm wide, bright green, upper surface is prominently ridged and the lower surface glossy. *Sheath* — is split, reddish at base. *Ligule* — is 1-2mm long, obtuse. *Auricles* — are narrow 1-3mm or longer. *Collar* — is distinct, broad. *Inflorescence* — has long, narrow flat spikes with awned spikelets placed edgewise to the continuous rachis.

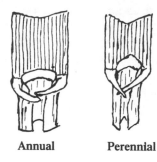

Annual   Perennial

Fig. 3.13
Ryegrasses x 3

Perennial ryegrass is similar to annual ryegrass only it is much finer in texture and has folded leaves in the bud-shoot. Blades are 2-6mm wide, sheath flattened to almost round, closed or split, reddish at base. Inflorescence like annual, spikelets awned.

Adaptation and culture — Annual ryegrass is less tolerant to temperature extremes than perennial. Under mild climatic conditions it may act as a winter annual or even short-lived perennial. Perennial ryegrass is a typical maritime climate with mild winters grass. It does not tolerate extremes, e.g., in northwest Germany and England it is a perennial grass and in New England, U.S.A. it is a short-lived perennial degenerating in 1-3 years. Ryegrasses grow best in fertile, low acidity or neutral soils. Used as a companion grass for slow establishing turf grasses, especially on slopes with erosion hazards or for temporary cover. They are quick germinating, aggressive and become clumpy. No more than 20% should be used in mixtures. Annual is more competitive. Ryegrasses are widely used as a winter grass for overseeding in the south as they die in the summer and in the north they are sometimes winterkilled. Normally, in the south they disappear in the spring before Bermuda regrowth. Clipping height is 1.0-2.0 inches. 3-4 lb. N per 1,000 sq. ft. is best. In ryegrasses, vascular bundles are tough and after mowing threads of cut leaf-edges are observable. The seeding rate of ryegrasses is 4-8 lb. per 1,000 sq. ft. Seeds are frequently used in low-grade, cheap, ready-made lawn mixtures where they provide a green cover quickly.

Common perennial ryegrass was developed in Oregon as a short-lived perennial grass with inferior summer performance. Breeders are working to develop turf-type varieties: wear resistance, leafy, lower growing, better density, more resistant to diseases (snow mold), finer texture, more shade tolerant and better summer performance are characteristics that need to be improved. 'Manhattan', 'Pennfine' are fine-textured and leafy perennial ryegrasses. Astor (Oregon A.E.S. 1964) and Gulf (Texas A.E.S. 1958) are annual ryegrass varieties. Newer ryegrass cultivars now available are 'Yorktown', 'Yorktown II', 'Prelude', and 'Barry'.

3.7 Timothy (*Phleum pratense* L.)

Fig. 3.14
Timothy x 3

Description — The leaves are rolled in bud-shoot. *Blades* — are 4-8mm wide, light green, not ridged, pointed, margins scabrous. *Sheath* — is round and split. *Ligule* — is obtuse to acute, 2-5mm long with a distinct notch at either side. *Auricles* — are absent. *Collar* — is broad, distinct. *Inflorescence* — has densely flowered, cylindrical, spike-like panicle. Timothy is a bunch grass, stems are erect from a swollen or bulb-like base, forming large clumps.

Adaptation, culture — Timothy is one of the most popular forage grasses, but it is not satisfactory as a lawn grass. It is sometimes found in poor-quality lawn seed mixtures. Its use for turf should be confined to rough and non-use areas where only occasional cutting is required. It grows best in fertile, well drained soils. It should be cut higher than 2 inches. Timothy is a slow growing grass and does not recover from mowing rapidly.

3.8 Orchard grass (*Dactylis glomerata* L.)

Orchard grass, like Timothy, is a forage grass, introduced from Europe.

Description — Leaves are folded in the bud-shoot. *Blades* — are sharply keeled below, 6-12mm wide, margins are rough. *Sheath* — is distinctly flattened, smooth, split partway, with hyaline margins. *Ligule* — is membranous, 3-10mm long, acuminate. *Auricles* — are absent. *Collar* — is broad, distinct and divided.

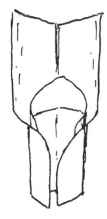

Inflorescence — has a panicle with spikelets crowded in dense clusters at the end of few, stiff branches. Orchard grass is a bunch type grass with a good root system.

Adaptation, culture — Orchard grass is tolerant to shaded areas. It does well on heavy clay or clay-loam soils that are well drained. It could be used in areas where occasional cutting is required. It is used mostly in orchards and shaded areas where other grasses will not survive. Used for erosion control.

Fig. 3.15
Orchard grass x 3

3.9 Wheat grasses (*Agropyron* spp.)

1. Fairway wheat grass (*Agropyron cristatum* (L.) Gaertn.)
2. Western wheat grass (*Agropyron Smithii* Rydb.)

Both of these wheat grasses are drought resistant, cool-season grasses that could be used for ground cover in the sub-humid and semi-arid cool regions where no irrigation is used.

1. Fairway wheat grass

Fairway wheat grass, also known as crested wheat grass, was introduced from eastern Russia and Siberia.

Description — Leaves are rolled in the bud-shoot. *Blades* — are pointed, tapering, bluish-green; upper surface conspicuously ridged, scabrous and soft pubescent, margins scabrous, 2-6mm wide. *Sheath* — is split, glabrous. *Ligule* — is membranous, truncate, lacerate 1-1.5mm long. *Auricles* —are long and claw-like. *Collar* — is divided. *Inflorescence* — has erect spike, glumes with awns. It is a light bluish-green, deep-rooted perennial bunch grass. It forms a fairly dense sod when seeded heavily and regularly.

Adaptation — Fairway wheat grass is a cold-resistant, cool-season grass well adapted to Canadian prairies, the northern Great Plains, the Intermountain Regions and to the higher elevations of the southern Great Plains where no irrigation is used. It withstands long, dry periods and heavy wear if not cut too closely. Usually it makes the most of its growth in the spring and fall. In the summer is goes into dormancy.

Fig. 3.16
Fairway wheat grass
x 3

Culture — it is used as a pasture-hay grass and also for lawns, general-purpose turf and for revegetation of semiarid plains in controlling water and wind erosion. Used also in athletic fields. Wheat grass is established usually by seed. It grows well on productive soils and likes low to medium maintenance fertilization.

No varieties are presently available for turf use.

2. Western wheat grass

Description — Leaves are rolled in the bud-shoot. *Blades* — are flat bluish-green, stiff, 2-6mm wide, somewhat constricted at the base, tapering, prominently ridged, scabrous on the upper surface, margins scabrous. *Sheath* — is round, split, prominently veined and somewhat purplish, truncate and ciliate. *Auricles* —

are claw-like, clasping. *Collar* — is medium broad, sometimes oblique. *Inflorescence* — has erect spikes. Western wheat grass is an erect, deep rooted perennial grass with long rhizomes. *Ligule* membranous, about 0.5mm long, truncate and ciliate.

Adaptation, culture — Adaptable to cool semi-arid northern and transitional regions. It withstands dry conditions well and is resistant to low temperatures. Although it grows under poor soil conditions, the grass responds well to fertilization and irrigation. It is rather tolerant to alkali soils. Where soil is favorable and moisture plentiful, western wheat grass may be found in almost pure stands. Western wheat grass is often used in mixtures with fairway wheat grass for the non-irrigated West Central Great Plains region for the same purposes as fairway wheat grass.

Fig. 3.17
Western wheat grass
x 3

W. wheat grass is propagated by seed and establishes itself slowly. The best time to plant is in early fall on a well prepared seedbed.

WARM-SEASON GRASSES

3.10 Bermuda grass (*Cynodon dactylon* Pers.)

Bermuda grass is a warm-season perennial grass widely distributed throughout the southern part of the United States and widely used for all kinds of turf. This grass was introduced in the United States around 1751 from the Western-Africa region and is well adapted to the South where rainfall is sufficient, and under irrigation in the southwest.

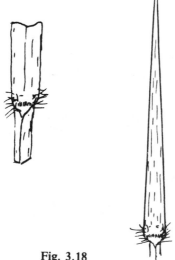

Description — Leaves are folded in the bud-shoot. They are born on stems which produce long internodes alternating with very short ones. *Blade* — is stiff, sharply pointed, 2-3mm wide, sparingly pubescent above, margins are rough. *Sheath* — is split, loose, round to compressed, with tuft of hair at the collar (throat). *Ligule* — has a fringe of hairs, .2-.8mm long. *Auricles* — are absent. *Collar* — is narrow and hairy on margins. *Inflorescence* — has 4 or 5 digitate spikes. All branches originating at the same point. Leaf blades of Bermuda are striped beneath, as compared to even colored zoysias. Bermuda grass blades usually are widest at the base (at collar-ligule) and awl-like tapering toward the tip. Zoysias leaf blades are widest in the middle tapering toward the tip and somewhat toward the base (collar-ligule area). Bermuda grass is spread by strong flat stolons and by scaly rhizomes. The root system is strong and deep. It is a perennial grass used for lawns, golf courses, athletic fields, cemeteries, and other turf areas. Between the different Bermuda grass varieties and selections there are considerable variations in blade and collar width, length of ligule, and shades of foliage color. Bermuda grass is one of the fastest growing southern turf grasses, and often invades flower beds or adjacent gardens as a weed.

Fig. 3.18
Bermuda grass
x 3

Adaptation — It is adapted to warm humid and warm semi-arid regions of the United States. It thrives best under warm to hot weather conditions. It is best adapted south of the Mason-Dixon line from Florida to California where the average daily temperature is above 75°F and stops growing below 60°F and turns brown at temperatures below 50°F. Foliage is easily killed by frost and regrows from rhizomes when the soil warms up.

Bermuda grass does not tolerate shade, poor drainage or high soil acidity. It is the most drought resistant grass but for normal growth needs water and can't be grown in arid regions without irrigation. Due to good wear tolerance and good recuperation, it is a good sports turf grass.

Culture — Cutting height for general purpose turf is 0.5-1 inch. It generally needs good, intensive management conditions, good fertilization, 4-8 lb. N per 1,000 sq. ft., requires irrigation, vertical mowing, top-dressing to prevent thatch formation. Bermuda grass turf (lawns) can be overseeded with ryegrass or other northern grasses in the fall. Bermuda remains thicker during the summer if not overseeded.

Bermuda grass is fairly resistant to diseases and insects. Most common Bermuda grass pests are leaf spot, brown patch, fusarium rot, armyworms, webworms, cutworms and nematodes.

Varieties (a) *Common Bermuda grass* is a coarse textured grass and it's the variety for which seed is available. Most improved varieties are sterile or nearly so and must be propagated vegetatively. C. Bermuda grass is widely used for home lawns, around public buildings, athletic fields or fairways. Seeds are small and 1-2 lb. per 1,000 sq. ft. is used. For vegetative propagation about 2 bushels of stolons or sprigs per 1,000 sq. ft. are used. Turf develops quickly.

The improved Bermudas are superior to common Bermuda grass in appearance, drought tolerance and they are preferred for most turf areas. These better quality Bermuda grasses are high maintenance grasses.

(b) *'Tifgreen'* and *'Tifdwarf'* were released by Georgia Agr. Exp. Station and USDA in 1956 and 1965, respectively. They are fine textured with good leaf density and low growth habit. Also, these varieties are rather hardy to low temperatures and can be used in the west and as far north as Washington, D.C. or Manhattan, Kansas.

(c) *'U-3'* (USGA Green Section and USDA, 1947) and *'Midway'* (Kansas Agr. Exp. Station, 1965), are known for cold tolerance and are widely used in turf production. 'Midway' is adapted in southwestern Kansas for lawn turf. 'U-3' has been grown successfully in the vicinity of Philadelphia, PA., Nebraska, Ohio, and Missouri.

Many more varieties with various degrees of cold tolerance, texture or vigor are on the market. Experiment stations are working toward developing better, more suitable varieties. Extension specialists and experiment stations should be consulted for the best varieties for different locations and needs.

3.11 Zoysias (*Zoysia* spp.)

1. Japanese or Korean lawn grass (*Zoysia japonica* Steud.)
2. Manila grass (*Zoysia matrella* (L.) Merr.)
3. Mascarine, Korean velvet grass (*Zoysia tenuifolia* Willd, ex Trin.)

Zoysias are warm-season grasses native to the Orient and Phillipine Islands. They differ in size, coarseness, aggressiveness (vigor) and winter hardiness. *Zoysia japonica* is coarse textured, more vigorous, and more cold tolerant; whereas *Z. tenuifolia* is very fine textured, the least cold tolerant and least aggressive. *Z. matrella* is intermediate in all respects.

Zoysia japonica Steud

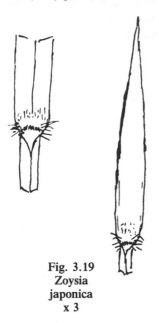

**Fig. 3.19
Zoysia
japonica
x 3**

Description — Leaves are rolled in the bud-shoot. *Blade* — is stiff, 2-5mm wide with few long hairs near the base, margins are smooth to rough and occasionally have long hairs near the base. *Sheath* — is round to slightly flattened, smooth but may have a tuft of hair above (at throat), and is split with hyaline margins. *Ligule* — has a fringe of hair about 0.2mm long. *Auricles* — are absent. *Collar* — is hairy at least at the margins. *Inflorescence* — has short, terminal spike-like raceme. It is a low growing perennial grass that spreads by above ground stolons and shallow rhizomes. In the vegetative stage of growth, characteristics are similar to Bermuda grass only the leaves in bud-shoot are more distinctly rolled. Zoysias leaf blades beneath are evenly colored when Bermuda grass is somewhat striped. Zoysias leaf blade is widest in the middle and somewhat tapering toward collar-ligule while the Bermuda blade is widest at the base (at collar-ligule area) and awl-like tapering toward the tip. *Z. matrella* identification-description characteristics are similar as *Z. japonica* only somewhat finer, e.g., leaf blades are 2-3mm wide only. They are very much alike and could be subspecies. *Z. tenuifolia* blades are involute and bristle-like (19, 26). Its more southerly distribution, greater heat requirements and late in the season bloom, compared with *Z. japonica* and *Z. matrella,* distinguishes it as a separate species. Besides, *Z. japonica* is deep rooted and *Z. tenuifolia* is a shallow rooted grass. *Z. tenuifolia* is a very low grower, and never gets higher than 2-3 inches. Thus, it could be considered more of a ground cover plant than a turf grass and is suitable around trees, shrubs, flower beds or between flagstones on a patio.

Adaptation – *Z. japonica* can be used as far north as Philadelphia, PA. *Z. tenuifolia* is suitable in warm coastal areas only. Zoysias usually turn the color of straw when the first killing frost occurs and remains off-color until next spring. In southern Florida and along the Gulf Coast it remains green all year long. *Z. japonica* can be grown as far north as Canada and survives temperatures as low as minus 10 to 20°F but the growing season there is very short. Drought and heat tolerance is very good. Zoysias are shade tolerant grasses. *Matrella* is more shade tolerant than the other two. In this respect they are equal to St. Augustine grass and superior to centipede grass or carpet grass. It becomes less shade tolerant as it moves further north.

Unlike Bermuda grass, zoysia is slow in establishing itself and in filling bare spots. It takes patience to get it established, but once established it is a joy for years to come: (a) makes beautiful turf, (b) makes dense sod and keeps out weeds, and (c) it is easily controlled around flower beds or shrubbery and never becomes a pest.

Zoysias grow best on good neutral (pH 5.5-7.0), well drained soils and it is a drought tolerant plant in humid regions. Like St. Augustine, it is rather tolerant to salt sprays and the resulting soil conditions. They are suitable for ocean front locations.

Zoysias are mostly used for lawns and general purpose turf in warm humid and transition zones. Due to the slow establishment, its usage for sports turf is somewhat limited.

Culture — Zoysia is usually propagated vegetatively by sprigs or plugs. It normally takes from 2 to 3 years to develop from plugs spaced 12 inches apart. To avoid weed encroachment, it is often sprigged or plugged into other grasses. Modern soil sterilization herbicides can be helpful in establishing this grass. The seed available is usually *Z. japonica.* Two lbs. of seed per 1,000 sq. ft. is used. A bad feature is its slowness in developing and therefore propagation by seed is not practical.

When established, zoysia is not a heavy feeder; 1 to 3 lbs. of N per 1,000 sq. ft. is enough. It is a tough grass and it is difficult to mow. Lawns should be clipped at 0.5-1.0 inches high. It grows slowly and does not need frequent mowing. To avoid thatch and puffiness, regular mowing below 1.0 inches is needed.

Zoysia is relatively free of disease and other pests. However, it recently was attacked by rust (*Puccinia zoysia* Diet.) (27). Zoysia is more resistant to insects than most other grasses. However it is sometimes attacked by billbugs, armyworms, sod webworms and cutworms.

'Meyer' zoysia (Meyer Z-52) was developed by USDA and USGA greens section in 1951. It is a selection of *Z. japonica*. In color and texture it resembles 'Merion' K. bluegrass and it is coarser than *'Emerald'* zoysia. It is good for general purposes in sun or shade.

'Emerald' zoysia was released by Georgia AES and USDA in 1955. It is a hybrid between *Z. japonica* and *Z. tenuifolia*. It is dark green and a fine textured grass. It looks like *Z. Matrella* but is faster in spreading and has a wider range of adaptation. It is comparable to the very finest of Bermudas. Best adapted in southeastern U.S. north to Maryland. Because of the slow growth, it is not recommended on heavy-duty areas.

'Midwest' zoysia is rather coarse grass. It was developed in Indiana in 1963 for the purpose of using it in mixtures with cool-region grasses in regions where climatic conditions do not favor either warm- or cool-season grasses.

3.12 St. Augustine grass (*Stenotaphrum secundatum* (Walt.) Kuntze)

A perennial grass, indigenous to the West Indies and common in Mexico, tropical Africa and Australia.

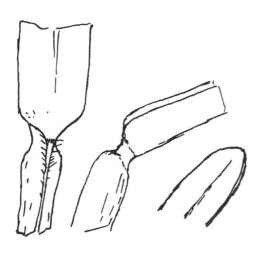

Front   Side view   Leaf tip
Fig. 3.20
St. Augustine grass x 3

Description — Leaves are folded in the bud-shoot. *Blade* — is somewhat petioled (constricted) above the ligule, 4-10mm wide, 8-15cm long (those arising from the stolons are much shorter) glabrous, flexuous and bluntly obtuse. *Sheath* — is compressed, keeled, split and slightly ciliate toward the summit along the margins. *Ligule* — is inconspicuous with a fringe of hair about 0.4mm long. *Auricles* — are absent. *Collar* — is broad and extending through petioled area. *Inflorescence* — short flowering culms bearing terminal and axillary racemes. It is a very coarse stoloniferous perennial grass with short flowering culms. Stolons are flat and up to 2-3 ft. long. The leaf blades are blunt, constricted at the juncture with the flattened sheath and exhibiting a half twist. The seedheads are coarse but infrequent. It is an aggressive plant and easily crowds out other grasses but does not spread in adjacent areas as a weed. St. Augustine grass is used as a forage grass in the Everglades where it furnishes more grazing than other grasses used there.

Adaptation — St. Augustine grass is the least winter-hardy of the southern warm-season grasses and it goes dormant when cool but recovers quickly. Adapted to warmer areas of warm humid regions. It can be grown successfully south of Augusta, Georgia and Birmingham, Alabama and westward to the coastal regions to Texas and the milder parts of California. This grass endures sun, shade and it is tolerant to close clipping. It is the best shade grass of the southernmost states. It is used for lawns and for general purpose turf. For sports turf, it is generally not used.

St. Augustine grass grows best on moist soils with good fertility and will withstand salt spray. Its drought resistance is below that of Bermuda grass, zoysia grass or Bahia grass. It is particularly well adapted to the muck soils of the Florida Everglades. Soil pH around 6.5 is the best but it grows well on acid as well as on alkaline soils.

Culture — Seed is not available commercially. St. Augustine grass is propagated vegetatively by sprigging, stolons or by spot sodding. It is one of the cheapest sods for Florida and the Gulf Coast and responds well to fertilization. Liberal applications of high-nitrogen fertilizers are necessary, especially on sandy light soils. Annually, St. Augustine grass should get 3-5 lb. N per 1,000 sq. ft. St. Augustine grass should not be mown closer than 1.0-1.5 inches high. It is best to mow this grass at a 1.5-3.0 inch height. Thatch can be a problem especially on well fertilized turf. Vertical mowing helps.

St. Augustine may suffer from brown patch, gray leaf spot (*Piricularia grisea* (CKE) Sacc.) and is especially subjected to insect problem, chinch bugs. Pest attacks often occur suddenly. It is also subject to a viral disease called St. Augustine decline.

There are few new varieties commercially released. *'Floratine'* is lower, finer in texture, has better density and has a blue-green color, and is used for lawns. *'Bitter Blue'* has blue-green color and is a more frost tolerant variety and is suitable for ornamental turf.

3.13 Centipede grass (*Eremochloa ophiuroides* (Munro) Hack.)

Centipede grass is a low-growing perennial grass that is a native of China and was introduced into the United States in 1919. Because of its low nutritive value, it is used chiefly for lawns and erosion control.

Description — Leaves are folded in the bud-shoot. *Blade* — is compressed or flattened, 3-5mm wide, short, blunt, keeled and ciliate with margins papillose toward base. *Sheath* — is glabrous with grayish tufts at the throat, very compressed with margins overlapping. *Ligule* — is membranous ciliate, cilia longer than the membrane, totaling about 0.5mm. *Auricles* — are absent. *Collar* — is broad, constricted by fused keel, tufted at the lower edge, pubescent. *Inflorencence* — has spike-like solitary recemes. Centipede spreads by thick, short noded leafy stolons that form new plants at each node. It is considered as an aggressive, low-growing grass and usually does not get taller than 3-4 inches. It is the intermediate between Bermuda grass and St. Augustine grass concerning width of leaf, stem size, density, color or shade tolerance.

Adaptation — Centipede grass adapts well to the southern United States, is more hardy to low temperatures than St. Augustine and is less hardy than Bermuda. It grows well in shade but not as well as zoysia or St. Augustine, but is much better than Bermuda grass. It also grows well in full sun.

Centipede grass is adaptable to a wide range of soil conditions and grows well in acid and unfertile soils with pH 4.3-5.8. Drought resistance is below that of Bermuda, St. Augustine or zoysia grass.

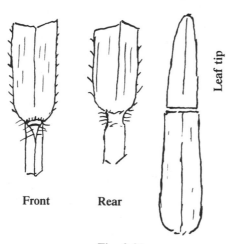

Front   Rear

Leaf tip

Fig. 3.21
Centipede grass x 3

Centipede grass is widely used for home lawns, church grounds and cemeteries in the deep south. It is not suggested for use on farm lawns; it may infest pastures and decrease their grazing value.

Culture — Centipede grass has low maintenance requirements and it is a good grass to use where only a minimum of care will be given. A moderate annual application of a complete fertilizer will improve the quality of a centipede lawn. 1-3 lb. N per 1,000 sq. ft. is needed for maintenance fertilization. Centipede is sensitive to nutrient imbalance, especially for its lack of iron. It is also sensitive to salt water spray.

Centipede grass establishes itself slower than most warm-season grasses with the exception of zoysias and is usually propagated vegetatively by sprigs or plugs. It can also be established by seed, but seed is rather expensive. A centipede lawn should be cut regularly at a 1-2 inch height. Although centipede is seldom damaged by diseases or insects, brown patch, dollar spot, nematodes and ground pearls can do damage. This grass is sensitive to organic arsonates and tolerant of triazine herbicides.

'*Oaklawn*' was released in 1965 by the Oklahoma A.E.S. and was selected for tolerance to drought and extreme temperatures. It is resistant to pests and grows in shade.

3.14 Bahia grass (*Paspalum natatum* Flügge)

Bahia grass is a coarse-textured grass native of tropical America. It is used more as a hay grass than for turf. There are few types of this grass each having morphological differences.

**Fig. 3.22
Bahia grass x 3**

Description — Leaves are rolled in the bud-shoot. *Blade* — is flat or folded at base, 4-8mm wide, usually sparsely ciliate at base (sometimes almost to summit). *Sheath* — is compressed, keeled, glossy, ciliate toward summit, overlapping. *Ligule* — is membranous, truncate, 1mm long. *Auricles* — are absent. *Collar* — is broad. *Inflorescence* — has 2, rarely 3 one-sided spike-like racemes. It is a perennial grass that spreads by stout, short rhizomes, and stolons which form dense, tough sod even on sandy soils. The root system is extensive, deep and once a sod is formed few other plants are able to encroach. Bahia is a tall growing grass with 1-2 ft. seed stalks. Bahia is largely an apomictic grass.

Adaptation — Bahia is adaptable to warm humid areas, grows as far north as North Carolina but is best adapted to Florida and lower coastal areas. It withstands drought and wear very well and grows in the shade. Bahia is tolerant to poor soils and low fertility but responds well to fertilization. It grows satisfactorily on sandy soils that dry quickly and hold nutrients poorly. Slightly acid soils with pH 6.5-7.5 are preferred. As a turf grass it is suitable for extensive areas like highways, airports, and large lawns with minimal maintenance expense.

Culture — Bahia can be propagated by seed and vegetatively by sprigs and plugs. About 3-5 lb. of seed per 1,000 sq. ft. is suggested. Seed germination usually is poor. Treatments with heat, acid or scarification may improve seed germination considerably. Light maintenance, fertilization with 2-4 lb. N per 1,000 sq. ft. is satisfactory. Bahia should be mown at 1.5-3.0 inch height, with no thatch build-up. A rotary mower is better for cutting seedheads than a reel mower.

Bahia is rather resistant to disease or insect pests. Few Bahia varieties are on the market. These are mostly forage grasses. 'Argentine', 'Paraguay', 'Pensacola', and 'Wilmington' are known varieties that can be used for turf production.

3.15 Carpet grass (*Axonopus affinis* Chase)

Carpet grass is a native of Central America and the West Indies.

Description — Leaves are folded in the bud-shoot. *Blade* — is obtuse, glabrous or ciliate at base, margins scabrous near apex, 4-8mm wide. *Sheath* — is compressed, glabrous. *Ligule* — has a fringe of hair, fused at base, about 1mm long. *Auricles* — are absent. *Collar* — is narrow, glabrous, occasionally with few hairs. *Inflorescence* — 2-5 racemes are on filiform stem. It is a low-growing coarse, sod forming perennial that spreads by stolons and seeds. Carpet grass has long, drooping and slender seed stalks which look like those of crabgrass. Because of its coarseness, carpet grass and St. Augustine look alike. The light green color of carpet grass helps to distinguish it.

Fig. 3.23
Carpet grass x 3

Adaptation — Carpet grass grows in southern humid regions and is most abundant on lowlands from coastal North Carolina to Florida and westward to Texas. It is best adapted to the southern part of the Gulf and Atlantic Coast states where the annual rainfall is 36 inches. It is not a drought tolerant grass. Carpet grass and centipede are alike concerning their tolerance to shade. It grows on acid (pH 5.2-6.7), non-fertile, wet sandy and sandy loam soils, where moisture is near the surface most of the year, and on soil too poor for other pasture plants. It is widely used to sod ditches, for erosion control and lawns.

Culture — Seeding is the cheapest method to establish carpet grass. It also can be propagated vegetatively by sprigs. The seeding rate is 3-5 lb. per 1,000 sq. ft. 2-3 lb. N per 1,000 sq. ft. per year is enough as a maintenance fertilization program.

Carpet grass is sensitive to iron deficiencies and it does not tolerate salt water sprays. It becomes chlorotic at pH 7 or above. It is rather resistant to diseases and insect pests. Brown patch is most common, seed rot and damping-off can be a problem in new seedings.

Tropical carpet grass (*Axonopus compressus* (Swartz) Beauv.) looks like *A. affinis* but is less winter hardy. It is found in Florida and southern Louisiana. It grows in partial shade, prefers rich organic soils and withstands temporary flooding. Use and cultural practices are similar to *A. affinis*.

3.16 Buffalo grass (*Buchloe dactyloides* (Nutt.) Engelm.)

Buffalo grass is a warm-season, native, fine-leaved, sod forming, perennial short-grass.

Description — Leaves are rolled in the bud-shoot. *Blade* — is pointed, drooping veined, pubescent on both sides, margins are toothed and glandular (with lens), 1-3mm wide. *Sheath* — is split, round. *Ligule* — has a fringe of hair, 0.5-1mm long. *Auricles* — are absent. *Inflorescence* — dioecious grass with stems bearing separate staminate and pistilate flowers. Pistilate heads 3-4mm thick, staminate culm with 2 or 3 spikes. It is a creeping, stoloniferous, gray-green perennial grass forming dense, matted growth 5-8 inches high. It is a fine-textured grass with drooping-curling leaves.

Adaptation — Adapted in warm semi-arid and sub-humid regions where no irrigation is available. It occurs in stands with blue grama in the central and southern Great Plains, particularly in western Kansas, Colorado and the high plains of Texas, Arizona and northern Mexico. It is a dominant grass of our prairies. Buffalo grass is a highly drought resistant grass. It is not tolerant to shade, therefore watering, fertilizing and high mowing, which encourages weeds, should be avoided. It is ideally suited for erosion control on the range

Fig. 3.24
Buffalo grass x 3

and pasture land that is not too sandy. It is used for lawns, parks, cemeteries, and athletic fields in warm and transition zones of semi-arid, sub-humid, non-irrigated areas. It grows best on heavier, fertile and well drained soils and is tolerant to alkali and intensive grazing.

Culture — Buffalo grass can be propagated by seed or vegetatively by plugs or by planting sod pieces in a well prepared seedbed. It should be planted in rows in order to facilitate weeding until it becomes established. Treated or stratified seeds may be sown in spring. Untreated seeds are better seeded in the fall. The sod should be planted as early as possible in the spring. Lawn turf should be mown at 1-2 inch height and 1-2 lb. N per 1,000 sq. ft. per year will fill the bill. At present, no varieties are available for turf purposes.

3.17 Blue grama (*Bouteloua gracilis* (H.B.K.) Lag. ex Steud.)

Blue grama is a native, warm-season, low-growing perennial bunch grass that generally grows with buffalo grass in the Great Plains.

Fig. 3.25
Blue grama x 3

Description — Leaves are folded in the bud-shoot. *Blades* — are flat to convolute, 1-2.5mm wide, tapering to a sharp point, somewhat twisted, curled, prominently veined above and below, scabrous or pubescent on upper surface especially near base, glabrous below. *Sheath* — round, split with hyaline margins, distinctly veined, and glabrous or sparsely pilose. *Ligule* — has a dense fringe of hair up to 0.5mm long. *Auricles* — are absent. *Collar* — is continuous, medium broad, distinctly yellowish green, with long hairs on inside of margins. *Inflorescence* — has 1 to 3 spikes (usually 2), spreading at maturity. It is a short densely tufted grass with short scaly rhizomes. Ground stems, under favorable conditions may root. Blue grama, a bunch grass, forms a rather dense sod especially if thickly seeded. Roots are shallow but extensive.

Adaptation — Blue grama is a drought and low temperature tolerant grass, well adapted, like buffalo grass to the southern region of the Great Plains. It is adaptable to a wide range of soils and grows in alkaline soils. Blue grama grows on much sandier soils than buffalo grass and it is well adapted for use on lands which cannot or should not be plowed. It is used in range seedings, conservation plantings, roadsides and as turf grass on some unirrigated areas of the Great Plains where low maintenance intensity is expected. It fits all areas of a golf course but the greens.

Culture — Seed is available but light and fluffy and it is difficult to distribute evenly. Seeding rate for pure stands is 1-2 lb. per 1,000 sq. ft. In areas where buffalo grass and blue grama are adaptable it is a practice to seed them together at a ratio of 1:2 and at 1 lb. per 1,000 sq. ft. For maintenance turf fertilization 1-2 lb. N per 1,000 sq. ft. can be used. Blue grama is less resistant to wear than buffalo grass and should not be clipped as close and as frequently as buffalo grass. Clipping height of 2-3 inches is suggested.

3.18 Weeping lovegrass (*Eragrostis curvula* (Schrad.) Nees)

A warm-season, perennial bunch grass with narrow weeping blades and fibrous roots. It was introduced from South Africa. Weeping lovegrass is propagated by seed which germinates and develops quickly. It grows up to 3-4 ft. tall and it is an excellent erosion control plant on non-usable areas in the southern Great Plains and in parts of the Southwest. It is a drought resistant grass but does not withstand frequent close cutting and therefore is not good for regular lawns. Sandy loams are preferred.

OTHER SPECIES

3.19 White clover (*Trifolium repens* L.)

White clover is a low growing, cold and humid region legume that spreads by stolons and provides green growth and very often was included in lawn mixtures before World War II. It withstands drought, unfertilized poor soils and continuous mowing below 0.5 inches. It should be seeded at a 1 lb. rate per 1,000 sq. ft. Applications of phosphorus fertilizers encourages clover growth. Clover indicates a sufficiency of lime in the soil.

White clover is considered undesirable in lawns since it is difficult to maintain a uniform stand. Clover does not blend well with grasses because of the darker color and different leaf texture. Under normal lawn cutting height it flowers and is distractive. It attracts bees. The leaves and stems are soft, juicy and stain clothing.

3.20 Dichondra (*Dichondra repens* Forst.)

Dichondra is a warm climate dicotyledonous plant, that spreads by seeds and vegetatively by creeping stems. Leaves are round, 1-2cm wide, and commonly pubescent. Corolla is campanulate, shorter than calyx, deeply 5-lobed.

Dichondra is widely distributed in moist soils of warm climate regions. It is often, like white clover, considered as a weed in lawns but in the south, especially in southern California, it is often used as a ground cover plant. Shade tolerance is good and tolerates slightly acid, low fertility soils and mowings at 1 inch or below.

Summary

Some characteristics of northern and southern grasses are presented in Tables 3.2, 3.3, 3.4 and 3.5.

Table 3.2 Characteristics of northern grasses

Grasses	Sod Forming	Leaf Texture	Establish-ment rate	Fertility requirements
1. Bent, colonial	Short stolons and rhizomes	Fine	Medium-fast	High
2. Bent, creeping	Stolons	Fine	Medium-fast	High
3. Blue, Kentucky	Rhizomes	Fine-medium	Slow	Medium
4. Blue, rough	Short stolons	Fine-medium	Slow	Low-medium
5. Fescue, red	Short rhizomes or bunch grass	Fine	Medium	Low
6. Fescue, tall	Bunch grass	Coarse	Medium	Medium
7. Redtop	Bunch grass and short rhizomes	Medium	Fast	Low-medium
8. Rye, perennial	Bunch grass	Medium	Fast	Medium

Table 3.3 Characteristics of southern grasses

Grasses	Sod forming	Leaf texture	Establishment	
			method	rate
1. Bahia	Short rhizomes	Coarse	Seed or vegetative	Medium-slow
2. Bermuda	Stolons and rhizomes	Fine-medium	Vegetative	Very fast
3. Carpet	Stolons	Coarse	Seed or vegetative	Medium
4. Centipede	Stolons	Medium-coarse	Seed or vegetative	Slow-meduim
5. St. Augustine	Stolons	Very coarse	Vegetative	Fast
6. Zoysia	Rhizomes and stolons	Fine-medium	Vegetative	Very slow

Table 3.4 Characteristics of northern grasses

	Shade tolerance	Drought resistance	Cold tolerance	Heat tolerance	Salinity tolerance	Wear tolerance
HIGH	Red fescue	Tall fescue	Rough blue	Tall Fescue	Creeping bent	Tall fescue
	Velvet bent	Red fescue	Creeping bent	Kentucky blue	Tall fescue	Perennial rye
	Rough blue	Kentucky blue	Canada blue	Colonial bent	Perennial rye	Kentucky blue
	Creeping bent	Redtop	Kentucky blue	Red fescue	Red fescue	Canada blue
	Tall fescue	Perennial rye	Colonial bent	Creeping bent	Kentucky blue	Red fescue
	Colonial bent	Colonial bent	Redtop	Perennial rye	Colonial bent	Colonial bent
	Redtop	Creeping bent	Red fescue	Redtop		Creeping bent
	Perennial rye	Rough blue	Tall fescue	Rough blue		
LOW	Kentucky blue	Velvet bent	Perennial rye			

Table 3.5 Characteristics of southern grasses

	Shade tolerance	Drought resistance	Cold tolerance	Salinity tolerance	Wear tolerance	Fertility requirements
HIGH	St. Augustine	Bermuda	Zoysia	St. Augustine	Zoysia	Bermuda
	Zoysia	Bahia	Bermuda	Zoysia	Bermuda	St. Augustine
	Bahia	Zoysia	Bahia	Bermuda	Bahia	Zoysia
	Centipede	St. Augustine	Carpet	Bahia	St. Augustine	Bahia
	Carpet	Centipede	Centipede	Centipede	Carpet	Carpet
LOW	Bermuda	Carpet	St. Augustine	Carpet	Centipede	Centipede

Vegetative characteristics of northern turf grasses

I. The bluegrasses (*Poa* spp.)

Leaves folded in the bud-shoot. Leaf blades have a characteristic median line (midrib): distinct light line on each side. Upper surface of blades not ridged. Sheath split. Membranous ligule present. Auricles absent.

(A) Kentucky bluegrass (*Poa pratensis*)

Blades 2 to 5mm wide, linear (parallel-sided), boat-shaped tip, dark green color. Lower surface of blades glossy. Ligule 0.4 to 1mm long, truncate. Sheath smooth. Rhizomes.

(B) Rough bluegrass (Rough stalked meadow grass) (*Poa trivialis*)

Blades 2 to 5mm wide, slightly tapering to boat-shaped tip with lower surface glossy. Lighter green than K. bluegrass. Ligules 2 to 5mm long, acute. Sheath somewhat flattened, rough to touch (on well developed older plants only). Short stolons.

(C) Canada bluegrass (*Poa compressa*)

Blades 2 to 4mm wide, boat-shaped but not glossy underneath, of bluish-green color, rather short. Sheath compressed (culms also compressed). Ligule 0.6 to 2.0mm. Wiry rhizomes.

(D) Annual bluegrass (*Poa annua*)

Blades 2 to 4mm wide, pale, short and somewhat tapering to subacute tips, not glossy. Ligule 1 to 3mm long, membranous, white, rounded to acute. It is able to produce seed stalks even under close turf mowing. No rhizomes or stolons.

II. Fescues (*Festuca* spp.)

(A) Leaves folded in bud-shoot. Blades narrow, bristle-like. Blade surface ridged. No auricles, sheath split. Fine grass.

(1) Red creeping and chewing fescues (*Festuca rubra*)

Blades 1-2mm wide, surface ridged, glossy below. Brownish red leaf sheath. Ligule 0.3 to 0.5mm, truncate. Auricles absent but with apparent enlargement tapering toward bristle-like blade.
Creeping r. fescue — short rhizomes
Chewing r. fescue — bunch grass

(2) Sheep fescue (*Festuca ovina*)

Blades 1-1.5mm wide, ridged. Similar to red fescue, with the exception that leaves are pale bluish-green. Ligule obtuse 0.2 to 0.4mm long. Bunch grass. Turf tufty.

(B) Leaves rolled in bud-shoot. Blades wide, 5 to 9mm, glossy. Coarse grasses.

   (1) Tall fescue *(Festuca arundinacea)*

   Sheath often reddish-purple at base. Blade 5 to 9mm wide, upper surface prominently ridged. Lower surface glossy, margins scabrous. Ligule 0.5 to 1.0mm long, truncate to obtuse, entire. Auricles 0.2 to 1.5mm long and hairy. Bunch grass.

   (2) Meadow fescue *(Festuca elatior)*

   Like tall fescue only less coarse (blades 4 to 8mm wide) and auricles not hairy.

III. Ryegrasses *(Lolium* spp.)

   (A) Annual (Italian) ryegrass *(Lolium multiflorum)*

   Very similar to tall fescue. Less coarse (blades 3 to 7mm wide), smooth leaf margins, narrower and longer glabrous auricles, 1 to 3mm long, ligule 1 to 2mm long. No stolons or rhizomes.

   (B) Perennial ryegrass *(Lolium perenne)*

   It is much finer in texture than annual ryegrass and has a folded bud-shoot. Blades 2 to 6mm wide. Sheath flattened to almost round, closed or split, reddish at base.

IV. The Bents *(Agrostis* spp.)

Leaves rolled in the bud-shoot. Sheath split. Auricles absent. Ligule membranous present. Blades sharp pointed, ridged on the upper surface, not glossy underneath.

   (A) Colonial bent grass *(Agrostis tenuis)*

   Blades 2 to 4mm wide. Blade margin may be smooth or scabrous. Ligule 0.4 to 1.2mm long, truncate, short stolons and rhizomes.

   (B) Creeping bent grass *(Agrostis palustris)*

   Blades 2 to 4mm wide. Ligule 1 to 3mm, toothed or rounded. Long, fine stolons.

   (C) Velvet bent grass *(Agrostis canina)*

   Blades 1 to 1.5mm wide. Ligule 1 to 3mm long. Stolons. It builds dense turf of light green color.

   (D) Redtop *(Agrostis alba)*

   Blades 4 to 7mm wide. Ligule 1.5 to 5mm long, rounded to acute, lacerate. Coarser than other bents. It has rhizomes or bunchy grass.

Identification key of northern turf grasses in vegetative stage of growth

I. Leaves folded in bud-shoot

(A) Auricles present, rather long. Blade surface ridged, glossy below, 2 to 6mm wide. Ligule 1 to 2mm long
     Perennial ryegrass *(Lolium perenne)*

(B) Auricles absent.

    (1) Leaf blades bristle-like, 1 to 2mm wide, ridged, dark green in color. Sheath thin, whitish, reddish tinted below, partway split. Ligule 0.5mm long. Auricles absent but with apparent enlargement tapering toward bristle-like blade.

        (a) Short rhizomes
         Creeping red fescue *(Festuca rubra)*

        (b) No rhizomes, bunch grass
         Chewing red fescue *(F. rubra* var *commutata)*

        (c) Leaves bluish-green, 0.5 to 1.5mm wide. Ligule less than 0.5mm long or obsolete. Sheath split. Bunch grass.
         Sheep fescue *(Festuca ovina)*

    (2) Blades flat, not bristle-like, surface smooth and has characteristic median line (midrib), light line on each side. Blade tip abruptly pointed, boat-shaped.

        (a) Blades underneath glossy

            (1) Blades 2 to 5mm wide, parallel-side, dark green color, glossy. Ligule 0.4 to 1mm long, truncate. Rhizomes.
             K. Bluegrass *(Poa pratensis)*

            (2) Blades 2 to 5mm wide, slightly tapering to boat-shaped tip with lower surface glossy. Light green color. Ligule long, 2 to 5mm, acute. Sheath somewhat flattened and rough to touch (retrorsely scabrous on well developed, older plants). Short stolons.
             Rough bluegrass *(Poa trivialis)*

        (b) Blades dull underneath, not glossy and rather short and slightly tapering toward the boat-shaped tip.

            (1) Blades 2 to 4mm wide, bluish-green. Sheath compressed (culms also compressed). Ligule short, 0.6 to 2.0mm. Wiry rhizomes.
             Canada bluegrass *(Poa compressa)*

            (2) Blades 2 to 4mm wide. Ligule 1 to 3mm long, membranous, white, rounded to acute. Annual or winter annual grass.
             Annual bluegrass *(Poa annua)*

II. Leaves rolled in the bud-shoot.

  (A) Auricles present, blade surface ridged, glossy underneath.

    (1) Blades 5 to 9mm wide, scabrous on margins. Ligule 0.5 to 1.0mm long. Auricles 0.2 to 1.5mm long and hairy. Bunch grass.
        Tall fescue *(Festuca arundinacea)*

    (2) Blades 3 to 7mm wide, smooth leaf margins. Auricles 1 to 3mm long. Ligule 1 to 2mm long.
        Annual ryegrass *(Lolium multiflorum)*

  (B) Auricles absent or rudimentary

    (1) Blades surface ridged, sharp pointed, not glossy underneath.

      (a) Blades 2 to 4mm wide. Ligule short (0.4 to 1.2mm long), truncate. Short rhizomes and stolons.
          Colonial bent grass *(Agrostis tenuis)*

      (b) Blades 2 to 4mm wide. Ligule long, 1 to 3mm, toothed or rounded. Long fine stolons.
          Creeping bent grass *(Agrostic palustris)*

      (c) Blades 1 to 1.5mm. Ligule long, 1 to 3mm. Stolons.
          Velvet bent grass *(Agrostis canina)*

      (d) Blades 4 to 7mm wide, ligule long, 1.5 to 5mm, rounding to acute, lacerate. Coarser than other bents. Rhizomes or bunchy grass.
          Redtop *(Agrostis alba)**

  (C) Blades not ridged, light green, bulbous base. Ligule 1.5 to 5mm long, obtuse to acute with distinct notch on either side.
      Timothy *(Phleum pratense)*

---

* Redtop is distinguished from timothy by the absence of a notch at either side of the ligule and by a prominent ridged upper surface of the blade.

Vegetative characteristics of southern turf grasses

A. Fine to medium textured grasses

  1. Bermuda grass *(Cynodon dactylon)*

      Leaves in bud-shoot are only slightly compressed and usually accepted as folded. Leaves are born on stems which produce long internodes alternating with very short ones. *Blades* 2 to 3mm wide and are widest at the base and gradually taper toward a sharp pointed tip. Blades sparingly pubescent above, margins somewhat scabrous, not glossy. Underneath blade midrib somewhat lighter in color and appears as stripe. *Sheath* is split, loose, round or compressed with tuft of hair at the collar (throat). *Ligule* — a fringe of hairs 0.2 to 0.8mm long. *Auricles* absent. *Collar* narrow. *Inflorescence* — 4-5 digitate spikes, all branches originating at the same point. Strong, flat, long stolons and scaly rhizomes. In Bermuda, leaf blades are well developed and expanded up to the stolon tips. This characteristic is helpful to distinguish Bermuda from zoysia. Although between different Bermuda varieties there are considerable variations, it is generally a fine to medium textured southern grass. Distinct characteristics: (a) fine textured grass, (b) leaf blades widest at the base and gradually tapering to the sharp extended tips, (c) midvein underneath leaf blade is lighter in color and produces a stripe, (d) leaf blades are well expanded up to stolon tips.

  2. Zoysias *(Zoysia* spp.)

      Leaves are rolled in bud-shoot. *Blades* stiff, 2-5mm wide with few long hairs near base. *Sheath* — round to slightly flattened, smooth but may have a tuft of hairs above (at throat), split with hyaline margins. *Ligule* — a fringe of hairs 0.2mm long. *Auricles* — absent. *Collar* hairy at least at margins. *Inflorescence* — short, terminal spike-like raceme. Stolons and rhizomes.

      Like Bermuda, zoysia is a fine-medium textured grass. Vegetative characteristics of both grasses are similar. Helpful points to separate them are: (a) Zoysia's leaf in bud-shoot distinctly rolled, (b) leaf blades beneath evenly dark green. Midvein in Bermudas are lighter and make stripes, (c) leaf blades at the end of stolons are poorly developed as compared with Bermudas, (d) leaf blade at base and at the half length toward the tip is of the same width and then tapering toward the tip. In Bermuda, blades are widest at the base and gradually taper toward the tip.

B. Coarse textured grasses

    In this group the most coarse grass is St. Augustine and the least coarse is centipede grass. Bahia and carpet grass are of intermediate type. St. Augustine, carpet grass and centipede are clearly folded in bud-shoot. Vernation (bud-shoot) of Bahia grass is not too clear, transitional. All these grasses have no auricles.

  3. St. Augustine *(Stenotaphrum secundatum)*

      Leaves folded in bud-shoot. *Sheaths* are greatly compressed, keeled, split and slightly ciliate toward the top and along the margins. *Blades* are 4 to 10mm wide, 8 to 15cm long (those arising from the stolons are much shorter), somewhat constricted (petioled) above the ligule, glabrous, flexuous and bluntly obtuse (boat-shaped). Leaf blades at constriction exhibit half twist. *Ligule* — inconspicuous, pubescent fringe of hairs about 0.4mm long. *Auricles* absent. *Collar* broad and extending through petioled area. *Inflorescence* — short flowering culms bearing terminal and axillary racemes. It is a very coarse, stoloniferous perennial grass. Stolons are flat and up to 2 to 3 ft. long.

4. Carpet grass *(Axonopus affinis)*

Leaves are folded in bud-shoot. *Sheath* — compressed, glabrous. *Blades* 4 to 8mm wide, obtuse, glabrous or ciliate at base, somewhat scabrous near apex. *Ligule* — fringe of hairs fused at base, about 1mm long. *Auricles* absent. *Inflorescence* — 2-5 racemes on filiform stem. Seed stalks are long, slender and drooping and look like those of crabgrass. It is a low-growing, coarse grass that spreads by stolons and seed. Because of coarseness and creeping stolons, carpet grass and St. Augustine look alike.

5. Centipede grass *(Eremochloa ophiuroides)*

Leaves folded in bud-shoot. *Sheath* glabrous with grayish tufts at the throat, very compressed with margins overlapping. *Blade* — 3 to 5mm wide, compressed or flattened, short, blunt, keeled and ciliate with margins papilose toward the base. *Ligule* membranous, ciliate, cilia longer than the membrane, totaling about 0.5mm. *Auricles* absent. *Collar* broad, constricted by fused keel, tufted. *Inflorescence* spike-like solitary racemes. Centipede spreads by thick, short-noded leafy stolons that form new plants at each node. It is a medium coarse grass. It is intermediate between Bermuda and St. Augustine concerning size, density or shade tolerance.

6. Bahia grass *(Paspalum notatum)*

Leaves folded or rolled in bud-shoot. *Sheath* compressed, glossy, ciliate toward the top. *Blade* flat or folded at base, 4 to 7mm wide, sparsely ciliate at base, upper surface ridged, glossy underneath. Blades are long (15-25cm), gradually tapering to sharp point. Midvein on the lower part of the blade surface usually whitish in color. *Ligule* membranous, truncate, 1mm long. Back of ligule row of hair, longer than ligule itself. *Auricles* absent. *Collar* broad. *Inflorescence* 2 or 3 one-sided spike-like racemes. Bahia spreads by seed and stout, short rhizomes and stolons.

CHAPTER 4
ADAPTATION OF TURF GRASSES

Climate, edaphic factors (soils), use of turf, grass texture, perenniality, maintenance requirements and susceptibility to various pests are the main factors which determine turf grass adaptation and usefulness.

4.1 Climatic factors

Grasses are adapted to various climatic regions which are determined by rainfall and temperature. Light also can play a role in the selection of a turf grass within a region of adaptability. It is possible to control moisture by irrigation, and therefore, temperature is a more important climatic factor than rainfall in most turf situations.

Temperature

Optimum growing temperatures for various turf grasses varies. Some tests indicate that ryegrass grows best at 59°F but temperature for growing Kentucky bluegrass shoots and roots is 70-75°F and 60°F, respectively (26). In Kansas (22) cool season grass roots start to grow when soil temperatures reach 40-45°F. Their shoots start to grow soon afterward. Bluegrass, a cool season grass, reaches maximum growth at 60°F. Bermuda does not begin growth until soil temperature approaches 60°F and growth continues unchecked by hot weather, if water and plant nutrients are available. It stops growth at 50°F. Zoysia needs higher temperatures for optimum growth than Bermuda grass. Concerning top growth, the optimum temperature range for cool-season grasses is 60-75°F compared to the optimum temperature range for warm-season grasses which is 80-95°F (1, 6, 24, 43). Optimum temperature for root or rhizome growth is somewhat lower. Roots of many northern turf grasses continue to grow as long as the ground is not frozen.

Extremes in climate are important, e.g., Rhode Island climate does not vary greatly from one season to another or from year to year. There could be climates of the same averages but with greater fluctuations from extreme to extreme. Average yearly temperatures in Rhode Island and southern Iowa are the same (50°F) but conditions for grasses are quite different (46). K. bluegrass as compared with colonial bent is superior in regions where temperatures vary and inferior in coastal areas where daily or seasonal temperature variations are smaller. However, both thrive in regions with the same average temperatures (10, 26).

Some cool-season grasses like K. bluegrass or perennial ryegrass need cool temperature (40-50°F) treatment to change from the vegetative stage of development into the reproductive stage of development. This treatment is called *vernalization*. Warm-season grasses do not need cold treatment and temperatures below 50-55°F will even inhibit flowering.

Optimum temperatures for physiological processes, like photosynthesis and respiration, are somewhat higher than the optimum temperatures for shoot or root growth. At optimum temperatures for shoot growth, carbohydrate accumulation is low and usually increases when temperatures fall below the optimum for shoot growth. Optimum temperature for respiration is higher than for photosynthesis and under high temperature stress carbohydrate reserves will decrease and accelerated root maturation and death will occur. New root initiation will be impaired. This is followed by a decreased rate of foliage growth. Direct kill of northern grasses usually occurs when temperatures reach over 100°F. Plant responses to high temperature are often complicated by related moisture, nutritional and disease relationships, e.g., bent grasses are rather tolerant to high temperatures but because of short roots are susceptible to wilt (6) when temperatures exceed 90°F.

During summer heat and drought, grasses may stop growth and turn dormant. K. bluegrass roots become dormant when soil reaches 80°F. Lack of water is the primary cause for summer dormancy. Under good transpirational conditions, grasses are kept cool and heat stress can be avoided. Syringing is helpful. It is an expensive procedure and is usually used on golf greens. Warm-season grasses demonstrate excellent heat hardiness, followed by tall fescue, K. bluegrass, bents and red fescues. Perennial ryegrass, redtop and rough bluegrass are the least heat tolerant northern grasses (Table 3.4).

Direct low temperature injury is caused by ice crystal formation within the plant and thus disrupting normal cell function and causing tissue death. Grasses usually recover if meristematic tissues in crowns or rhizomes are not killed. Plants in a dormant stage of growth are significantly hardier to low temperature than when they are actively growing. Low temperature kill usually occurs in late winter or early spring. In the fall or early winter, grasses are more tolerant to low temperatures. Differences in low temperature hardiness between turf grasses have been observed. Differences even between varieties of the same species can be found. Low temperature hardiness with least susceptible grasses first and most susceptible last are as follows (Tables 3.4 and 3.5): rough bluegrass, creeping bent grass, Kentucky bluegrass, Canada bluegrass, colonial bent grass, redtop, red fescue, tall fescue, zoysia, perennial ryegrass, Bermuda grass, Bahia grass, carpet grass, centipede and St. Augustine grass. The degree of injury or absolute kill is usually affected by the rate of freezing, rate of thawing, length of time frozen, tissue hydration level, and maintenance practices (24).

Artificial soil warming has been investigated. The main objectives were to maintain green grass color and to protect against frost. Cool-season grasses need 35-40°F and warm-season grasses need 60-65°F to retain color. Various methods and devices can be applied for subsurface soil warming. The use of heating in turf maintenance is very limited at present.

Ice cover over turf in winter may injure or even kill grasses. Accumulation of toxic gases like CO_2 or cyanide gas are basic causes of injury. Lack of O_2 also occurs. Perennial grasses may tolerate ice cover as long as two months. Due to frost heaving in the spring, grass roots may lose contact with soil and die by desiccation. This often occurs in organic muck soils. Rolling with a heavy roller is helpful.

Light

Light energy from the sun is converted by the process of photosynthesis into chemical energy and serves for plant growth and development. Only about 1-2% of solar energy is absorbed and utilized by turf grasses. Light is needed for photosynthesis. Photosynthetically active green grass leaves and stems are important in this photochemical process. Dense stands, i.e. good cover, is needed in turf grass culture. *LAI* — leaf area index is defined as the total quantity of leaf area present per unit of soil area, i.e. ratio of leaf area per unit of soil area over which they grow.

Light is usually beneficial in grass seed germination. Crabgrass and goose grass seed need light for germination. In thickly seeded turf grasses competition for light is strong and weaker seedlings die. On the other hand in thin seedings light and bare spaces encourage weeds to germinate and establish.

Photoperiod. Day length is an important factor in plant growth and development. Generally, cool short days are influential in inducing changes from vegetative to reproductive stages in cool season grasses. In zoysias these changes are induced by short photoperiods and warm weather conditions. Besides photoperiod, temperature, nutrients and other environmental factors may also be influential in inducing turf grass flowering. In

Bermuda grass a long photoperiod is needed for maximum flowering but this grass is able to produce flowers over a wide range of day length (57). Photoperiod affects total grass growth: when days are longer, there is more time to absorb sun energy and to synthesize carbohydrates and this results in larger plants and higher yields. Prostrate growth, increased tillering and reduced shoot growth is expected under short day conditions (1, 34).

Intensity. Shading. Normal light intensity favors photosynthesis and carbohydrate reserves thus root-shoot ratios increase. During periods of low light intensities, carbohydrate synthesis may be so low that root carbohydrates may be utilized for normal plant growth and development. Under low light intensity plants are more succulent and thus more susceptible to diseases. High light intensity favors reproductive development and low light intensity favors vegetative development. Normally, low light intensities are needed for chlorophyll production. At high light intensities, its breakdown may occur. In the fall, light intensity is high and at temperatures below minimum for growth, synthesis of chlorophyll is impaired and causes discoloration of Bermuda grass of zoysias (55, 56).

Decreased light intensity by tree shading weakens turf grasses due to competition for water and plant nutrients. Increases in relative humidity, decreased air movement and temperature fluctuations also occur under shade.

Light intensity can be a factor in turf grass adaptation. Some grasses are rather tolerant to shade while others do not grow well in shaded areas. Red fescue and rough bluegrass are cool-season grasses well adapted to shaded areas. Under good maintenance bent grasses will stand shading well (Table 3.4). Tall fescue and ryegrass will stand some shading in southern parts of the cool humid region or in the transition zone area. K. bluegrass, a cool-season grass, is the least suitable in shaded areas. From the warm-season grasses St. Augustine grass and zoysias are best adapted to shaded areas. Centipede and carpet grass are medium and Bermuda grass is least suitable to shaded areas.

Shade may compensate for latitude: K. bluegrass grows much better in the south when shaded.

Water

Average yearly precipitation in the United States is about 30 inches. About 70% of this amount is lost to the air because of evaporation and transpiration, and the rest, 30%, is lost to streams, lakes and rivers. Seasonal distribution is important. In the northeastern region, distribution is rather uniform throughout the year, whereas in the Great Plains total precipitation is half as much but 85% of it falls during the growing season (16, 46). Temperature and moisture interact and it is difficult to separate their effects. Water loss from soil by evaporation or transpiration by plants will be higher during dry hot periods than during cool humid days. Wind increases the transpiration rate. *Evapotranspiration* (water loss from soil by evaporation + transpiration) from actively growing grasses is 1-2.5 inches weekly. Of course this will vary between a coastal foggy-humid area and the desert.

Irrigation plays an important role in turf grass management. The availability of water should be considered when selecting grass species. Where water is limited, red fescue alone or in mixtures with K. bluegrass should be used. Bermuda grass is drought resistant because it is a deep-rooted plant. Red fescue is rather shallow rooted grass but transpiration is relatively low due to narrow rolled leaves. For more about water-plant relationships, see Chapter 11.

4.2 Soils (Edaphic factors)

Soil conditions may be modified or altered to suit turf production or to compensate for unfavorable climatic conditions. It is easy to change soil acidity, fertility, or moisture conditions. By adding organic matter as peat, one is even able to change texture and aeration properties of a soil. Soil fertility is easily changed by applying proper fertilization programs.

There are relatively narrow differences among common lawn grass species in their adaptation to soil conditions. Red fescue, for example, will survive longer on acid light sandy soils than K. bluegrass. The fescues have comparatively low moisture requirements in contrast with other species (bluegrasses, bents) in their region of adaptation, but they will make their best growth where available moisture supplies are good. Broadly speaking, fertile soils that are permeable and of good water holding capacity with relatively rapid subsoil drainage are best suited for all important species of turf grasses. Excellent turf can also be maintained on soils that are far from ideal, especially where climatic conditions are favorable and management good. For a more complete discussion of soils, see Chapters 6 and 7.

4.3 Use of turf grasses

Main turf grass uses are:

1. *Lawns:* a) home lawns, b) lawns around institutions and industries, c) cemeteries, and d) parks.

2. *Intensive use areas:* a) golf courses, b) athletic fields, and c) playgrounds.

3. *Miscellaneous grass areas:* a) erosion control, b) airfield, c) highways, d) ski slopes, road and river banks.

Lawn, cemetery and park turf should be fine textured while highway banks can be coarse textured. Bermuda grass should not be used for cemetery turf because labor costs required to clip and clean around markers is high. Heavy duty turf areas, like athletic fields or putting greens of golf courses, should be able to stand wear. As such, wear resistant grasses should be used. Southern grasses are more wear tolerant than cool-season ones. Zoysias, Bermuda grass, Bahia grass, tall fescue and perennial ryegrass are the most wear tolerant turf grasses. The least tolerant are creeping bent grass, redtop, colonial bent grass, centipede grass and rough bluegrass. Medium tolerant are: Kentucky bluegrass, Canada bluegrass, red fescue, St. Augustine grass and carpet grass (Tables 3.4 and 3.5).

4.4 Other factors

In selecting grasses for lawns or other turf areas, the following factors should also be taken into consideration.

1. *Maintenance.* Management practices are important considerations in selecting grasses. Grasses should be selected to fit management. Under intensive care, colonial bent grass or Merion K. bluegrass will provide first class lawns. The same grasses under low maintenance will be failures. Also, the ability to withstand specialized management, e.g., height and frequency of cutting should be considered. Defoliation causes poor shallow root systems. Continuous use of nitrogen also adds to this. Foliage develops at the expense of the roots. Thus plants are weakened, food reserves of the root are low, and the power of the plant to absorb plant nutrients and water from deeper soil layers is decreased considerably.

2. *Appearance, texture, density.* The need for proper mixes and blends of turf grasses that form a high quality turf having good color and density varies depending upon the function of the area.

3. *Longevity,* i.e. turf established for permanent or temporary use only.

4. *Resistance to diseases* and other pests.

4.5 Grasses for various regions

The United States can be divided into climatic regions where the best grass species used for turf can be established. The map (Figure 4.1) indicates these regions (16, 26, 35). Within a region, because of mountains or southern versus northern slopes of valleys, climatic conditions can differ widely and the most suitable grass species or varieties also can differ. It must be remembered that no sharp boundaries for various grasses can be fixed. Under good maintenance, species — even those not well adapted — will produce good turf, whereas under poor maintenance, they will fail.

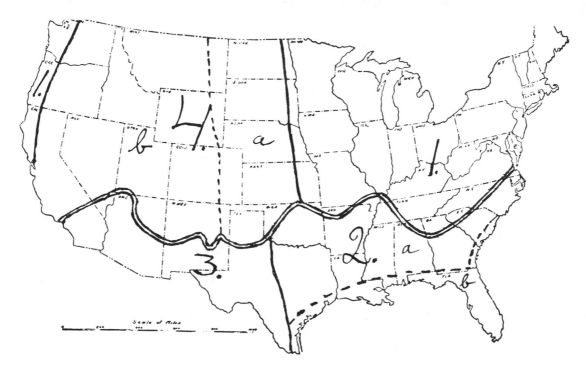

Figure 4.1 Map showing turf grass adaptation regions
≈ Transition zone between northern and southern turf grass

Region 1. Northern cool and humid region. This region includes the northeastern part of the United States between the Atlantic Ocean and the northern Plains in the west. The southern borderline goes roughly along the northern borderlines of North Carolina, Tennessee, Arkansas and Oklahoma. Also included in the same region of adaptation are the Northwest Pacific coastal areas (Figure 4.1). Roughly, the average yearly precipitation of this region is 30-45 inches. In the western areas of this region along the Plains, the yearly precipitation is 20-30 inches only, whereas in the northwest Pacific coastal areas it is 30-80 inches. The average January and July temperatures are 15-38°F and 65-75°F, respectively.

The *major grasses* are:

(a) Kentucky, Canada, rough bluegrasses
(b) Colonial, creeping, velvet bent grasses and redtop
(c) Red, chewing and tall fescues
(d) Perennial and annual ryegrasses.

Along the southern boundaries of this zone (transition zone) Tall fescue is well adapted for general purpose turf use. Bermuda grass and some zoysias can also be used.

Region 2. A warm humid region and including the southeastern areas below the transition zone, the Gulf Coast areas including the eastern half of Texas in the west. Average yearly precipitation is 35-55 inches with the Gulf coastal area 60-70 inches. Average January and July temperatures are 40-70°F and 75-80°F, respectively. This region can be divided into northern (a) and southern (b) areas.

The *major grasses* of the *northern 2a* region are:

(a) Tall fescue, (b) Kentucky bluegrass, (c) Bermuda grass and (d) zoysia grasses. Tall fescue is generally better adapted than K. bluegrass in this region.

The *major grasses* of the *southern 2b* region are:

(a) Bermuda grass, (b) Zoysias, (c) St. Augustine grass, (d) carpet grass and (e) Bahia grass.

Region 3. A warm, semi-arid and arid region including the southwestern part of the United States. Yearly precipitation is 5-20 inches. Average January and July temperatures are roughly 30-50°F and 75-90°F, respectively.

The *major grasses* of this region are:

(a) Bermuda grass and (b) zoysia grass. Almost no carpet grass, centipede grass or St. Augustine grass is used in this region. Bermuda grass and zoysia grass need irrigation for normal growth. Due to good root system Bermuda grass is preferred under limited irrigation and it is considered as the major turf grass of the region.

Without irrigation, buffalo grass and wheat grass are used where regular mowings are part of the maintenance. On roadsides or for general conservation purposes without regular cuttings, sideoats grama, weeping lovegrass and wheat grass are used.

Region 4 consists of the North Great Plains (a) and Intermountain region (b). It is also called the West Central and Intermountain region. It is a sub-humid, semi-arid and arid region. Annual yearly precipitation is 10-25 inches. In some intermountain areas yearly precipitation may drop to 5 inches. Average January and July temperatures are 5-25°F and 60-80°F, respectively. The region has the greatest diurnal or seasonal temperature variations. Grasses are subjected to the widest temperature fluctuations in the country.

Grasses. Bermuda grass can be used only in Kansas-Oklahoma region and zoysia along the southern borderline of the region. Otherwise cool humid region grasses are used:

(a) Kentucky bluegrass, (b) fine-leaf fescues (red, sheep, hard), (c) creeping and colonial bent grasses, (d) buffalo grass, (e) blue grama, and (f) wheat grasses. For lawns K. bluegrass and fine-leaf fescues are the most popular. K. bluegrass is the No. 1 grass for utility turf, including lawns. Irrigation is needed and without it buffalo grass, blue grama and wheat grass should be used. In the cooler areas, especially at higher elevations of this area, fine-leaf fescues are better adapted. Very few fine fescues are used in the southern parts of the region. In shaded areas K. bluegrass and fine fescue mixtures are adapted. For golf course putting greens, bent grasses are used. Bermuda is used very little for lawns and for golf putting greens. Zoysia is used more in the eastern portion between the 35th and 40th parallel (i.e., Oklahoma and Kansas).

Summary

Factors determining grass adaptation

1. *Climate* — temperature, moisture and light
2. *Soil properties* — some species grow well on sandy dry soils and some prefer heavy wet soils
3. *Use of grasses* — home lawns, athletic fields, playgrounds, golf courses, airfields, highways, grass for erosion control, etc.
4. *Miscellaneous other factors* — grass texture, longevity, density, susceptibility to pests.

The United States can be divided into northern and southern zones as far as grass species used for turf establishment are concerned. Again, both regions can be divided into humid and semi-arid regions. Bluegrasses, fescues and bents are the major turf grasses of the northern zone. In the semi-arid region of this zone they need regular irrigation. Zoysias, Bermuda grass, Bahia grass, St. Augustine, centipede and carpet grass are typical grasses of the southern zone. In the semi-arid region Bermuda and zoysia are the major grasses and need regular irrigation.

In the northern and southern semi-arid-arid regions without irrigation wheat grasses, buffalo grass, blue grama, weeping lovegrass can be used for low maintenance turf areas. Tall fescue, K. bluegrass, red fescue, Bermuda grass and zoysia are the major grasses of the transitional zone between the north and south.

CHAPTER 5
GRASS SEEDS

5.1 Introduction

The easiest way to establish a lawn is by seed. Seeds are formed as a result of fusion of the male cell egg (pollen from anthers of grass flower) and the female portion of the flower, (egg) pistil. After pollination a single ovule in the carpel is fertilized and develops to form an endospermic fruit (''seed'') called a caryopis. In the majority of grasses the caryopis remains enclosed within by the lemma and palea even when mature. This is apparent in fescues, ryegrasses, bents, timothy. Caryopis of wheat and rye are without lemma and palea. Thus the fruit of the grass is a ripened floret, consisting of caryopis or grain usually enclosed in the two chaffy scales, the lemma and palea (Figure 2.15). In most of the species the spikelets are several-flowered and a joint of the axis (rachilla) persists at the base of the palea and is often an important diagnostic feature. In the species having one-flowered spikelets the rachilla is lacking or merely a rudiment, as in bents for example. The palea usually has two nerves or keels. The caryopis lies in the palea with the point of attachment (hilum) toward it.

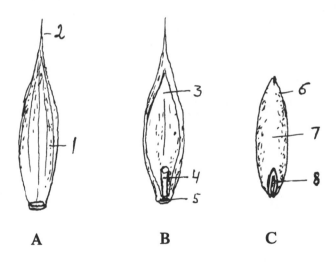

Figure 5.1 A-back view of a floret: 1-lemma, 2-awn
B-front view of a floret: 3-palea, 4-rachilla, 5-callus
C-caryopis: 6-seed coat, 7-endosperm (food reserves) and 8-embryo

The major parts of a grass seed (Figure 5.1) are: a) seed coat, b) food reserves — endosperm, and c) embryo. The embryo is a rudimentary plant with a root, stem and leaf regions in the undeveloped stage. Endosperm is the food storage for seed needed immediately after germination until a seedling develops roots and leaves and thus is able to absorb food from the soil and assimilate carbohydrates with the help of leaves.

5.2 Glossary of selected terms pertaining to seeds and seed identification.

Apex — tip, point, summit; extreme point or distal end.

Awn — bristle-like appendage arising from the lemma.

Callus — a hard protuberance or calloused area. In the grass family it is a hard swollen area at the base of the floret or point of insertion of the lemma or palea, often the hairs.

Carpel — a simple pistil, or one member of a compound pistil.

Caryopsis — a one-seed fruit with the pericarp and seed coat fused into one covering, as in corn and other grains.

Dorsal — back; relating to the back or outer surface of a part of an organ.

Fruit — a fruit is a matured (ripened) ovary of a plant, together with any intimately attached parts that developed with it from flower.

Geniculate — abruptly bent (awns).

Glabrous — without hairs or pubescence.

Glumes — the pair of bracts at the base of a spikelet in grasses.

Lemma — the outer bract of the flower of grasses, sometimes referred to as the flowering glume.

Nerves — ribs or veins in the chaffy structures of grasses.

Ovary — the part of the pistil that contains ovule or ovules; it ripens to form the fruit.

Ovule — the body within the ovary of the flower that becomes the seed after fertilization and development.

Palea — the tiny upper bract which with the lemma encloses the flower in grasses.

Pericarp — the covering of a seed that is derived from the ovary wall. It may be thin and intimately attached to the seed coat as in a kernel of corn; fleshy, as in berries, or hard and dry as in pods and capsules.

Pistil — the seed-bearing organ (female) of the flower, composed of stigma, style, and ovary.

Rachilla — a short stalk arising at the base of the seed and directed upwards.

Sinus — the space between the margin of lemma above the point of attachment to the rachilla.

Ventral — front; relating to the inner face of an organ; opposite of dorsal.

5.3 Seed descriptions (29,47)

1. Tall fescue and meadow fescue

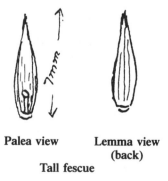

Palea view   Lemma view
(back)

Tall fescue

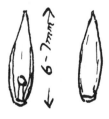

Palea view   Lemma view
(back)

Meadow fescue

Figure 5.2 Tall and meadow fescue seeds

Tall fescue has its lemma long-pointed or short awned, rarely awnless. The lemma of the meadow fescue is short-pointed, awnless, glabrous. In harvesting and milling awns of tall fescue may be broken off. The rachilla and callus of both are similar. *Both fescues have a club-shaped rachilla.*

In tall fescue the surface lemma and palea is granular, darker in color, and pubescent, whereas in meadow fescue it is glabrous, straw-colored and glazed.

2. Ryegrasses

Seeds of ryegrasses and the tall and meadow fescues are rather similar but can be distinguished by the character of the rachilla, shape of the seed and the position of the hairs on the keels of the palea.

The rachilla of ryegrass is flattened usually with an angular tip. The apex of the rachilla is not expanded and lies flat against the palea. In fescues the rachilla is cylindrical; the apex is expanded into a disk and tends to stand away from the palea.

Perennial ryegrass seed is narrowly oblong, not markedly thickened through the middle and the palea is not transversely wrinkled. Lemma is awnless and 6-7mm long.

In annual (Italian) ryegrass the lemma is awned, occasionally awnless and 6-7mm long.

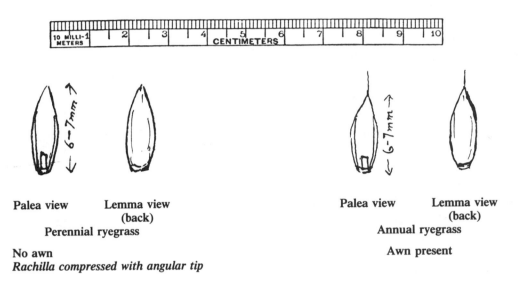

Palea view   Lemma view   Palea view   Lemma view
         (back)   (back)
Perennial ryegrass   Annual ryegrass

No awn   Awn present
Rachilla compressed with angular tip

Figure 5.3 Ryegrass seeds

3. Red fescues, creeping and chewing

The seeds of red fescues are about ⅔ the length of ryegrass and ½ the width. Awns are present. The lemma and palea surfaces may be glabrous or pubescent. The lemma margins are slightly inrolled over the palea.

Seeds of creeping and chewing fescues are too similar to be identified with certainty in all cases.

Red fescue   Sheep fescue

Figure 5.4 Red and sheep fescue seeds

4. Sheep and hard fescues

Seeds are similar to red fescue seeds but slightly smaller in size, duller and more opaque in appearance. It may be possible to identify bulk samples but not individual seeds.

5. Bluegrasses

The seed of bluegrasses are equally three-sided in cross sections, pointed at both ends, with a shallow groove or sinus on one side where the rachilla is located. The grooved surface is called the palea and the opposite sides together make up the lemma which usually has veins or nerves running lengthwise. Poas have five-nerved lemmas, keeled along the heavy mid-nerve and often finely pubescent. The dark brown caryopsis is compressed laterally with a blunt keel on the back above the embryo and a more or less pronounced groove on the opposite side.

Palea view   Lemma view
                 (back)
Kentucky bluegrass

Grain broadest in the
middle of lemma

Palea view   Lemma view
                 (back)
Canada bluegrass

Grain broadest in the
upper half of lemma

Figure 5.5 Kentucky bluegrass and Canada bluegrass seeds

In Kentucky bluegrass varieties, except Merion, rough bluegrass, and annual bluegrass, the intermediate nerves of the lemma are distinct to the base. In Canada bluegrass and Merion K. bluegrass, the intermediate nerves of the lemma are lacking or obscure.

Texture and color of lemma as well as presence of hairs on the edge of palea, may serve to distinguish species and varieties of bluegrasses.

6. Bents and redtop

Spikelets are one-flowered, seeds very small, 2mm or less in length, and rachilla obscure or lacking. Commercial seed lots have tendency to be hulled. Infrequent presence of awns variously attached and twisted; palea may be absent, much reduced or well developed; grains are soft or hard; and lemma is dull, shiny, or translucent — all these are characteristics used to separate species and varieties of *Agrostis*. They are the most difficult to separate of the grasses.

Determination of individual *Agrostis* spp. seeds requires 40X magnification. Bulk distinctions can be made using a 10-power binocular microscope. Seeds of bents and redtop are similar.

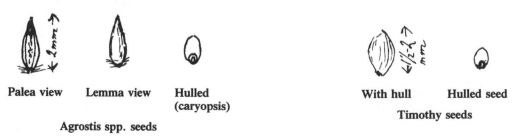

Palea view   Lemma view   Hulled
                            (caryopsis)

Agrostis spp. seeds

With hull   Hulled seed

Timothy seeds

Figure 5.6 Agrostis spp. and timothy seeds

7. Timothy

Spikelets are one-flowered, seed about 2mm long, oval in shape, with surface reticulated, and rachilla lacking. In commercial lots some hulled seeds are usually present.

8. Orchard grass

The lemma is compressed laterally and curved to one side toward the top, ciliate on the keel, lightly five-nerved, short awned, and 7-8mm long, including awn. It has a light straw color and the grain (caryopsis) is soft.

Palea view

Figure 5.7 Orchard grass seed

9. Bermuda grass

Side view   Palea view

Figure 5.8 Bermuda grass seed

Spikelets are one-flowered and seed is a spikelet without glumes or a hulled caryopsis. Florets are compressed laterally with the dorsal side arched, and the ventral side nearly straight. Lemmas are firm, and the upper half of the keel nerve is pubescent. The floret of common Bermuda grass is about 2mm long and ¾-1mm wide. The caryopsis is light brown and the apex pointed. Caryopsis is 1-1½mm long and ½mm wide.

10. Zoysia

Zoysia spikelets are one-flowered. First glume is lacking and the second glume is stiff, hard and lustrous, short awned or awn pointed and completely infolds the thin lemma and palea. Thus the seed unit is a spikelet. Z. japonica seeds are broadly ovate, short pointed or short awned, dull brownish, commonly with a purplish tinge, 3½-4mm long, and 1½mm wide. Z. matrella seeds are narrowly elliptic or lance shaped and short awned, bright yellowish, straw-colored, 3-3½mm long, and 1mm wide.

Zoysia japonica   *Zoysia matrella*

Figure 5.9 *Zoysia japonica* seed   Figure 5.10 *Zoysia matrella* seed

11. Centipede

Caryopsis   Inflorescence joint

Figure 5.11 Centipede grass seed

Centipede belongs to the sorghum tribe. As with other sorghums, inflorescence of centipede breaks up into joints. The length of the joint is 3-3½mm and the width is 1½mm. The glume of the fertile sessile spikelet is smooth, glabrous, broadly winged at the summit and with 5 to 6 projections on the margins toward the base. The entire joint is rarely present in commercial seed and the seed unit is usually a hulled caryopsis. The caryopsis is oval, flattened, dorsal ventrally, reddish brown and finely striate, 2mm long, and 1-1½mm wide.

12. Carpet grass

The single-flowered spikelets of the carpet grass disarticulate (disjoint) below the glume and the fertile floret with its persisting glume and sterile lemma is the unit called the seed. The first glume is lacking and the sterile lemma does not bear a sterile palea. Fertile florets are without the attached glumes and sterile lemmas are not commonly found in cleaned seed.

Axonopus affinis and *A. compressus* are very similar. Spikelets are 2-3mm long, sparsely long hairs along the margins, midnerve of glume and sterile lemma are wanting or faint. Glume and sterile lemma are obtuse or short-pointed, equally or slightly exceeding the grain.

Palea view
A. affinis

Palea view
A. furcatus

Figure 5.12 Carpet grass seeds

St. Augustine grass *(Stenotaphrum secundatum)* grass seeds are similar in appearance with carpet grass seeds. First glume is present, short, spikelet is 4-5cm long, and the second glume and sterile lemma are equal, glabrous and long-pointed, exceeding the fertile lemma; the midnerve is obscure or lacking.

14. Bahia grass

Spikelets are one-flowered. The first glume is usually wanting, second glume and sterile lemma are about equal, thin and papery; the fertile lemma is stiff and hard. Papery glumes are not persistent and the fertile lemma is strongly convex on the back. The lemma is fertile, oval, stiff, smooth and glossy, often slightly wrinkled transversely and 3-nerved.

Common Bahia has a spikelet length of 3½mm with a width of 2½-2¾mm.

Pensacola has a spikelet length of 3mm with a 1½-2mm width.

Lemma view   **Palea view**   **Side view**   **Caryopsis**
Bahia grass

Figure 5.13 Bahia grass seed

15. Buffalo grass

Buffalo grass hulled seed

Figure 5.14

Buffalo grass is a dioecious plant. The pistilate spikelets are borne in hard whitish burlike heads. These burs are called seed. Each bur consists of 2-6 spikelets held together by a thickened base and surrounded by thick, hard overlapping second glumes, each of which terminates in three rigid, usually green-tipped, accuminate lobes. As a rule not all of the spikelets in a bur contain caryopsis. Seed samples sometimes consist of caryopsis that have been hulled by processing. A hulled seed is brownish, 2½-3mm long, oval or broadly elliptic and markedly thicker at one end.

16. Fairway wheat grass

The lemma is smooth, glabrous or minutely pubscent and compressed laterally throughout. Hairs on the keels of the palea are wide-spaced, short and stout. Lemmas are awned. Awns are about ½ the length of the lemma. Lemma length is 5-6mm, excluding awn and the width is ¾mm.

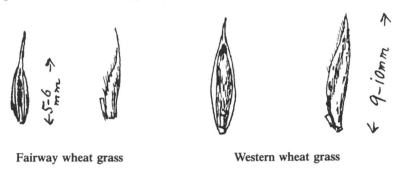

Fairway wheat grass   Western wheat grass

Figure 5.15 Wheat grass seeds

17. Western wheat grass

The lemma is glabrous or sparingly scabrous on nerves toward the top. Lemma is rounded or slightly flattened on the back; if keeled only slightly so. Rachilla hairs are short and oppressed. Lemma is narrowly lance-shaped or elliptic. Sinus is V-shaped, occasionally U-shaped. The rachilla flares out at the top and lies against the keels of the palea which are often grooved down the center. The apex is deeply V-notched and lemmas are 9 to 10mm (excluding awn) long and 1½mm wide.

18. Grama

A spikelet consists of one fertile floret with rudiments of one or more florets above it, the entire spikelet falling from the glumes which remain on the rachis. Lemma of the fertile floret is keeled on the back, glabrous or sparingly long — pubescent at the callus and along the sharply keeled back, lustrous lateral nerves exerted as short awns. Length (excluding awns) is 4mm and the width is ½mm. Caryopsis is thick and 3-angled.

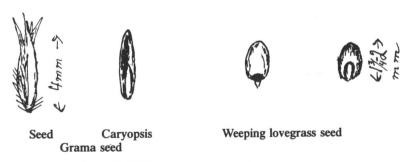

Seed   Caryopsis   Weeping lovegrass seed
      Grama seed

Figure 5.16 Grama and weeping lovegrass

19. Weeping lovegrass

The spikelets of weeping lovegrass are several-flowered, disarticulating above the glumes. The lemmas are 3-nerved, the lateral nerves sometimes obscure. Lemmas and paleas are rather delicate and easily detached so that processed seed consists entirely of a hulled caryopsis. Caryopsis is oval, light brownish, smooth or striate and the embryo areas are black. Length is 1¾ to 2mm and the width is 1mm or less.

5.4 Seed quality

Major turf grasses are perennial plants forming a lasting turf area. Establishing any turf area is a very expensive proposition. Seedbed preparation, fertilization, liming, seeding and maintenance of new seedlings until the first mowing adds up to $3,000.00 or more to establish an acre of home lawn. Seed usually costs around 5% of this total. Therefore, in establishing any turf area the seed used should be of the best quality.

Seed, being the product of sexual fertilization, have the mixed heredity of both parents. Seeds may inherit some properties from the mother and some from the father plant, i.e., seeds of one generation may differ somewhat from the other. In using seed for propagation of turf one may expect some minor unpredictable variations.

Kentucky bluegrass is an apomictic plant, i.e., seeds can be formed from mother cells without sexual fertilization. Because of this characteristic Kentucky bluegrass varieties are easier to keep pure and uniform than those species which are reproduced by pollination.

The Federal Seed Act and the State Laws regulate sale, transportation and distribution of seed. The Federal Seed Act, enacted by the United States Congress in 1939, applies to imported seed and to seed in interstate commerce. State seed laws regulate sales, transportation and distribution of seed in the state. There is considerable variation in detail among the various states in seed laws. Normally, seed laws and regulations require that seed sold in the state should meet minimum quality requirements and should be labeled.

The most important feature describing any seed quality may be listed: 1) species, variety, strain; 2) % purity; 3) % germination; 4) % weeds. Normally, seed laws and regulations require that the above mentioned quality features must be indicated on the labels. The label must include (in mixtures), fine textured and coarse textured grass seeds. Seed tagging regulations vary between various states in the Union.

Species, variety and strain

It is most important to select the right species of grass in establishing a lawn or any turf area. The factors of adaptation that should be considered in selecting grass species have been already discussed. Of course, the best varieties or strains of the best species should be chosen. The term variety denotes an assemblage of cultivated individuals which are distinguished by any characters (morphological, physiological, cytological, chemical, or others) significant for the purposes of turf culture, and which, when reproduced (sexually or asexually) retain their distinguishing features.

Seed must be adapted to the area — it must be winter hardy and resistant to common local diseases. If it is to be seeded as a mixture, it must be compatible with the other varieties used in the mixture. A poor choice here can make all other standards meaningless. Seed growers and scientists of experiment stations of various states are working to develop better adapted grasses to climatic, and management conditions and grasses that are resistant to pests. One should use the most suitable variety of the best grass species.

At present Oregon State is the major world producer of turf grass seeds (bluegrass, bents, fescues, ryegrasses). Other producers are Denmark, Netherlands, New Zealand and Canada.

So-called *foundation* seed is a primary source of seed of a genetically identified variety from which all increases are made, (i.e. foundation seed is seed developed and produced under the supervision of the breeder himself, the certifying agency or the agricultural experiment station). Foundation seed is normally released for surveillance to other growers whose crop is called *registered* seed. Registered seed is the progeny of foundation seed that is so handled as to maintain satisfactory genetic identity and purity and that has been approved and certified by the certifying agency. In *certified* seed production, field and after harvest seed is inspected and the tag gives a guarantee that (genetically), it is of indicated variety, and origin but does not guarantee purity or germination.

Purity and weed seeds

Purity is the percentage of pure seed by weight of the kind named. When the variety name is also given, the pure seed represents the proportion that is pure seed of that variety. If we have an indication on the label that the seeds are, e.g. creeping red fescue seeds with purity 92 percent, one should know that in a bag weighing 100 lbs., 92 lbs. are red fescue seeds of the creeping strain. In this case the rest or so-called impurities, i.e., 8 lbs. or 8% by weight may be made up of: (a) other crop seeds: (b) inert matter (chaff, dirt, sand, pieces of broken seed, etc.); and (c) weed seeds.

The purity expressed in percent is not as important as the kind of impurities. Seed which is 99% pure may be highly undesirable if 1% are noxious weed seeds. Seed 90% pure may be satisfactory if the 10% impurities are not noxious weeds. "Other crop seeds" include also: bent grass, tall fescue, redtop, rough bluegrass and ryegrass. These species in some mixtures may be objectionable and can be considered as weeds. The percentage of weed seeds include seeds of noxious weeds, even though the presence of noxious weed seeds usually has to be shown separately on the label.

Noxious weeds are plants defined under the State Law as being particularly injurious. The name and occurrence of seeds per pound of the contents of the containers is shown on the label. In most states it is illegal to sell seed that contains seeds of certain noxious weeds. The Massachusetts Seed Law lists the following weed seeds as noxious.

a. Prohibited noxious weed seeds:

Canada thistle (*Cirsium arvense*)
Field bindweed (*Convolvulus arvensis*)
Quack grass (*Agropyron repens*)

b. Restricted noxious weed seeds:

Dodder (*Cuscuta* spp.)
Horse nettle (*Solanum carolinense*)
Wild mustard (*Brassica* spp., including *B. Juncea, B. Kaber, B. nigra*)
Wild garlic and wild onion (*Allium* spp.)
Perennial saw-thistle (*Sonchus arvensis*)
Corn cockle (*Agrosthema githago*)
Buckhorn plantain (*Plantago lanceolata*)
Wild radish (*Raphanus raphanistrum*)
Bedstraw (*Galium* spp.)
Annual bluegrass (*Poa annua*)

Germination

The germination percentage represents the proportion of the pure seed that will germinate. A label stating germination 90% does not mean that 90% of the contents of the bag will germinate but that 90% of pure seeds present in the bag are expected to germinate. This is termed "pure live seed".

For a seed to germinate it needs *moisture*, suitable *temperature* and *air*. The seed absorbs water and if other conditions are suitable the cells of the embryo become active. Cell division starts and the seed germinates. Some seeds may be viable but dormant. *Dormancy* is a resting stage of a seed. It may be caused by many reasons. Sometimes the seed coat is impervious to water and the seed does not germinate. Soaking or scratching the seed coat may be helpful to get the seed germinated. There may also be physiological or biochemical reasons for dormancy, e.g., seeds may carry inhibitors which have to undergo chemical modification before the embryo is able to sprout. Seed testing laboratories grow seeds under favorable conditions to measure germination. A number of conditions affect the performance in the field, as compared to the laboratory, e.g., the size of the seeds, the condition of the seedbed, the natural time taken for germination, and the vigor of the seedlings.

Germination is the quality of seeds that is most certain to change. The germination of seeds that are stored in places of high moisture and high temperature may drop in a few weeks. The same seeds stored in dry, cool rooms may lose very little germination in several months. The laws governing the labeling of agricultural seeds requires that the date of germination test be indicated on the label. The laws usually prevent the sale of seed with an old germination test. Most laws allow 9 months, i.e., germination determinations should be done at least every nine months. The Federal Seed Act prohibits interstate shipment if the test is more than 6 months old.

Other things being equal, the heavier the seeds of a grass, the better the germination and the more vigorous the young seedlings can be expected. There is more food in the endosperm of the heavier seeds than in the lighter ones. Seed sizes vary greatly among the grass species. The larger and heavier the seed of a species, the fewer seeds there are in each pound or bushel. The larger the seeds the more seed one has to use in order to get the same number of seedlings — plants per square foot or acre. In Table 5.1 the data of average seed number per pound and the average quality (germination, purity) for the major grass seeds used in turf production are presented.

The term "pure live seed" or "real value" is used often to express the quality of seeds, even though it is not usually shown on the label. "Pure live seed" is the percentage of the contents of a bag of seeds that is pure seed that will germinate. This value is determined by multiplying the percentage of pure seed by the percentage of germination and dividing by 100, e.g., if purity is 90% and germination is 80%, the "pure live seed" will be:

$$\frac{90 \times 80}{100} = 72\%$$

This means that 72% of the contents of the package consists of pure seed that can produce plants.

5.5 Seed treatments

Seeded grasses can be susceptible to attack by a wide variety of fungi. The grasses may fail to appear above the ground due to "damping off", seed rot or dying just after emergence. Various *disinfectants* and *fungicides* can be used to treat or coat seeds before seeding. Damping off is caused by soil borne fungi and therefore seed disinfection cannot eliminate these pathogens surrounding the seed and seedlings. In practice, damping off of grass seedlings seldom creates significant damages. It usually is not difficult to get good healthy grass seedlings without treatments. In cases where seedling is done during hot humid periods, seedling injury may be possible. Use thiram or captan against soil-borne diseases to help prevent this.

Sprouting grass seed inside and then seeding outside may hasten seedling development somewhat. Pre-sprouting is usually done by mixing seed with damp soil, peat, sand, vermiculite or soaked and kept in polyethylene bags. Of course, presprouted seed must be sown within a few days no matter what soil or weather conditions are outdoors. Seeding presprouted wet seed can create handling difficulties. The practicability of this treatment for wide use is questioned.

Treating seed with plant *growth regulators* such as gibberellins has been investigated. So far no practical methods have been developed. Using seed of the best quality and of the well adapted varieties in a well prepared seedbed is still the most practical way to establish a lawn.

Sample label required for turf seed mixtures

F. M. Crook Seed Company
26 Orchard Street
Hadley, Massachusetts 01035

No. 5 Lawn Seed Mixture

Lot 27-14

TREATED WITH THIRAM
DO NOT USE FOR FOOD, FEED OR OIL PURPOSES

Purity	Component	Germination
Fine textured grasses:		
37.50%	Pennlawn red fescue	80%
20.72%	Kentucky bluegrass	82%
17.04%	Merion K. bluegrass	84%
Coarse kinds:		
15.79%	Perennial ryegrass	85%
5.25%	Redtop	91%
Other ingredients:		
0.28%	Weed seeds	
3.20%	Inert matter	
0.22%	Other crop seeds	

Restricted noxious weeds:

Contains 22 buckhorn plantain seeds per pound

Tested June 1982

Net weight 5 pounds

Table 5.1 Quality characteristics of major turf grass seeds

Grass	Seed per pound	Average		Seeding rate lb/1,000 sq ft
		Purity %	Germination	
COOL-SEASON GRASSES				
Bent grass, colonial	8,000,000	95	90	0.5-1
Bent grass, creeping	8,000,000	95	85	0.5-1
Bent grass, velvet	9,000,000	90	85	0.5-1
Bluegrass, Canada	2,200,000	90	85	1-2
Bluegrass, Kentucky	2,200,000	90	80	1-2
Bluegrass, rough	2,500,000	90	80	1-2
Fescue, red	500,000	95	80	3-4
Fescue, sheep	600,000	90	80	3-4
Fescue, tall	200,000	95	90	5-8
Redtop	5,000,000	92	90	1-2
Ryegrass, annual	220,000	98	90	4-8
Ryegrass, perennial	220,000	98	90	4-8
Wheat grass, fairway	300,000	90	85	0.5-1
Wheat grass, western	125,000	85	80	1-2
WARM-SEASON GRASSES				
Bahia grass	200,000	72	70	3-5
Bermuda grass (hulled)	1,800,000	97	87	1-2
Buffalo grass (treated)	290,000	85	50	0.5-2
Carpet grass	1,300,000	92	90	3-5
Centipede	400,000	50	70	0.3-1
Grama, blue (unhulled)	800,000	40	75	1-2
Lovegrass, weeping	1,500,000	95	85	1-2
Zoysia	1,300,000	95	50	1-2

5.6 Seed mixtures

On any turf area comparatively large numbers of miscellaneous plants will be found but usually over 80-90 percent will be made up of one, two or three grass species. Also a complicated lawn grass mixture, consisting of many species, seeded in an area would finally show two or three grasses dominant in the sward; only the best adapted species would survive. Competition between seedlings is a continuous process. Plants compete for plant nutrients, light, water and space. Competition is for the growth factor which is in minimum. The principle of plant establishment and competition is that the first plant to occupy any area tends to exclude others. Keenest competition occurs when competing plants are alike in their needs for environmental factors. Therefore, one would expect fiercer competition between various varieties of K. bluegrass than between K. bluegrass and red fescue in a turf. Plants which are successful in competition demonstrate: (a) ready and uniform seed germination under adverse conditions, (b) rapid development of seedlings and large photosynthetic surface, (c) a large number of stomata and (d) a good root system with many fibrous roots near the surface (32). The turf grass seedling that establishes first has optimal surroundings for growth. Due to management practices or the plant itself these environmental conditions change, e.g. during a drought period seedlings with better root systems have a better chance for survival. Competition is a rather complex phenomena and it is difficult to pinpoint which factor was decisive in the establishment and survival of a seedling. In selecting a grass or grasses in a mixture, environmental as well as management practices should be taken into consideration.

Some 30-50 years ago, it was not uncommon to use complicated mixtures for agricultural pastures, meadows or turf areas. Advancement in agricultural sciences and better knowledge of grasses has shown that the simpler mixtures composed of species suited to definite requirements are best. In cases where soil and seedbed conditions are uniform and maintenance can be well adjusted, a single turf grass species may be advantageous to use (monoculture, monostand). Mixtures (polyculture, polystand) are advantageous when the area is large and not uniform with regard to soil texture or shading conditions. In that case, using the proper mixtures, one grass will become dominant under drier conditions, another under wet or more shady conditions. Using large numbers of species in a mixture for safety's sake may run one into trouble because in some cases the least desirable grass may survive, making patches and thus creating an unevenness in the sward. The seed mixture must, therefore, be simple and it must consist of species which are capable of intermingling to form a uniform sward. Matching the texture and color of grasses used in a mixture is desirable to avoid a spotty appearance. K. bluegrass and red fescue blend or melt well and produce a good looking uniform sod. On the other hand K. bluegrass and ryegrass don't melt well because of leaf color and different growth pattern.

Northern cool region

In the northern cool humid region (Fig. 4.1) the most widely used mixture is that of Kentucky bluegrass and red fescue. These two turf grasses blend excellently and are widely used in various proportions in home lawns, especially where a wide range of soil and environmental conditions exist.

The following is suggested as a guide in selecting a lawn mixture for a northern cool region wide range of conditions.

I.	Grasses	% by weight	seeding rate
	Kentucky bluegrass	40 to 70%	4 lb/1,000 sq. ft.
	Red fescues (creeping, chewing)	60 to 30%	

If light sandy soils, a shady area and poor maintenance conditions are anticipated, a higher percentage of red fescue (within limits indicated) should be used; and contrary to this, if area is sunny and maintenance good, K. bluegrass should be favored and even 10 to 30% of K. bluegrass can be substituted for by using Merion K. bluegrass.

For sunny areas plus good soil and maintenance conditions, Merion K. bluegrass alone or in mixtures with other K. bluegrasses (common, Newport, Prato, Park, etc). A seeding rate of 2 lb. per 1,000 sq. ft. is suggested.

The blending of several bluegrass varieties: strains which possess different plant growth, leaf type, color, thatch, and disease characteristics — is becoming more common. A blend is suited to a broader area of adaptation and disease tolerance is better than using a single variety. Only where lawns can be carefully managed: fertilizer, watered, and constantly protected from disease infections — will a single variety or strain produce as good a lawn as would normally be expected from a mixture.

Mixture II for shaded areas with poor drainage is suggested in the northern cool region.

II.	Grasses	% by weight	Seeding rate
	Kentucky bluegrass	20 to 30%	
	Red fescues (creeping, chewing)	70 to 40%	4 lb/1,000 sq. ft.
	Rough bluegrass	10 to 30%	

Decrease percentages of grasses in mixtures I and II as shown and add 15 to 20% of ryegrass seeds under the following conditions:

a) area is sloping and subject to erosion
b) poor time for seeding, such as mid-summer and
c) dry, hot weather conditions are anticipated without irrigation.

Ryegrasses, whether annual or perennial, are short-lived grasses. They are characterized by quick germination and rapid growth and thus may be helpful in establishing a lawn under the above mentioned adverse conditions. Because of their rapid growth they can be competitive with other fine turf seeded species and therefore the proportion of ryegrasses should be limited to 20 percent by weight of the total mixture. Ryegrasses can be used for temporary cover to prevent erosion, combat weeds or add organic matter to the soil at a 4-8 lb. rate per 1,000 sq. ft. This type of lawn is generally turned under prior to establishing a permanent lawn. Annual (Italian) ryegrass is usually used, but perennial ryegrass can also be used. There is also a so-called common ryegrass which is a mixture of annual and perennial ryegrass. Annual ryegrass is a larger plant and produces heavier growth than perennial ryegrass.

Redtop can be used in place of ryegrass in seed mixtures as a companion plant for a quick temporary cover. It is a short-lived, fast growing grass. Seeds are very small and should not exceed 3-5 percent in mixtures.

K. bluegrass, red fescue and bents are the so-called *fine* turf grasses. Tall fescue, redtop, annual ryegrass, timothy and orchard grass are *coarse* grasses. Perennial ryegrass is of intermediate type. Some new varieties of perennial ryegrass are finer in texture and could be considered as fine grasses. Coarse grasses are not suited to lawn grass mixtures for permanent stand. They make excellent cover where rapid establishment is essential, where coarse texture is satisfactory and where minimum maintenance will be given, such as highway banks, dams, etc.

Colonial bent grass is a typical cool and humid region grass which is adapted and used as a lawn turf grass in areas west of the Cascade Mountains in the western parts of Washington and Oregon. Although bent grasses do not melt too well with K. bluegrass or red fescue, in this region even mixtures with red fescue are recommended for lawns (13). The high rainfall, coupled with acid and cool soils provide an environment that is ideal for colonial bents. The Atlantic shore areas of New England are regions where bent grass can be used in lawn mixtures (37). Bent grasses require close, frequent mowing, thatch control and generally intense maintenance practices.

For *hard use, heavy duty,* utility turf in northern cool humid regions: (a) tall fescue mixtures with K. bluegrass and red fescue, (b) K. bluegrass alone, or (c) mixtures of 2-3 varieties of K. bluegrass can be used (Table 5.2). Tall fescue is a coarse, deep rooted and not demanding turf grass. In northern regions it can be used for heavy duty areas as well as for low maintenance, secondary use turf (highway banks, roadsides) alone or together with other grasses. Tall fescue for heavy duty areas like athletic fields, playgrounds, etc., should be seeded in pure stands or at least 70%, well fertilized (3-4 lbs. N/1,000 sq. ft.) and maintained at 2-3 inch height. Its coarse texture will be reduced considerably under this maintenance. Tall fescue should not be used in regular lawn mixtures. It persists and makes clumpy, non-uniform lawns. In backyards where they are used as playgrounds, it could be used but it should be the dominant grass (over 70%) and thickly seeded (4-8 lb./1,000 sq. ft.).

With irrigation, grasses adapted to the cool humid region are used in the northern Great Plains and intermountain region (Fig. 4.1). In Idaho, Washington and other northwestern states even red fescue alone is grown as a lawn grass. It starts.earlier than K. bluegrass in the spring and is a tougher grass that tolerates shade better.

In Table 5.2 some turf grass seed mixtures for northern humid region are presented.

Table 5.2 Some examples of turf grass seed mixtures for northern cool region

	% by weight	Seeding rate
A. Home lawns:		
1. Wide range of conditions:		
a. Kentucky bluegrass	25	
Merion Kentucky bluegrass	25	2-4 lb/1,000 sq. ft.
Red fescue	50	
b. Kentucky bluegrass	30	
Merion Kentucky bluegrass	10	4 lb/1,000 sq. ft.
Red fescue	40	
Perennial ryegrass	20	
2. For better conditions:		
c. Kentucky bluegrass	60	2 lb/1,000 sq. ft.
Merion Kentucky bluegrass	40	
d. Merion Kentucky bluegrass	100	2 lb/1,000 sq. ft.
3. Shaded areas:		
Normal soil moisture conditions-		
e. Kentucky bluegrass	40	2-4 lb/1,000 sq. ft.
Red fescue	60	
Poor drainage conditions-		
f. Kentucky bluegrass	25	
Red fescue	50	2-4 lb/1,000 sq. ft.
Rough bluegrass	25	
B. Heavy duty areas (playgrounds, athletic fields, parks):		
g. Kentucky 31 tall fescue	80	5-7 lb/1,000 sq. ft.
Merion Kentucky bluegrass	20	
h. Kentucky 31 tall fescue	80	
Kentucky bluegrass	10	5-7 lb/1,000 sq. ft.
Red fescue	10	
i. Merion Kentucky bluegrass or blends of 2-3 K. bluegrass varieties	100	2 lb/1,000 sq. ft.
C. Sloping areas (slopes, banks, dams, highways):		
j. Kentucky 31 tall fescue	75	
Perennial ryegrass	25	5-7 lb/1,000 sq. ft.
Also No. "h" is satisfactory		
D. For temporary use (summer cover, erosion):		
k. Ryegrass (best)	100	5 lb/1,000 sq. ft.
l. Buckwheat	100	5 lb/1,000 sq. ft.
m. Oats	100	5 lb/1,000 sq. ft.
n. Rye (for winter cover)	100	5 lb/1,000 sq. ft.

Transition zone

In the transition zone (Fig. 4.1) neither cool-season nor warm-season grasses are well adapted. Here northern grasses survive warm long summers but usually do not produce an attractive lawn all year round. On the other hand, southern warm-season grasses grow during the warm summer months and with the first frost turn brown and stay dormant until the next spring. Mixtures of warm- and cool-season grasses can be used. In September, northern grasses can be seeded in an established, warm-season sod. On the other hand in places where cool-season grass sod is established, warm-season grasses may be introduced as plugs/sprigs in May-June. K. bluegrass with Bermuda grass for sport fields or with zoysia for lawns is preferred. Tall fescue with Bermuda grass or with Bahia grass are also used. Generally, Bermuda grass for sport fields and zoysia grass for home lawns are preferred. In such a mixture matching the texture and color of grasses is desirable to avoid a spotty appearance. In Kansas (22) Meyer zoysia and Merion K. bluegrass are considered the best mixture available. These two grasses are most complimentary in texture, color and growth habits. In practice, mixtures of cool-season grasses and warm-season grasses in the transition zone do not produce good turf. Due to cold conditions for southern grasses and too warm conditions for northern grasses, turf thins out and degenerates.

Tall fescue is rather well adapted for transition zone lawns (21, 48). It is especially suited for larger lawns and parks where a uniform wear-resistant cover is more important than very fine texture. Tall fescue is a drought and high temperature tolerant grass and stands well in warm seasons and can be considered, even in the deep South, as a turf grass for playgrounds, athletic fields and heavy duty areas. In the South most of the northern fine turf perennials like bluegrasses, bents or red fescues, turn into winter annuals, but tall fescue stays as a perennial grass. If clipped closely, it forms a very dense, tough, deep rooted turf. Tall fescue should be seeded alone at 4-8 lbs. per 1,000 sq. ft. rate, well fertilized and cut at 2-2.5 inches. Of course, in the transition zone pure warm-season grasses (Bermuda, zoysia) or pure cool-season grasses are widely used.

Warm humid regions

Most of the southern grasses are propagated vegetatively but some of them can be propagated by seed also, e.g., Bahia grass, Bermuda grass, carpet grass, centipede grass, buffalo grass, blue grama, weeping lovegrass and some species of zoysias. Mixtures of grasses are usually used throughout the Central and Northern latitudes of the United States. Single species of grasses are more often planted in the southern than in the northern part of the country.

The most widely used grasses in the warm humid regions are Bermuda grass, zoysias, St. Augustine grass, centipede grass, Bahia grass and carpet grass. All of them are perennial grasses. Under intensive maintenance conditions in sunny areas, improved fine leaf Bermuda grass (Sunturf, Tifgreen, Tifway or Tifdwarf) produce fine high quality turf. Under less intensive maintenance conditions common Bermuda grass, zoysia grass and St. Augustine grass should be used. Under low maintenance conditions Bahia grass and centipede grass are best suited. Bahia grass, especially, is adapted to rough turf like industrial areas, roadsides and airfields. For such a turf common Bermuda grass is widely used also. Bermuda grass and zoysia grass are wear tolerant plants and need a good water supply for normal growth. In shaded areas St. Augustine grass and zoysias are the best. In northern parts of the region, especially in the transition zone, tall fescue is used. It tolerates shaded areas well. Bermuda grass and carpet grass are the least shade tolerant southern grasses.

In the South where winters are mild, northern grasses can be used as temporary winter grasses. During the summer months they die or may survive and thus they can be carried into the next fall-winter season. This is possible in Piedmont. The use of cool-season grasses in the South for winter cover of southern turf is called winter *overseeding*. Bermuda grass turf is suited for winter overseeding. Dense growing, aggressive southern grasses such as St. Augustine grass, zoysia grass, centipede grass, Bahia grass, carpet grass are not too compatible with other grasses and are much less used for overseedings. In these winter overseedings it is important that in the fall or spring transition from one to another dominant specie should be fast and smooth. Experience shows that using not a single specie of cool-season grasses but rather a mixture of them does a better job. For general turf overseedings ryegrass, K. bluegrass, bent grasses, red fescue and rough bluegrass can be used. For sports Bermuda grass turf overseeding K. bluegrass, ryegrass and tall fescue should be preferred.

Mixtures in northern parts of the southern warm region and in the transition zone can be used. In the northern Piedmont, mixtures of 2-3 K. bluegrass varieties plus up to 5% of redtop are used in sunny areas. In shaded areas (a) K. bluegrass with red fescue and redtop, (b) K. bluegrass with tall fescue, or (c) tall fescue alone are preferred. Mixtures of southern grasses and northern grasses that would persist — one dominating in winter and another in summer — is wishful and overseeding would not be needed. Tests indicate that some varieties of Bermuda grass with bent grasses are encouraging.

Semi-arid and arid regions

Southern and northern sub-humid, semi-arid and arid regions include adaptation regions 3 and 4 (Fig. 4.1). In most cases under intensive maintenance and irrigation (athletic fields, model lawns, golf course tees, greens) perennial cool- or warm-season grasses are used. Without irrigation for low maintenance lawns, road-sides, roughs of golf courses, airports, ski slopes, wheat grasses and, more in the southwest, buffalo grass with blue grama and weeping lovegrass can be used. Common Bermuda grass, as a deep-rooted plant, can be included in southern areas with better deeper soils.

5.7 Some practical hints

Researchers at agricultural experiment stations are working toward developing new and better varieties of turf grasses. The best varieties available should be used. Therefore, in choosing a grass or mixture of grasses, consult your county agricultural agent or your state agricultural experiment station. Examine the analysis tags on the seed container before you buy.

It is best if one decides what seeds and in what proportion he is going to seed and then buys the needed seeds separately, mixes them, and then seeds. This is practical, especially when larger turf areas need to be seeded. Buying seeds separately is cheaper.

There are many good ready packed lawn seed mixtures available on the market. Their value depends on the proportion of well adapted permanent grass seeds present. When small amounts are needed, these prepacked mixtures should satisfy any discriminating buyer.

5.8 Seeding rates

Seed quality and size usually determines the amount of seeds needed for an area unit. Too much seed slows grass seedling development. Because of excessive seedling competition, seedings cannot develop until some factor, usually disease, thins out the population so that surviving individuals have enough space to grow. On the other hand, too little seed results in thin stands with bare spaces between. While grass slowly fills in, the area is open for weed invasion. Madison (25) showed that the best turf establishes and forms sod which starts with fewer seedlings than final numbers of plants and reaches into mature density by growth and tillering (Fig. 5.17). His results indicate that 1-2 lbs. of Kentucky bluegrass and 1 lb. of bents are the most practical rates of seed to use for 1,000 sq. ft. areas in turf establishment. Normally we should aim for 10 to 20 viable seeds per square inch for K. bluegrass and red fescues and because of higher mortality, 20 to 30 seeds for bents. If soil and weather conditions are below optimum, to be on the safe side it is better to increase seeding rate. Under optimum conditions, when the seedbed is clean and no competition is expected, the seed rate can be slightly decreased. Bunch type grasses seeded thinly do not fill bare spots as fast as grasses spreading by rhizomes or stolons. Therefore, thicker seeding of bunch type grasses may improve the chances of getting good sod.

In Table 5.1 seeding rates for various turf grasses are presented.

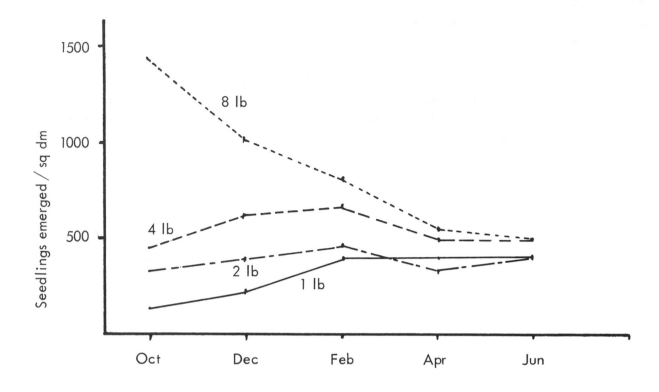

Figure 5.17 Population density of K. bluegrass at germination is a function of seeding rate, but populations converge to a common level with time (25).

Summary

1. The most common method to establish a lawn is by seed.

2. At present, for the most part cool-season grasses are established by seed and most of the warm-season grasses are established vegetatively. The major parts of a grass seed are: a) seed coat, b) food reserves (endosperm), and c) embryo. The embryo is the rudimentary plant with root, stem and leaf regions in an undeveloped stage.

3. Tall fescue and ryegrass seeds are alike. The form of rachilla is the most outstanding feature for their identification. Fescue has a club-shaped rachilla and ryegrasses have a rachilla with an angular tip. Perennial ryegrass seeds have no awns and annual ryegrass has awns.

4. The most important features in describing grass seed quality are: a) species, variety, strains; b) purity; c) germination and d) weeds. For turf production certified seed should be used. The production of certified seed is supervised by the government or professional agencies. On the label (tag): a) varieties, strains; b) purity, c) germination and d) impurities are indicated. As impurities are usually included: a) other crop seeds, b) inert matter and c) weed seeds. The most important impurity is weed seeds. The noxious weed seed number per pound or ounce should be indicated. Seed germination usually needs to be checked every six or nine months. "Pure live seed" is the percentage of the contents of a bag of seeds that is pure seed that will germinate.

5. The practicability of grass seed treatments with fungicides before seeding to protect them from damping off and other diseases is questioned. Also, the value of seed presprouting or treating with growth regulators is questioned.

6. K. bluegrass, red fescues and bents are fine turf grasses. Tall fescue, redtop, timothy and ryegrasses are coarse turf grasses. In the northern cool region for home lawns the best grasses are Kentucky bluegrass and red fescues (creeping or chewing types). In the shade under moist conditions up to 30% in mixtures of rough bluegrass can be used. For athletic fields pure seedings of Merion K. bluegrass, pure seedings of tall fescue and its mixtures with K. bluegrass and red fescue can be used. For temporary lawns ryegrass is suggested. In cool humid regions west of the Cascade Mountains and in New England close to the Atlantic shore, colonial bent can be used for home lawns under intense maintenance.

7. In the southern warm region turf grasses are: 1) Bermudas, zoysias, St. Augustine, centipede, carpet grass, Bahia, and tall fescue. For shaded areas St. Augustine and zoysias can be used. In the South usually single species are planted to establish a lawn. For overseeding in the South the following grasses can be used: ryegrasses, bluegrass, bent grass, fescues.

Problems

1. A lawn seed mixture is made up of 50% Kentucky bluegrass and 50% creeping red fescue. If this mixture is seeded at the rate of 4 lb./1,000 sq. ft., how many pounds of each grass seed will be needed for 20,000 sq. ft.?

2. A seed mixture is made up of 30% K. bluegrass, 20% Merion K. bluegrass, 35% red fescue and 15% annual ryegrass. If this mixture is seeded at 4 lb./1,000 sq. ft., how many pounds of each grass will be needed for 1,000 sq. ft. of lawn?

3. Write a mixture for a well-drained shaded area. Indicate how much seed is needed of this mixture for 1,000 sq. ft. and calculate how much seed of each species is needed for 1,000 sq. ft. and 2 acre lawns.

4. How many seedlings should be expected per sq. inch from seeding 3 lb. of red fescue per 1,000 sq. ft.?

5. If you seed 2 lb./1,000 sq. ft. of Merion bluegrass on a front lawn, how many seedlings can you expect per sq. inch in the lawn?

6. Write a mixture for a moist, shady lawn. Indicate how much of your proposed mixture you will use for 1,000 sq. ft. and calculate how many seedlings of each grass you expect per sq. inch.

NOTE: For problems 4, 5 and 6 use necessary data from Table 5.1, page 64.

CHAPTER 6
SOILS

6.1 Generalities

Soil is the natural medium which terrestrial plants grow, therefore soil can be defined as the part of the outer crust of the earth's surface in which plants grow. The soil is termed "the edaphic environment" of plant life. Soil consists of many types of small particles. The majority are decomposed parent rock fragments and can be imagined as rock dust. In decomposition of parent rock (or in formation of soils), the following factors play a role:

    a. the nature of the parent material,
    b. climate (temperatures, rainfall, etc.),
    c. topography or relief,
    d. organisms (flora and fauna),
    e. time.

These factors are interrelated and one or more of them may be dominant under different conditions. Because of these interrelationships, we have great variations in soils. Thus, soil can be defined as the outer crust of the earth surface which is medium for plant growth and whose characteristics have resulted from the forces of climate and living organisms acting upon parent material as influenced by surface relief, over a period of time. Thus, with changes occurring continuously in a soil, soil can be considered dynamic.

The soil is composed of solids, liquids and gases. The solids are in the inorganic and organic form. The inorganic forms are the various clay minerals and the oxides of iron and aluminum. The organic forms are the decomposed plant and animal matter. The liquid portion is water with dissolved salts and the gas portion is mostly air and CO_2. By having various proportions of solids, liquids and gases, we have different soil types.

A rich and crumbly topsoil is of prime importance when establishing a good lawn.

    a. Grasses need a well prepared, reasonably fine and firm seedbed.
    b. Lawn grasses should be well supplied with oxygen, water and plant nutrients.
    c. Soil conditions must be favorable for the development of beneficial soil micro-organisms. Micro-organisms play an extremely important role in plant nutrient changes, availability to plants, and to all other biological processes of soil.
    d. The soil must be free from compounds and conditions detrimental to normal growth of plants, i.e., high acidity, alkalinity or the presence of chemical compounds or salts which may injure grasses or interfere with the normal absorption of plant nutrients. Ideal soil conditions seldom exist where one needs to establish a fine turf grass. Therefore the knowledge of soil properties, their improvement as well as the knowledge of soil and plant relationships are needed.

6.2 Soil texture

For a soil to be in good physical condition for plant growth, air, water and solid particles must be in the right proportions at all times. The solid portion of a soil consists of mineral and organic matter. Mineral praticles are usually classified as follows:

sand   2.0-0.05mm in diameter
silt   0.05-0.002mm in diameter
clay   smaller than 0.002mm in diameter

U. S. Department of Agriculture, Bureau of Plant Industry, Soils, and Agricultural Engineering

GUIDE FOR TEXTURAL CLASSIFICATION

May 1, 1950

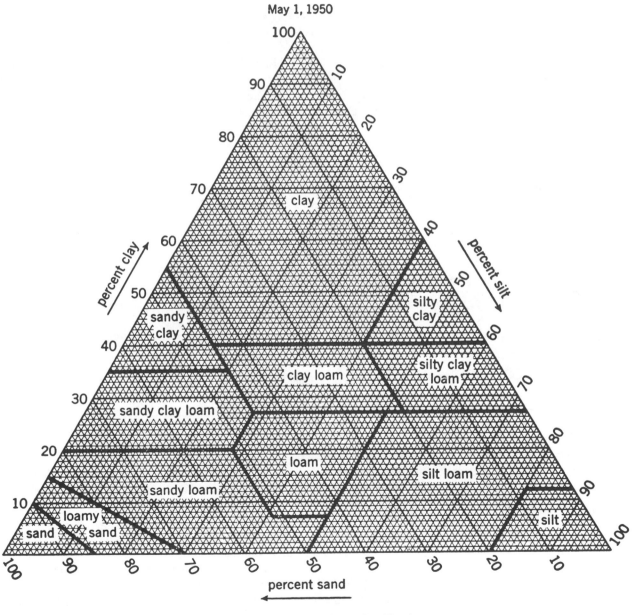

Fig. 6.1 Guide for textural soil classification

Sand particles usually settle in the water fast and feel gritty when smeared. Silt particles settle out of the water in an hour or so. They smear as a rough, irregular surface. Clay particles produce a smooth, slick smear. The separation of soil particles into sand, silt and clay is done by mechanical soil analysis. *Texture* is the relative proportion of various soil particles. *Soil texture usually refers to the relative percentage of sand, silt and clay in a soil.* Very seldom is soil completely sand, silt or clay. Normally, natural soils are mixtures of these three ingredients in various proportions. The textural name is usually determined from mechanical analysis. The equilateral triangle has been adapted to determine a textural name of a soil (Fig. 6.1).

If the mechanical analysis of a soil is sand-40%, silt-40% and clay-20%, then in the following lines of the triangle, we find the point where all three lines intersect. The point indicates loam, i.e., the textural name of our soil is loam. Loams are crumbly mixtures, not very sticky but yet not as quick to dry as sand. Loams are good soils to establish a lawn. Clay particles are small and when they are loose and wet the spaces between particles are small, form capillars and are usually filled with water. Clay soils often have very little air space. On the contrary, sandy soils have too many larger pores filled with air. Loamy soils with 40-60% sand, 20-30% clay and 20-30% silt are most desirable. In these soils air and water spaces are well distributed and adequate. The more common soil textural names, listed, in order of increasing fineness are: sand, loamy sand, sandy loam, loam, silt loam, silt, sandy clay loam, clay loam, silty clay loam, sandy clay, silty clay and clay. Lawns are most easily grown on loam or sandy loam soils. These soils are usually quite fertile, hold ample supplies of water, and have good drainage and air movement. Soil texture of sandy loam to light clay loam provides adequate moisture holding capacity but still allows proper internal drainage and air movement. It is less susceptible to soil compaction than the clay soils and is not as droughtly as the sandy soils. Under a good water supply sandy soils should be preferred over silty or clayey ones. Aeration in such soils is good and there are no compaction problems.

Surface area of soil particles in a soil is associated with the soil texture, e.g., 1 gram of clay has about 50 times more surface area than the same weight of very fine sand, and 10 times more than silt. Physical and chemical soil properties are influenced by surface area: the larger the particles the less chemically active in absorption, adsorption and exchange of plant nutrients or applied pesticides.

6.3 Organic matter, micro-organisms, colloids

Organic matter of a soil consists of plant and animal residues, living plant roots and microscopic organisms. Plant residues, especially roots, account for most of the soil's organic matter. Highly decomposed organic matter is termed *humus*. Humus is dark colored, odorless, more or less stable and a uniform material. Humus has a high capacity to store moisture and plant nutrients.

Good quality topsoil for a lawn should have at least 2% organic matter. Prairie soils often have about 7% and typical Kentucky bluegrass soils have about 3-4% organic matter. In desert and coastal areas soil organic matter content is close to zero. Soils containing 15-20% or more organic matter in the upper 1 ft. layer are called organic soils. Muck soils are well decomposed organic soils.

Organic matter is needed by soil micro-organisms as a source of food (carbon). The temperature and moisture conditions which favor microbial activity will also favor organic matter decomposition. Organic matter is mainly composed of carbohydrates, proteins, fats, water soluble compounds and organic acids combined with some minerals. Various micro-organisms break down these organic compounds into decomposition products and use them as food or form new compounds within their bodies. These microbes in turn die, decompose and can become available as nutrients for plants. In this way nitrogen containing organic compounds can be changed into ammonia $\rightarrow$ nitrites $\rightarrow$ nitrates. If a growing crop is present, the nitrate will be absorbed by roots or leached through the soil profile. When a lack of oxygen exists aerobic microbes are replaced by the anaerobic micro-organisms. Generally, it is important to keep the soil well aerated so that aerobic organisms will prevail in the soil. Anaerobic microbes are responsible for the loss of nitrogen through the process of denitrification ($NO_3 \rightarrow NO_2 \rightarrow N_2O + N_2\uparrow$).

Humus contains a high percentage of very fine particles called *colloids* which strongly affect the physical properties of soil (i.e. structure). The chemically active fraction of soil solids is confined primarily to clay and humus particles which are smaller than 0.0002mm in diameter, known as colloids. Colloidal clay is crystalline, whereas humus is amorphous. The nutrients added to soils from commercial fertilizers and those released by the weathering process are held by colloidal clay and organic matter particles of soils. These colloidal particles have a negative charge and are able to attract plant nutrients or soil applied pesticides (e.g., herbicides) that have a positive charge, such as calcium (Ca^{++}), magnesium (Mg^{++}), ammonium (NH_4^+) and potassium (K^+), thus reducing their loss by leaching. It is this property which accounts for cation adsorption in soils. An example of this mechanism is shown in Fig. 6.2.

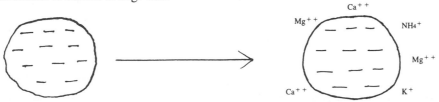

Fig. 6.2 Colloidal particle
with negative charges

Attracted plant nutrients possessing
positive charges (Ca, Mg, NH₄, K) and thus
their losses by leaching are reduced.

This phenomenon is known as the cation exchange capacity (CEC). The CEC is the amount of cations that a soil can adsorb, or very simply, the amount of nutrients that the soil can hold. Such an attraction may affect soil applied pesticides also, e.g., pre-emergence soil applications of herbicides may be at least partly bound to the colloidal particles and thus their availability to kill weeds can be decreased appreciably. Therefore in heavy soils or in soils with a high content of organic matter (muck soils) higher herbicide rates are usually used compared to light sandy soils.

6.4 Soil structure

Soil structure (tilth) can be defined as the way soil particles are held and grouped together into aggregates. Silt and especially clay particles are very small and if they stay as individual separate particles they build a soil with very small pores making the soil compact when wet or very loose like dust when dry. This is structureless soil. Single soil grains can be bound in units without a definite pattern of aggregation. In a soil with good structure loose soil particles are bound together into clusters, crumbs, aggregates or peds of various sizes. Naturally formed aggregates are fairly water-stable and are called peds. The majority of crumbs usually are 1 to 3mm in diameter. Such a soil retains good structure even if wet and it remains porous with adequate air and water space. On the other hand, a soil with poor structure has soil particles which are loose and not aggregated into crumbs but stuck one to the other, thereby compacting and eliminating most pore space. These soils are compact and impervious to water and air. Such soils are slaking; individual particles are loose, and do not adhere. Such soils puddle and form crusts readily.

Organic matter, lime and generally good conditions for biological activity play a very important role in creating a good soil structure. Organic matter serves as a nuclei in binding loose soil particles in larger crumbs and aggregates. Alternate shrinking and swelling, freezing and thawing also are very important in breaking single soil particles and aggregating them into stable crumbs, thus creating a good soil structure. These latter factors are especially important in heavy clay soils which are inclined to form heavy lumps. In heavy soils if the particles are not aggregated into crumbs and if they are loose, they seal up the pores between aggregates. Such a soil has poor aeration and poor drainage qualities. Also, in forming aggregates, adsorbed cations play an important role. Ca, Al and H ions favor soil flocculation, whereas sodium ions favor dispersion thus contributes to poor physical soil conditions. Sodium replaced by Ca helps to improve soil structure.

The proper use of mechanical implements during cultivation or aerification may be helpful in obtaining a good soil structure.

6.5 Soil, air and water

During respiration, plant roots absorb oxygen (O_2) and give off carbon dioxide (CO_2). Grass roots must have oxygen and therefore the soil should be properly aerated and ventilated. Respiration is an important physiological process. Uptake of plant nutrients and water is directly controlled by the rate of respiration. Plants must have a constant supply of fresh air from the atmosphere flowing to the surface of every living and growing root to replace carbon dioxide-laden soil air which is constantly building up around the roots. Therefore, soil air usually has more carbon dioxide and less oxygen than atmospheric air.

The exchange of air in soils takes place through the spaces between the solid particles of the soil. The larger spaces between soil particles serve as the air spaces through which a soil "breathes". It is through these large openings that rain or irrigation water runs into the soil and is distributed to the smaller or capillary spaces. The capillary spaces are the spaces in which water is held in the soil. Water drains readily from large soil pores due to gravity and these pores are usually filled with air. Small pores are able to hold water against gravity by capillarity and comprise the capillary or water pore space. Soils of finer texture have larger numbers of small capillary pores, larger particle surface and therefore are able to store more water than sandy soils of coarser texture. An ideal soil of good texture and structure should have by volume about 50% solid matter, 25% small pores or water space and 25% large pores or air space.

The size and character of soil pores may be changed by compaction. In building a lawn the use of heavy machinery should be avoided especially when the soil is wet. This compacts the soil to the point where the percentage of air space is greatly reduced. When preparing the seedbed one should avoid working soil into dust or fine powder. Such a soil loses structure by reducing the proportion between solid matter and pore space, resulting in a poor soil media for turf grass growth.

6.6 Improving Soils

Soil quality should be judged chiefly by its ability to provide good aeration and water-holding capacity and not so much on its fertility. A fertility problem can be solved by proper fertilization and liming. The amount of moisture which is available to plant roots that a soil can hold is determined by its texture, aeration and organic matter. A sandy light soil generally has sufficient aeration but, low water-holding capacity. This is because it has too few small water-holding pores but plenty of large air spaces or noncapillary pores. Just the opposite is true for a heavy soil. In light sandy soils not only water-holding capacity is poor but also the plant nutrient holding capacity is poor. The colloidal fraction in these soils is very low and soluble plant nutrients are readily leached underground or washed away. Fine material is needed to increase plant nutrient and water retention and coarse material is needed to increase water infiltration, air spaces and prevent compaction in heavy utility turf areas. Good quality soil should have sufficient organic matter in it to give the structure aeration and water-holding capacity that will make lawn establishment easy. Besides, organic matter is needed for micro-organisms and increases their activity in a soil.

Materials and methods. To improve light sandy soils we can use organic matter and clay, clay loam or any heavy soil. To improve heavy clay soil we can use organic matter and sandy loam, sand or any light soil. Thus organic matter is the universal soil conditioning material used to improve water and nutrient retention of sandy soils and aeration and water infiltration of heavy soils. Good aeration enables plant roots to use the large amount of water which such soils are capable of absorbing and holding.

Peat, well-rotted manure and fine sewage sludge can be used as organic matter for soil improvement at the rate of 2 to 4 cubic yards per 1,000 sq. ft. They should be thoroughly mixed into the first 5-6 inches of soil. There are a number of other waste materials like sawdust, raw straw, cocoa shells, buckwheat hulls, peanut hulls, rice hulls, spent mushroom soil, etc. which can be used as a source of organic matter. Manure, compost, rotted sawdust and sewage sludge may be spread 1-2 inches deep. Often 2-4 bales of peat or peatmoss for each 1,000 sq. ft. is suggested. These materials are satisfactory soil additives if they are composted. Sawdust, if not composted, should be 7-10 years old. One also can add organic matter to the soil by turning under a *green manure* crop 4 to 6 weeks before seeding the grass. In the northern part of the states, spring plantings of soybeans, sweet clover, red clover, sudan grass or ryegrass provide green manure for turning under in August. In the southern part of the United States fall plantings of crimson clover, hairy vetch, winter rye, or ryegrass provide good green manure for turning under prior to spring lawn seeding or planting. These crops also provide a cover for the soil during the fall and winter. If large amounts of sawdust, shredded straw or green manure are used 1 lb. of N per 1,000 sq. ft. should be added as food for micro-organisms working on decomposition.

Besides organic matter, light sandy soils as well as heavy clay soils can be improved by adding proper mineral soil. Sandy soils can be improved by applying a 2 to 3 inch layer of clay loam topsoil and on the other hand, heavy clay soils can be improved by applying a 3 to 6 inch layer of sand or a 6 inch layer of sandy loam topsoil. Since a layer of sand or sandy loam soil 3 to 6 inches thick is required to improve clay soil, the benefits usually do not justify the expense. These applied topsoils *should be well mixed* by rototilling or disking to a depth of 5 to 6 inches.

Improved heavy soils should always have proper subsurface drainage. Due to good water-holding capacity they easily get compacted so proper drainage is needed.

In preparing of seedbeds for heavy duty turf areas like athletic fields, sports fields or golf courses, radical and complete soil modification may be needed. Often a topsoil mix (root zone mix) is prepared which may be completely different from the original topsoil of the area. Usually underneath the topsoil mix is an 8-12 inch thick subsoil layer of coarse sand. For aeration and drainage this coarse subsoil should be connected with a proper drainage system. Topsoil or root zone mixes of various depths are prepared by using organic matter and soil having good water infiltration and good water and plant nutrient retention. The USGA Green Section has worked out specifications and procedures for root zone mix preparation.

Summary

1. Soil is the outer crust of the earth's surface in which plants grow. Soil is a product of decomposed parent rock. Soils differ. In soil formation the nature of the parent rock, climate, topography (relief), organisms and time play an important role.

2. Soil is composed of solids, liquids and gases. Solids can be inorganic or of an organic origin. Liquids are water with dissolved salts. Gases are composed of air and CO_2.

3. In establishing a fine turf area it is important to have:

    a. fine and firm seedbed,
    b. grasses supplied with air, water and plant nutrients,
    c. soil conditions favorable for the development of beneficial soil micro-organisms,
    d. soil free from conditions and compounds detrimental to normal turf grass growth.

4. Soil texture refers to the relative percentage of sand, silt and clay in a soil. Soil structure can be defined as the way soil particles are held and grouped together. In a soil with good structure loose particles are bound together into clusters, soil crumbs, aggregates or peds of various sizes. The majority of crumbs are usually 1 to 3mm in diameter.

5. Organic matter of a soil consists of plant and animal residues. Decomposed, decayed organic matter forms humus. The chemically active fraction of soil solids is confined primarily to clay and humus particles which are smaller than 0.0002mm in diameter, known as colloids. Plant nutrients and various pesticides added to soil may be attracted and held by colloid particles of soils.

6. An ideal soil of good texture and structure should have about 50% solid matter. 25% small pores or water space and 25% large pores or air space by volume. A sandy light soil generally has sufficient aeration but low water-holding capacity and heavy soils have a good water-holding capacity and poor aeration.

7. To improve light sandy soils one can use organic matter and heavy soil. To improve heavy soil one can use organic matter and any light soil. Organic matter as well as mineral soils added should be mixed with the upper 5-6 inches of soil.

CHAPTER 7
FERTILIZERS AND LIME

7.1 Introduction

Justus von Liebig (1803-1873), a German agricultural chemist, proposed the chemical theory of plant nutrition. He showed that the plant needs chemical elements for normal growth and development. He also believed that by analyzing crop plant ash it is possible to formulate a fertilizer that would supply all essential elements for the next crop. Thus, he laid the foundation for a modern plant nutrition theory. Liebig also coined the *Law of Minimum:* crop yield is limited by that one factor which is least available to the plant in comparison to each of the other factors.

There are 16 elements that have been determined to be essential for plant growth and reproduction. These essential plant food elements come from air, water, soil and fertilizers.

From air and water: carbon (C), hydrogen (H), oxygen (O), and nitrogen (N). Ninety to 95 percent of all plant substance is comprised of these elements.

From soil and fertilizers: a) *major* (primary) nutrients are: nitrogen (N), phosphorus (P), potassium (K); b) *secondary* nutrients are: calcium (Ca), magnesium (Mg), sulfur (S); c) *micro* nutrients are: iron (Fe), boron (B), manganese (Mn), copper (Cu), zinc (Zn), molybdenum (Mo), and chlorine (Cl).

The primary or major plant nutrients are needed by crops in large amounts. The secondary nutrients and especially the micro nutrients are required by plants in very small quantities. They may be deficient or unavailable in soils and thus have to be added. Research is being conducted by plant physiologists to determine whether additional elements are necessary for normal plant growth. Sodium (Na), iodine (I), cobalt (Co), and possibly selenium (Se), are required by animals but have not been shown to be essential for plants. Boron and molybdenum have not as yet, been established as necessary for animals.

Soil is the source of 13 of the 16 elements essential for plant growth. Twelve of the 13 elements originally come from parent rock from which the soil developed. Whereas the original source of all nitrogen was the air. Plants can use atmospheric nitrogen only when it is chemically or biologically fixed in the soil. Nitrogen is also a constituent of most organic matter and is highest in amount in cool, humid regions which favor an accumulation of soil organic matter. Organic matter may vary from zero in sandy coastal soils to 7% in prairie soils and even much higher in muck soils. The less rainfall the higher the percentage composition of total phosphorus, potassium, calcium and magnesium in the surface soils. The phosphorus available to plants in soils is normally 0.03 to 0.1 percent; potassium ranges from almost nothing in leachable soils to 2.5 percent in good prairie loam.

7.2 Nitrogen

Nitrogen plays a very important role in plant life. It is an indispensable part of proteins, chlorophyll, amino acids, nucleic acids, enzymes and vitamins. Young actively growing plant tissues have a higher content of nitrogen. Of the main plant nutrients, nitrogen is needed in the largest amount.

Nitrogen is the key element in turf production. It is primarily responsible for vegetative growth and color. Constant liberal supplies are essential for good leaf density and satisfactory root development under sod. If it is in short supply, poor leaf color and root development and a thin sod results. Excess, on the other hand, renders the grass plant oversucculent, turgid, and soft due to the formation of thinner cell walls, and therefore susceptible to drought, cold, disease attack and other pests.

Deficiency symptoms (31). A sickly yellowish green color, distinctly slow and dwarfed growth, drying up or "firing" of leaves which starts at the bottom of the plant and proceeds upward. In grasses, the firing starts at the tip of the bottom leaves and proceeds down the center or along the midrib. Stunted shoot growth and increased seedhead formation was observed in Bermuda grass (16).

Fertilizers

Nitrogen may be added to soil in (a) synthetic inorganic, (b) natural organic and (c) synthetic organic forms. Each type has certain advantages and disadvantages.

Synthetic inorganic nitrogen forms are highly soluble and release nitrogen quickly. Because they possess salt type properties, care must be taken in application, especially during active growth periods, to prevent burning. Applications of more than 1 lb. of N per 1,000 sq. ft. applied as inorganic nitrogen may burn grass or cause excessive succulent growth. Such a grass has low resistance to diseases and adverse conditions. Nitrogen in this form may also be lost quite easily due to leaching. The soluble nitrogen carriers require more frequent application than organics but they are usually much less expensive per pound of actual nitrogen. Some of these carriers possess acidifying properties which can result in a markedly increased soil acidity with continued use. Ammonium sulfate is particularly acidifying to the soil, while ammonium nitrate is less effective in this respect (Table 7.1). Carriers such as calcium nitrate and sodium nitrate have a basic effect. That is, they can cause soil acidity to decrease. As such, they increase the soil pH level.

Solid N materials or liquid forms could be used as nitrogen solutions. They can be applied as individual materials or as mixtures with carriers of one or more of the other primary plant nutrient elements (phosphorus, potassium). Water soluble inorganic N fertilizers can be manufactured as granules coated with resinous materials. In this form N release is slower, and residual effects longer. According to thickness of coating, fertilizers can be prepared with longer or shorter residual effects.

Natural organic. The nitrogen in natural organic carriers is combined in organic compounds. Soil microorganisms must break down the organic structure to release the nitrogen into an available form so it can be taken up by roots. These microbes are not very active when soil temperatures are below 55-60°F and therefore, the release of nitrogen during the cool-season is limited. As a result it may be necessary to use inorganic soluble nitrogen for quick response at this time. Since the natural organics are not soluble, leaching and burning problems are negligible and fewer applications will be required per year. However, the cost per pound of nitrogen may be three or more times that for soluble materials. The rate of release of nitrogen from various organic carriers can be quite variable so the user should be familiar with the product. Besides, natural organic fertilizers are impure and many minor elements are supplied. Furthermore, these fertilizers are beneficial to soil structure. They are bulky to store and transport and may have a foul smell. In hot-wet weather conditions, nitrification (i.e., decomposition) may be rather rapid.

Synthetic organic urea and calcium cyanamid (Table 7.1) are water soluble and act like inorganic synthetics. They also have a high potential for gaseous ammonia loss. Calcium cyanamid has 37% calcium. It is best to use it as a preplant application when establishing turf. It also works as a herbicide and fungicide also.

Ureaform (UF) is synthetically prepared material providing slow release properties. The advantages and disadvantages are similar to those for natural organics. Initial turf grass response is better than from natural

Table 7.1 Nitrogen fertilizers

Material	Analysis N-P$_2$O$_5$-K$_2$O	Lbs needed for 1 lb N	Salt index	Effect on soil pH
Synthetic inorganic				
1. Ammonium chloride, NH$_4$Cl	26-0-0	3.8		Acidifying
2. Ammonium nitrate, NH$_4$NO$_3$	33.5-0-0	3.0	105	Acidifying
3. Ammonium sulfate, (NH$_4$)$_2$SO$_4$	20.5-0-0	4.8	69	Acidifying
4. Anhydrous ammonia	82-0-0	1.2	47	Acidifying
5. Calcium nitrate, Ca(NO$_3$)$_2$.4H$_2$O	15.5-0-0	6.4	52	Basic
6. Potassium nitrate, KNO$_3$	14-0-0	7.1	74	Basic
7. Sodium nitrate, NaNO$_3$	16-0-0	6.2	100	Basic
8. Monoammonium phosphate, NH$_4$H$_2$PO$_4$	11-48-0	9.1	30	Acidifying
9. Diammonium phosphate, (NH$_4$)$_2$HPO$_4$	18-46-0	5.6	34	Acidifying
Natural organic				
10. Castor pomace	6-1.5-1.5	16.7		
11. Cotton seed meal	7-3-2	14.3		
12. Corn gluten meal	8-0.4-0	12.5	Average 3.5	
13. Dried blood	13-2-1	7.7		
14. Fish scraps	7-6-0	14.3		
15. Hoof & horn meal	14-1-0	7.1		
16. Manure, cattle, dried	2-1.5-2	50.0		
17. Sewage sludge, activ. milorganite	5.5-4-0.5	18.2		
18. Soybean meal	7-1.5-2.5	14.3		
19. Tankage, animal	7-10-0.5	14.3		
Synthetic organic				
20. Cyanamide, CaCN$_2$	20.6-0-0	4.8	31	Basic
21. Urea, Co(NH$_2$)$_2$	45-0-0	2.2	75	Acidifying
22. Ureaform, (UF)	38-0-0	2.6		Acidifying (slowly)
23. Flowable liquid ureaform (methylol and methylene ureas)	30-0-0	3.3	4	Basic
24. IBDU (isobutylidene diurea)	31-0-0	3.2		Acidifying (slowly)

organics and residual effects are also better than for natural organics. Ureaform nitrogen is released by bacteria (best a pH 6.0-6.5). Generally, ureaform performs better on low maintenance turf.

IBDU (isobutylidene diurea) is a comparatively new slowly soluble synthetic nitrogen fertilizer. The mode of N release depends solely upon the presence of water. Initial turf grass response and residual effects are similar to UF.

Slowly available natural organic and ureaform nitrogen fertilizers are especially useful in maintenance fertilization of turf grasses. They work slowly, are not leached and one or two applications can supply nitrogen for the entire growing season. Besides, these slow working nitrogen fertilizers can be applied in larger quantities without danger of burning the grass. Normally a single application of ureaform is not sufficient to supply the nitrogen needed for the whole growing season, except when very high rates are used.

Salt index

High concentrations of soluble salts added to soil may increase the salt concentration of the soil solution and increase the osmotic pressure which may be injurious to the plant due to decreased water availability to the plant. Thus, high salt concentrations in the soil solution may cause so-called physiological drought and damage plants. The salt index was proposed (33) as a means of expressing the effects of various fertilizers upon the soil solution and consequently upon the tendency of a fertilizer to injure crops by undue osmotic pressure in the soil solution. Salt index: ratio of increase of osmotic pressure produced by a fertilizer material to that produced by the same weight of sodium nitrate ($NaNO_3$), based on a salt index of 100. In tables 7.1, 7.2 and 7.4 are presented salt indexes (33) of some fertilizers used in turf management. Organic slowly available nitrogen fertilizers have low osmotic value, low salt indexes (average 3.5) and cause little salt damage.

7.3 Phosphorus

Phosphorus is a necessary element of all living plant tissue. It is an important constituent of DNA, RNA, some enzymes and ATP. It is vital for energy transfer processes and respiration processes. In the seed it is important in the formation and development of good reserves. Phosphorus is particularly important in stimulating the quick development of a good root system in newly seeded grasses. Phosphorus is rather mobile in plants and can be stored and reused later. Phosphorus also increases the wear tolerance of turf grasses and clover. Where clover is a problem, phosphate applications should be limited to minimum needs.

Deficiency signs (31). Leaves turn dark green, then purplish by red anthocyanin pigments during cool weather. Leaves show a tendency to roll. Thin, slow growing sod. Seedlings are more likely to be deficient than mature sod. Different grasses respond only slightly differently to phosphorus deficiencies.

Phosphorus is taken up by plants as phosphoric ions (i.e. HPO_4^{-2} or $H_2PO_4^-$). Soil with a high proportion of silt and clay particles contain more phosphorus than light sandy soils. P is quickly fixed in the soil in the form of insoluble salts and it is not lost by leaching: phosphate ion readily combines with iron and aluminum to form an insoluble, fixed, unavailable form. Soil reactions (Fig. 7.1), organic matter and other soil conditions influence the availability of phosphoric acid to plants. It redissolves slowly following precipitation. Adding lime or sulfur may be helpful in releasing fixed phosphorus for plant use. Iron phosphate is insoluble in soil and at high levels of phosphorus in soils, iron supply for plants may be poor. Phosphorus may interfere with zinc uptake also. Arsenic can replace phosphorus in some reactions (26) and vice versa. High phosphorus supply may decrease effectiveness of arsenical pesticides. Surface applications of phosphate fertilizers work down into the soil to the root zone at an exceptionally slow pace. Therefore, it is important to enrich the topsoil with phosphoric acid before seeding a lawn. See Figure 7.1 for the effects of soil Ph on P availability.

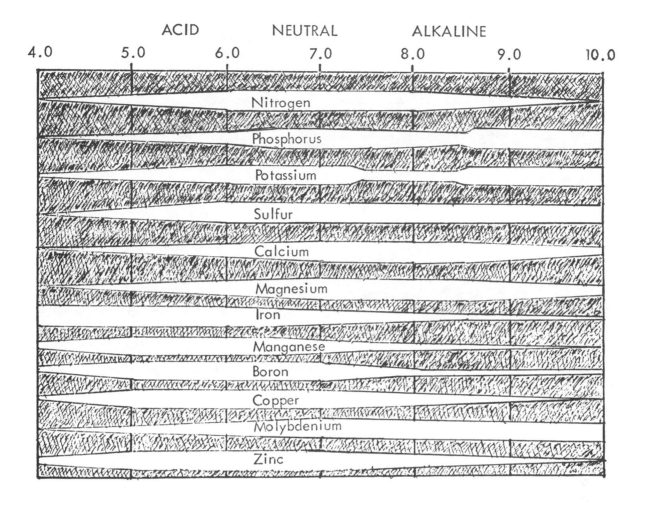

Figure 7.1 Soil pH and availability of plant food elements. The wider bar, the greater the availability. Source: Truog, University of Wisconsin (9, 44).

Fertilizers

Phosphorus naturally occurs in a number of soil minerals along with various inorganic and organic compounds. In the United States about 40% of our rock phosphate supply is in Florida and Tennessee, with 60% in the Rocky Mountain states. Superphosphates are the most important commercial source of phosphoric acid. Common superphosphate usually has 20% phosphoric oxide (P_2O_5), and the more concentrated triple phosphate may have up to 48-50% of phosphoric oxide (Table 7.2). Ammonium phosphates are quick acting fertilizers. Their phosphate fraction is completely water soluble. They should be used with caution, otherwise they may burn turf badly. They should be watered in or applied on turf in mixtures with other materials. Basic slag is a by-product of the steel industry. It is a slow working basic (alkaline) fertilizer best applied to acid muck soils. Rock phosphate is rather insoluble and should be used on acid soils rich with organic matter. Bone meal is an organic source of phosphoric acid. It contains about 22-25% P_2O_5, 4% nitrogen and is a slowly available insoluble tricalcium phosphate. In organic materials, phosphoric acid becomes available to grasses only after microbial decomposition. It is a good source of phosphorus for maintenance as well as for seedbed preparation.

Table 7.2 Phosphorus fertilizers

Material	Percent		Lb needed for 1 lb		Salt index	Effect on soil pH
	P_2O_5	P	P_2O_5	P		
1. Superphosphate	20	8.8	5.0	11.4	8	Neutral
2. Superphosphate, conc.	48	21.0	2.1	4.8	10	Neutral
3. Monoammonium phosphate	48	21.0	2.1	4.8	30	Acidifying
4. Diammonium phosphate	46	20.0	2.2	5.0	34	Acidifying
5. Rock phosphate	25	11.0	4.0	9.1		Basic
6. Basic slag	10	4.4	10.0	22.7		Basic
7. Bone meals	22	9.7	4.5	10.3		Basic

The phosphorus in fertilizers is guaranteed in the form of phosphoric oxide (as pentoxide P_2O_5), but erroneously called "phosphoric acid". Although phosphorus and potassium have been expressed in the oxide form for many years, the use of this form is actually incorrect because these nutrients in fertilizers are not in the form of P_2O_5 or K_2O as usually is indicated on the bag. Conversion factors in elemental forms are presented in Table 7.3.

Table 7.3 Oxide-elemental conversion factors for phosphorus and potassium

% or lb		Factor	Converted to % or lb	
P_2O_5	x	0.43	=	P
K_2O	x	0.83	=	K
P	x	2.29	=	P_2O_5
K	x	1.20	=	K_2O

7.4 Potassium

Potassium is a major plant nutrient but not a constituent of plant organic materials like proteins, chlorophyll, fats or carbohydrates. It acts as regulator of physiological plant processes. It appears to be of importance in production and movement (within the plant) of carbohydrates and proteins. It has catalizing properties concerning water supply within the cell, transpiration and enzymatic actions. It is helpful in producing energy and plant structural materials and increases vigor and disease resistance to plants. It helps produce a strong, stiff stalk and thus reduces lodging. It increases plumpness of the grain and seed and is essential to the formation and transfer of starches, sugars and oils. Potassium has been associated with increased winter hardiness of turf grasses. It also imparts winter hardiness to turf legumes and other crops. There is evidence that potassium plays a role in resistance to disease pathogens. It is apparent that plants often accumulate more potassium in their tissues than is needed. In plant tissue, K can be as high as 4-6% on dry matter basis. For normal turf grass growth, potassium-nitrogen should be supplied in a 1:2 ratio.

Deficiency symptoms (31). Symptoms show up on older leaves as a marginal browning. These dead areas may fall out, leaving ragged leaves. In grasses, firing usually starts at the tip of the leaf and proceeds down the edge, leaving the midrib green. Also, dwarfed growth, drooping of the leaves, and increased tillering can be observed.

Like phosphorus, most of the soil potassium is retained on the finer soil particles. In loam and heavier clay soils there is more potassium than there is in light sandy soils. Sands, muck and peat soils are low in potassium and need regular fertilization with this element. Potassium is soluble but held on colloids or held as part of soil minerals. Soil minerals release K slowly. Soil K is usually released and available in spring but later in the growing season it is depleted and plant needs should be supplemented by fertilization. The regular use of potassium is necessary, especially on light sandy soils because these soils are naturally poor in potassium and leaching is a great avenue of K loss.

Fertilizers

Potash (K_2O) is potassium oxide. Large deposits of potassic salts, mostly potassium chloride, are found in Germany, America, Spain, Poland, Russia and other countries. They are the source of potassic fertilizers. In fertilizers, potassium content is usually expressed in terms of potash (K_2O). The most common potassium fertilizers are presented in Table 7.4. Potassium chloride is known as muriate of potash and is usually 95% pure KCl, equivalent to 60% K_2O. Other potash carriers are sulfate of potash and sulfate of potash-magnesia. Cotton hulls, unleached hardwood ashes and tobacco stems can also be used as potassium carriers. In Table 7.4 salt indexes are presented for some of the K carriers.

Table 7.4. Potassium fertilizers

Material	Percent		Lb needed for 1 lb		Salt index	Effects on soil pH
	K_2O	K	K_2O	K		
1. Potassium chloride, KCl	60-62	50-52	1.7-1.6	2-1.9	116	Neutral
2. Potassium sulfate, K_2SO_4	50-53	42-44	2-1.9	2.4-2.3	46	Neutral
3. Potassium nitrate, KNO_3	44-46	36-38	2.3-2.2	2.8-2.6	74	Basic
4. Potassium Mg-sulfate, $K_2SO_4.2MgSO_4$	20-26	17-22	5.0-3.8	5.9-4.5	43	Neutral
5. Potassium carbonate, K_2CO_3	53-70	44-58	1.9-1.4	2.3-1.7		
6. Potassium metaphosphate, KPO_3	40	33	2.5	3.3		
7. Hardwood ashes	3-8	2.5-7	33-12.5	40-14		
8. Tobacco stems	6	5	16.7	20		

7.5 Secondary and micro nutrients

Major fertilizer materials usually contain other essential plant food elements in addition to N, P and K.

Calcium is required by plants as a nutrient as well as being associated with the lime requirements of a soil. In turf grass composition (concerning quantity), Ca is third after N and K. It affects the soil physical and chemical properties. This fact is often more important than calcium as a plant nutrient.

Calcium is a structural element, participates in cell wall and chromosome structure, promotes early root formation and growth, improves plant strength and vigor and neutralizes poisonous compounds produced in plants. It does not move in plants and therefore first deficiency symptoms appear on young plant tissue. It appears first as a reddish brown color between the vein of younger leaf margins. Later, leaf tips curl, wither and die. Leaves have a wrinkled appearance. Short and many-branched roots are a result of Ca deficiencies.

Calcium is usually supplied with lime, superphosphate and other phosphatic materials. Cyanamide, a nitrogen fertilizer, also contains appreciable quantities of calcium.

Magnesium is a constituent of living cells and it is an essential part of *chlorophyll*. Magnesium is involved in many enzyme reactions, phosphorus uptake and metabolism, acts as a carrier of phosphorus, carbohydrates and promotes formation of oils and fats. Magnesium is mobile in plants and first *deficiency* symptoms usually appear on older leaves as loss of green color. The veins of leaves remain green. Leaves may have sharply defined pale green stripes changing to a cherry red.

Light sandy acid soils are usually more often deficient in magnesium than heavy soils. Magnesium requirements are met most readily by the use of dolomitic limestone, magnesium sulfate, and seed meals. Readily soluble magnesium sulfate (Epsom salts) is used to correct deficiencies quickly by applying 2 lbs. per 1,000 sq. ft.

Sulfur is a constituent of certain amino acids and it is involved in protein synthesis and oxidation-reduction reactions in plants. It also is important in nitrogen fixation by legume nodules. Sulfur does not move readily in plants and *deficiency* symptoms first appear on younger leaves as a gradual "firing", starting at leaf tips. Scorching may extend to the base of the blades. Veins of some grasses don't get chlorotic. Slow stunted growth may occur.

Superphosphate, ammonium sulfate, potassium sulfate and gypsum can be mentioned as a source of sulfur. In industrial areas the plant may obtain sulfur from contaminated air.

Micro nutrients or so-called trace elements are required in very small quantities but they are needed for normal plant growth. Unsatisfactory plant growth may occur, especially on sandy and muck soils, due to the lack of one or more of these elements. Regular fertilizers, like superphosphate or barn manure contain trace elements in appreciable quantities. In some cases they may be applied as a spray to the growing plants. With some of these elements the range between beneficial and detrimental amounts is very narrow and therefore should be used carefully.

Generally, deficiencies of micro elements are rare in turf. Very light sandy soils or overlimed soils may develop iron deficiencies. This may occur more often in arid regions or, as with centipede grass, in warm southern regions. Pale yellowing plants, even under good nitrogen fertilization, is a symptom to look for. Chelated iron or iron (ferrous) sulfate can be used as a foliage spray for correction. Follow the manufacturer's recommendations when using chelates. In cases of copper, manganese or zinc deficiencies sulfates of these elements can be used. Borax for boron and sodium molybdate for molybdenum will provide help.

Since micro element deficiencies on turf grasses are rare and difficult to diagnose visually, a suspected deficiency should be verified by plant analysis before trying to correct it.

7.6 Complete fertilizers

Most fertilizers sold in the United States, except organics, are mixtures of fertilizer materials containing nitrogen, phosphorus and potassium. Such mixed fertilizers usually are called complete fertilizers. Major nutrients in a complete fertilizer are always given in percentage form in N-P-K order on a fertilizer bag. For example, a 20-10-10 fertilizer contains 20% nitrogen, 10% phosphoric acid (P_2O_5), and 10% potash (K_2O). The remaining 60%, known as the carrier, is considered inert, although it often contains valuable secondary nutrients such as calcium, magnesium, sulfur or minor elements. This complete fertilizer possesses a 2-1-1 ratio. Complete fertilizers of 16-4-8 and 15-5-10 analysis would possess 4-1-2 and 3-1-2 ratios, respectively.

Percentage composition of a mixed fertilizer is called *analysis* (grade). 20-10-10 analysis has a total of 40% of plant nutrients. *Low* analysis is when total plant nutrients in a complete fertilizer is less than 20% (e.g. 8-6-4). *Concentrated* fertilizer has more than 30% of total nutrients. *High* analysis will be represented by 20-30% of total plant nutrients.

Fertilizer recommendations usually are expressed in pounds of N, P_2O_5, and K_2O per 1,000 sq. ft. or per acre, e.g., when establishing a lawn in New England 2 lb. of N, 2-6 lb. of P_2O_5 and 2 lb. K_2O are recommended in preparing the seedbed before seeding. The recommendation requires that nitrogen, phosphorus and potassium be applied in a 1-3-1 ratio. If possible, it is best to choose a complete fertilizer having the same nutrient ratio, e.g., 5-15-5, 5-12-4, or 10-30-10. If we divided the percent nitrogen into 100 we would get the number of pounds of respective fertilizers needed to supply one pound of N per 1,000 sq. ft. Twice this would supply the recommended amount.

$$\frac{100}{5} \times 2 = 40 \text{ lb of 5-15-5}$$

$$\frac{100}{4} \times 2 = 50 \text{ lb of 4-12-4}$$

$$\frac{100}{10} \times 2 = 20 \text{ lb of 10-30-10}$$

Also we can compute by using simple proportions, e.g., how many pounds of 5-15-5, 4-12-4 or 10-30-10 fertilizers do we need to get 2 lb. of nitrogen?

$$\frac{100}{5} = \frac{x}{2} \quad x = \frac{100 \times 2}{5} = 40 \text{ lb of 5-15-5}$$

$$\frac{100}{4} = \frac{x}{2} \quad x = \frac{100 \times 2}{4} = 50 \text{ lb of 4-12-4}$$

$$\frac{100}{10} = \frac{x}{2} \quad x = \frac{100 \times 2}{10} = 20 \text{ lb of 10-30-10}$$

As we see, the recommended rates are exactly supplied by 40, 50, and 20 lbs. of fertilizers, respectively.

The recommended proportions of N, P_2O_5 and K_2O do not always correspond to the ratio of these nutrients carried by mixed complete fertilizers on hand or in supply. In such a case, the rate of application for maintenance fertilization should be based upon needs to supply recommended nitrogen. In establishing a lawn for seedbed preparation in many regions the right amount of P_2O_5 should be mixed in and recommendations should be based on phosphorus needs. If necessary, individual fertilizer materials like ammonium nitrate, superphosphate or muriate of potash can be used to supplement the needed nutrients of any complete fertilizer.

7.7. Soil tests. Liming

Plant nutrient elements in a soil can be: a) soluble and readily available, b) insoluble but available when needed by growing plants, and c) fixed and not available (for the time being) for growing plants.

Plant nutrient deficiencies can often be detected by the appearance of grasses. Rapid chemical tests of various types are available to determine fertilizer needs. State agricultural experiment stations, county agents and commercial companies offer soil testing services. The farmer or home owner can buy a kit and make his own soil analysis. Determinations usually include the pH value and quantities of organic matter, and available P_2O_5 and K_2O present.

Simple soil tests for nitrogen are not reliable. Testing methods usually measure the quantity of soluble nitrogen in the soil. Grass roots absorb the nitrogen as soon as it is formed, so a soil test may show a deficiency when really the supply is satisfactory. Secondly, high levels of nitrogen may be shown one day but may be leached shortly afterward by heavy rains. In a grass sod nitrogen is steadily exhausted and it is always advisable to supply it. It is a good practice to have soils tested by a reliable institution. They have the facility to determine the *total* available N of a soil.

Soil tests are usually used to determine the amounts of available phosphorus and potassium. Fertilization recommendations are often based on these findings. Phosphorus is a very stable element in the soil and is not subject to leaching. Potassium is held in soil by clay complexes and organic matter and is not readily lost by leaching. Determination of results are of practical value only when they are interpreted by a person who knows the soil, who has had fertilizer experience with turf, and who understands the problem of its maintenance. In some cases soil may be loaded with phosphorus but fixed and not available due to the acidity, alkalinity, or lack of organic matter in the soil. In such a case tests may indicate the need of phosphorus but actually what such a soil needs is lime or organic matter.

Of course, fertilizer levels should be higher where clippings are removed and active growth is maintained by liberal irrigation practices. Soil tests for acidity and alkalinity are most valuable and applicable for practice. The degree of acidity or alkalinity of a soil is called the *soil reaction* and is designated by the term pH. The pH scale ranges from 0 to 14 and it is based upon the logarithm of acid ions. For the pH scale, the dividing point is 7. Figures below 7 represent increasing acidity; the ones above, increasing alkalinity.

In wet cool regions soils are usually acidic. Water increases the leaching of basic Ca and Mg salts. High organic matter contents produce organic acids. Due to leaching and organic matter, the soil surface is more acid than lower soil horizons. In arid regions due to Na content, soils are alkaline (Fig. 7.2). The best phosphorus availability to plants is at pH 6-7.5. Iron, manganese, copper and zinc are unavailable in alkaline soils (Fig. 7.1).

Most lawn grasses grow best in the pH range of 6.0-7.5. As a general rule, if the pH values are below 5.0, liming is needed. On the other hand, if the pH is above 7.5 acidifying fertilizers or an application of sulfur or gypsum ($CaSO_4$) should be applied. Ryegrasses and bluegrasses do not tolerate marked acidity. They grow best at soil conditions close to neutral. Wheat grass, buffalo grass and grama grass are well adapted to semi-arid regions and tolerate alkaline soil conditions. On the other hand bent grass and fescues tolerate slight soil acidity. Sheep fescue and centipede grass usually prefer acid soil conditions with a pH of 4.3 to 5.8. On neutral or alkaline soils centipede frequently becomes chlorotic from lack of iron.

7.8 Lime materials

Lime is obtained from deposits of limestone rock or produced as a by-product of the chemical industry. The common liming materials are:

a) Calcic limestone or calcite, composed largely of calcium carbonate ($CaCO_3$). It is ground limestone and most widely used for liming acid soils.

b) Dolomitic limestone. Domomite is calcium and magnesium carbonate ($CaMg(CO_3)_2$). It is ground limestone high in magnesium. Pure dolomite contains 26.6% Ca and 13.1% Mg.

Table 7.5. Soil reaction range for good growth of turf grasses (1, 26, 30, 38)

Grasses	pH range
Cool-season grasses	
1. Wheat grass, fairway	6.1-8.6
2. Bluegrass, Kentucky	5.8-7.5
3. Bluegrass, rough	5.8-7.2
4. Bluegrass, Canada	5.7-7.2
5. Ryegrass, annual & perennial	5.8-7.4
6. Bent grass, colonial & creeping	5.6-7.0
7. Fescues, red & chewing	5.6-6.8
8. Fescue, tall	5.5-7.0
9. Bluegrass, annual	5.5-7.0
10. Bent grass, velvet	5.2-6.5
11. Redtop	5.0-6.5
12. Fescue, sheep	4.5-5.8
Warm-season grasses	
1. Bahia grass	6.5-7.5
2. St. Augustine grass	6.3-7.8
3. Grama grass	6.1-8.6
4. Buffalo grass	6.1-8.0
5. Bermuda grass	5.7-7.0
6. Zoysia grass	5.5-7.0
7. Carpet grass	5.2-6.7
8. Centipede grass	4.3-5.8

c) Burned lime or quicklime is calcium (CaO) or magnesium (MgO) oxides obtained by burning limestones. They are water soluble, faster in action, caustic and should not be used, especially on sandy soils.

d) Hydrated (slaked) lime $Ca(OH)_2$ or $Mg(OH)_2$ is obtained by adding water to burned lime. They are hydroxides of Ca or Mg. In this form lime is somewhat water soluble and their action in neutralizing is more rapid than that of ground limestone. Hydrated lime and ammonia fertilizers react together and subsequently release ammonia gas which is toxic to grass. They should not be applied at the same time; two weeks apart is all right.

Other materials for correcting acidity may be mentioned: marl, coral, oyster shells, slag. Marl is clay mixed with calcite ($CaCO_3$). Slag is a by-product of the iron industry and consists of calcium silicates.

100 lbs. of pure limestone, 74 lbs. of hydrated lime and 56 lbs. of burned lime have the same neutralizing value. In a dolomitic lime $CaCO_3$ plus $MgCO_3$ should not be less than 90%. $MgCO_3$ has slightly greater neutralizing power than $CaCO_3$. In practice these elements exist as a mixture of Ca and Mg carbonate which is more insoluble and is harder to grind than pure Ca carbonate. Thus, in the field, the higher neutralizing value of MgO from high magnesium limestone is offset by decreased rate of reactivity. In practice, CaO and MgO in liming materials should be given equal weight as far as their neutralizing values are concerned. Finely ground limestone acts faster than coarsely ground limestone. For turf use at least one-half should pass a 100-mesh screen, and all should pass a 10-mesh screen.

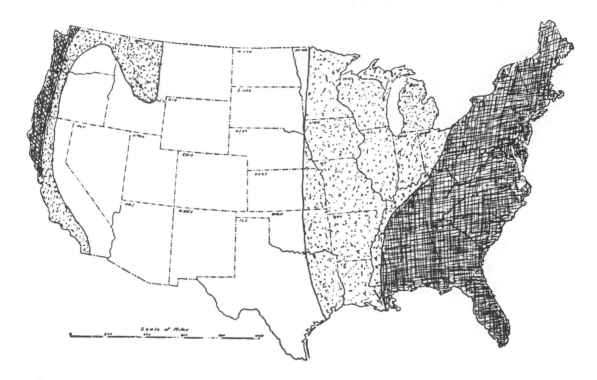

Figure 7.2 Soil acidity regions
        Shaded areas are acid and require liming.
        The darker the area the more acid (National Limestone Institute 1953)

Rate and application

The rate of applying lime is determined partly by the texture of soil. Due to the differences in cation exchange and buffering capacities more lime is needed on a loam or clay soil than on a sandy soil to produce the same change in pH. Some acid soils are deficient in magnesium and dolomitic limestone which contains not less than 20 to 30 percent magnesium should be used.

As a rule in establishing lawns in acid regions (Fig. 7.2) in the United States 50 lbs. of limestone on light sandy soils and 100 lbs. of limestone on heavier loam soils should be applied for each 1,000 sq. ft. area. If acidity soils tests are available, the following rates are suggested:

	Pounds limestone for 1,000 sq. ft.	
Soil pH	Light soil	Heavier soil
over 6.2	0	0
5.2-6.2	25-50	50-75
under 5.2	50-75	100-150

In determining limestone rates the needs of various grasses for optimum growth conditions should be taken into consideration: bluegrass, Bermuda grass or ryegrasses need more lime than fescues or bent grasses. When establishing a lawn, lime should be applied to the seedbed before seeding and mixed in 5 to 6 inches deep. As turf grass maintenance, lime applications in the late fall, winter or early spring are most effective.

If the soil is too alkaline, e.g., pH is above 8.0, one should lower the pH. Too high a pH interferes with nutrient availability (Fe, Mn, Cu, Zn, B) and may be detrimental to grass. Ammonium sulfate and iron sulfate are the most practical to use to lower a high pH in soils. Elemental sulfur at 3-5 lbs. per 1,000 sq. ft., sulfuric acid or aluminum sulfate can also be used. Acidifying fertilizers can be helpful and practical to use (See Tables 7.1, 7.2) or gypsum ($CaSO_4$) can be spread over the surface at 30-50 lb/1,000 sq. ft. and mixed in 4-6 in. deep.

7.9 Soil samples

Soil samples must be truly representative. Variations in soil, topography and turf grasses determine the number of composite samples to collect. Each composite sample should consist of at least five or six cores of uniform diameter and exactly 3 inches long, i.e. all samples should be taken to exactly the same 3-inch depth in an established lawn. The 3-inch depth should be measured below the surface thatch of turf. Samples should be about 5-6 inches deep in preparing the seedbed for new seedings. Small, inexpensive soil sampling probes are available from lawn supply houses. Each sample should be air dried before placing in clean containers for shipment. Label the outside of each sample with a soft lead pencil, giving the pertinent information. Include information about drainage, kind of grass, maintenance, irrigation and fertilization practices. Soil should be tested every three to four years.

Summary

1. Nitrogen (N), phosphorus (P) and potassium (K) are major or primary plant nutrients.

   Calcium (Ca), magnesium (Mg), and sulfur (S) are secondary plant nutrients.

   Iron (Fe), boron (B), manganese (Mn), copper (Cu), zinc (Zn), molybdenum (Mo), and chlorine (Cl) are needed in very small amounts for plant growth and are called micro nutrients.

2. Nitrogen is the key element in turf production. It is primarily responsible for vegetative and continuous growth. Constant liberal supplies are essential in turf management. Nitrogen may be applied in inorganic, organic or as a synthetic organic. Inorganic is soluble and fast acting. Organic and synthetic organics are slow working, do not burn grass and can be applied in larger amounts. These are especially important in turf grass maintenance fertilization.

3. Phosphorus and potassium are present in heavier soils in larger quantities than in light soils. Phosphorus is readily fixed in the soil in an insoluble form. Surface applications of phosphate fertilizers work down into the soil to the root zone at a very slow pace. Where needed, phosphorus should be applied to the seedbed before seeding a lawn. Nitrogen and potassium needs can be met by applications to the established turf sod.

4. Mixtures of fertilizer materials containing N, P and K are called complete fertilizer. Major nutrients in a complete fertilizer are given in percentages of $N-P_2O_5-K_2O$ on a fertilizer bag.

5. The most valuable and applicable soil tests are for acidity-alkalinity and for available nitrogen, phosphorus, and potassium.

6. To decrease soil acidity calcic and dolomitic limestones are used. Dolomitic limestone contains magnesium and should be used in soil where magnesium is needed.

CHAPTER 8
ESTABLISHING LAWNS. SEEDING

A new lawn can be established by seeding, sodding, or vegetatively by using sprigs, plugs, stolons and rhizomes. In any case, a successful turf establishment depends upon good seedbed preparation. This is the foundation for a lawn and a good foundation is the key to success in any building program. It is concerned primarily with the creation of good conditions for grass growth in the upper surface layer of soil.

8.1 Grading and drainage

The construction of a new lawn is very often associated with the building of a house. As a rule the top 4 to 6 inches of soil should be pushed to one side and piled for later distribution after the building and subsoil grading operations are completed. Subsoil is the layer which underlies the immediate topsoil or loam. When a new house is planned, topsoil should be separated from the subsoil when digging the basement or foundation. Before starting rough grading building debris such as boards, paper boxes, bricks, cans, wire pieces, tree stumps, etc. should be removed. This debris should not be buried in the subsoil. Buried debris will create pockets and depressional areas which will cause trouble in the future in maintaining a satisfactory lawn. Stones larger than 1-2 inches in diameter should be removed from the 3-5 inch upper soil zone. They may interfere with turf aerification (coring). Good surface drainage is important in lawns and especially in athletic fields where rapid surface drainage is needed. Poor soil aeration, shallow root systems and increased soil compaction result in turf areas that are consistently too wet.

Good surface drainage by providing proper slopes and grades in relation to the house, other buildings on the property, walks, driveways and parking lots is of first importance. The soil should slope gently away from the foundation of the house so water (from rain or melting snow) will readily be removed. There should not be any high spots that will dry out rapidly or be scalped by mowing and no low spots in which water will stand and make puddles. Steep slopes are very difficult to establish and maintain. The lawn should be planned without steep slopes or terraces, if possible. It is better to build retaining walls than steep slopes or terraces. One or two percent slope, i.e., a 6 to 12 inch drop in 50 linear feet is adequate for good surface drainage. The slope should not exceed a 3-4 feet drop in 50 linear feet.

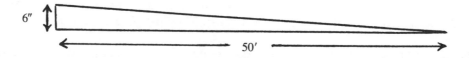

Figure 8.1 One percent slope

A system of tile drains is required when natural drainage is inadequate. If the subsoil is poorly drained or has a history of water logging, surface drainage will be inadequate. Drain tile installed at about 20-foot intervals, 3-4 feet below the surface may be used. In drainage line should fall 6 inches per 100 feet (at least 3"/100'). The herringbone system of design is the most satisfactory. It resembles a tree in outline (Fig. 8.2). The main tile line represents the trunk of the tree and the laterals correspond to the branches. The main should follow the general direction of the slope. The lateral lines should make a 45 degree angle with the main line and should not be more than 20 feet apart. A 3-4 inch tile for laterals and a 4-6 inch size for the main is satisfactory. Plastic or burnt clay tiles are used. In some cases an intercepting system (Fig. 8.2) or even 2-4 inch slits 2-4 feet deep and filled with gravel or crushed stones up to soil surface can serve the purpose. For closed low spots, dry wells can be satisfactory. Direction, seepage area, etc., may vary from place to place and in many cases professional help may be needed to lay tile properly with an accurate consistent slope and appropriate main drains and outlet. Consult your county agricultural agent, experiment station or tile dealer for advice.

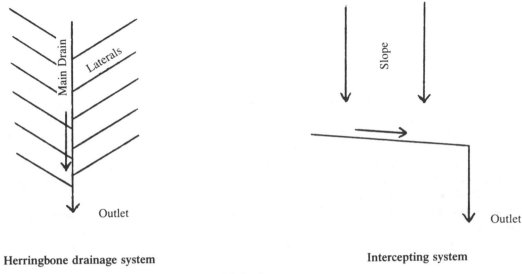

Herringbone drainage system   Intercepting system

Figure 8.2 Drainage systems

If topsoil has been pushed to one side and piled and if trucks and other heavy vehicles have driven over the planned lawn area the subsoil has probably been packed. Topsoil never should be placed on packed and uneven subsoil. Hard and uneven subsoil should be loosened by harrowing, disking or rototilling about 5-6 inches deep. The roots of turf grasses need a firm seedbed but not compacted soil with poor aeration and water movement conditions. If subsoil is evenly loose, tillage may not be required before distributing topsoil. Hard and uneven soil should be loosened and a rough grade established.

8.2 Improving soil

In some cases additional topsoil or "loam" may be needed. One should be extremely cautious when buying it. It should be of good texture and structure, clean from debris, toxic salts, and especially not contaminated with seeds, stolons or rhizomes of noxious weeds. The prescribed amount of topsoil, e.g., 4-6 inch layer, over subsoil is not a must for establishing a good lawn. If the subsoil is uniform and of good quality a 1 to 3 inch layer of good topsoil may do the job. In many instances it is more practical to add organic matter and till it into the existing soil than to buy topsoil. In some cases building a lawn from subsoil alone may be feasible and even preferable especially when top soil is infested with noxious weed rhizomes, stolons or seeds. A good subsoil well fertilized, limed and enriched with organic matter in many cases will provide a satisfactory seedbed for a lawn. Grass itself furnishes over 50 lb. of organic matter through decomposing roots yearly per 1,000 sq. ft. of lawn. Usually it takes more time for grasses to establish but with good care the lawn improves itself and develops into a good turf area.

Lawn soil should be improved in cases where subsoil or even topsoil is too heavy, sticky or too light and "bottomless" before seeding. We can improve both by adding organic matter and sand to the heavy soils and organic matter and loam clay to sandy soils. These soil improving additives should be applied when preparing the seedbed with lime and basic fertilizers before application of starter fertilizer and seeding. If, for the improvement of soil, undecomposed organic matter (sawdust, raw straw, ground corncobs or tobacco stems) are used, an extra 20-40 lb/A N of a nitrogenous fertilizer should be added as food for bacteria working on decomposition. For more details on soil improvement see Chapter 6.

If planned, underground irrigation lines or sprinkler irrigation should be installed at this time.

The surface of a prepared seedbed of a lawn before seeding should be at least one inch lower than the surface of adjacent walks or driveways. After a lawn is established the surface will then be on the same level as the walkway and grass scalping will be avoided.

8.3 Seedbed preparation with chemicals*

It usually is cheaper to control all kinds of pests in the soil before seeding a lawn than later after the turf is established. Soil infested with nutsedge (*Cyperus* spp.), quack grass (*Agropyron repens*), japanese bamboo (*Polygonum cuspidatum*), or other troublesome pests should be eliminated before seeding. At the present time there are a lot of good chemicals to do the job. It is important to use a chemical which does the job and decomposes fast without leaving residues in the soil which may injure or kill grass seedlings. Potent soil sterilants like diuron, monuron (substituted urea compounds) or simazine, atrazine (triazines) have long lasting soil residue effects and should not be used. Nutsedge is becoming the most troublesome perennial weed in some parts of the United States. This weed spreads mostly by underground tubers (nuts) and it is almost impossible to eradicate in a short time with available herbicides. Methyl bromide, a soil sterilant-fumigant kills most weeds, seeds, tubers, rhizomes, stolons, fungi and nematodes. It does not leave any residual effect; grass seed can be sown 2-3 days after treatment. The following is a list of soil sterilants, fumigants and herbicides which may be used in sterilizing the seedbed before establishing a lawn. Every year new and better chemicals are developed by agricultural chemical industries. Always consult the agricultural county agent and state agricultural experiment station for the latest news and developments.

List of chemicals for seedbed cleaning:

Herbicide-sterilants:

1. Glyphosate (Roundup; N-(phosphonomethyl glycine) — A nonselective translocated into roots with visible effects in 7-10 days. Best results on unmown plants. Good for control of quack grass. Use 2-4 lb./A of active ingredient. Seeding can be done 3-7 days after application.

2. Cacodylic acid (hydroxydimethylarsine oxide) is a nonselective postemergent contact herbicide. Cacodylic acid is used at 5-20 lb./100 gallon spray to wet the tops well for good kill. It is not absorbed by roots and can be used under the trees. Seeding can be done 5-7 days after application.

3. Paraquat (1,1-dimethyl-4, 4-bipyridinium salt) is a contact herbicide, kills the plant tops; rhizomes are not killed. Used at ½-1 lb. active ingredient per acre. Breaks down in soil and there is no residue problem but it is not safe for the operator and all precautions indicated on the container should be carefully followed. Seeding can be done 1-2 days after application.

4. Dalapon (2,2-dichloropropionic acid) and amitrole (3-amino-s-triazole). Dalapon is effective against grassy weeds like quack grass, Bermuda or Dallis grass. Treat as label indicates and when grass is growing rapidly. Reseed 4-6 weeks later. The cooler the weather the longer the wait.

---

* For more detailed information on chemicals, see the chapter on weed control.

Amitrole is used for broad-leaved and grassy weed control and when both kinds of weeds are present it can be used as a mixture with dalapon. Useful in nutsedge control. Seeding can be done a couple of weeks after application.

5. Calcium cyanamide ($CaCN_2$) is a nitrogen fertilizer. Safe to use for temporary soil sterilization, kills many weeds when used 50-75 lb./1,000 sq. ft. Cyanamide should be applied when soil temperature is over 55°F. It should be worked into the soil 2-3 inches deep. Treated area should be kept moist (water) for 3-6 weeks before seeding or planting. Better results on heavier soil.

Fumigants-sterilants:

1. Methyl bromide (Dowfume MC). Volatile and very active fumigant. It kills living plants, most seeds, rhizomes, stolons, insects, nematodes, fungi. Poisonous. In southern warm regions, while establishing zoysia lawns, it is practical to use for killing nut grass, Bermuda grass, carpet grass, or Johnson grass. It should be used under a gas-proof cover like polyethylene film. Usually applied on prepared seedbed when temperatures are above 65°F. Soil should be kept moist for several days before treatment. Grass seed can be sown 2-3 days after treatment.

2. Metham (Vapam, SMDC) (Na-methyldithiocarbamate). Liquid, soil fumigant, easy to use. For best results soil should be kept moist several days before treatment. (Rates) 6-9 lb. active ingredient per 1,000 sq. ft. Seeding can be done 3-4 weeks after treatment. Apply as label indicates.

3. Vorlex (chlorinated hydrocarbons and methyl isothiocyanate). Soil fumigant-sterilant. Use as label indicates.

All these chemicals should be applied exactly as the label indicates. Most pesticides are poisonous, follow the safety precautions indicated on the label. Soil sterilants-fumigants such as methyl bromide should be used and applied by experienced persons, professionals.

In summary: *If a soil is infested with noxious pests (weeds, insects, nematodes, etc.) it is more practical to postpone seeding (even for a year or two) and eradicate them completely than to establish a lawn and try to control them afterwards.*

8.4 Lime. Basic fertilizers.

Rough grading, drainage and seedbed cleaning are the initial steps in establishing a lawn. The next important step is liming and fertilization. It is advisable to have the soil tested. As we have already discussed soil tests are especially important to find the needs for liming. If the pH is lower that 6.2, soil should be limed before seeding turf grasses. Over much of the northeastern part of the United States lime would be useful, but a pH test is the only sure indicator of whether or not it is needed for a given lawn. If no tests were done, 100 lb. of ground limestone should be applied per 1,000 sq. ft. on heavier soils and somewhat lower rates on light soils. This will meet the average requirements in most parts of the United States. If pH values of soil are known to raise about one unit, one could use 100 lb. of ground limestone for each 1,000 sq. ft. of lawn. Rates of hydrated lime should be lower. Hydrated lime should not be applied on growing grass unless flushed from the foliage. Hydrated lime should be applied separately from the fertilizers.

Before seeding a lawn, a complete fertilizer containing all three major plant nutrients should be used. Although we apply a complete fertilizer, the most important factor at this time is to apply enough phosphorus to the seedbed. This is the last chance to get phosphorus down into the root zone, for P does not move through the soil as readily as potassium. Potassium and nitrogen fertilizers are more soluble and can be applied to an established sod thus supplying these plant nutrients when needed.

Of course, soil fertility varies greatly and phosphorus as well as other main fertilizer needs may differ considerably from place to place or from region to region in the United States. Chemical soils tests should be made before any fertilizer is added. Also, the need to consult extension specialists for advice cannot be over-emphasized. Most soils of Idaho do not need the addition of phosphorus and potassium. Again fertilization needs may depend on the mixture or grass we plan to have in our lawn, e.g., in the south a seedbed for a Bermuda grass lawn should be better supplied with plant nutrients than a centipede grass lawn. In Washington state, west of the Cascades, a colonial bent grass lawn will need higher fertility levels than in the provinces east of the mountains for a red or sheep fescue lawn. In most cases in northern, southern, or western regions of the United States 2 to 6 pounds P_2O_5, 2 to 3 pounds potash (K_2O) and nitrogen as inorganic fertilizers per 1,000 sq. ft. of seedbed are practical rates to apply. These are basic fertilizers used in establishing a lawn. These fertilizers, besides being plant nutrients for the future turf grasses, are also soil nutrients important for micro-organisms and directly or indirectly affecting soil biological processes and structure. Too high rates of nitrogen in basic fertilization is not practical: young seedlings do not utilize very much and rapidly released N may be lost through leaching or volatilization.

Lime as well as basic fertilizer should be uniformly spread over the graded surface and well incorporated 4 to 6 inches deep into the soil. When large amounts of lime and phosphate need to be applied it is advisable to apply one-half of the amount on graded subsoil and the rest with basic fertilizer on top of the seedbed. In each case, lime and fertilizers should be worked into the soil 4-6 inches deep. Generally, after an application of fertilizers, incorporation should not be delayed longer than a couple of days. Both lime and fertilizers can be applied the same day if incorporation follows in a day or so. In order to prevent rapid phosphorus fixation in soil it is advantageous to apply lime as early as possible and before basic fertilization. Of course, applied lime should be incorporated 4-6 inches into the soil. Effective incorporation of lime and basic fertilizers can be obtained by thorough disking, harrowing, plowing, rototilling or even spading. Soil modifying (improving) materials used can be incorporated along with lime or basic fertilizer in a single tillage operation. The next table (Table 8.1) gives the amounts of fertilizers needed to supply approximately 2-3 lb. of N, and K_2O and 2-6 lb. of P_2O_5 to the seedbed of a lawn either 1,000 sq. ft. or an acre in size. The best is a complete fertilizer which has an analysis ratio 1-1-1, 1-2-1 or even 1-3-1 where soil enrichment with phosphorus is needed. If phosphorus is not high enough in the analysis, then it should be additionally supplemented e.g., superphosphate.

Table 8.1 Basic inorganic fertilizers for seedbed preparation in establishing a lawn.

Fertilizer	Amount in lb per		Ratio supplied
	1,000 sq. ft.	acre	
1. 8-8-8	25	1100	1-1-1
2. 10-10-10	20	880	1-1-1
3. 5-10-5	40	1760	1-2-1
4. 10-20-10	20	880	1-2-1
5. 5-5-5 and 20% superphosphate	40 10	1760 440	1-2-1
6. 5-15-5	40	1760	1-3-1
7. 10-10-10 and 20% superphosphate	20 20	880 880	1-3-1

The limestone, basic fertilizers and any soil improving additives should be mixed well into the top 4-6 inches of soil. Mixing all these added ingredients into the seedbed is the most important step in insuring deep rooting of the grasses.

8.5 Final grading. Firm seedbed.

In final grading slopes should be checked, larger stones and foreign materials removed and the soil surface levelled. The seedbed should be firm and compact. For firming the seedbed a heavy (250-300 lb.) roller or cultipacker can be used. If a water balast roller is used it should be filled ½ to ¾ full. A roller 1.5 ft. in diameter and 2 ft. long, outside measurements, holds approximately 25 gallons and when filled with water it weighs about 275 lb. The soil is best worked when it is damp — neither dry nor wet. Alternately raking and rolling the area until footmarks cannot be seen readily or they are less than a quater inch deep. When making a firm seedbed high spots should be taken off and the low ones filled in. The surface, now prepared, will stay for many years so the extra care is worth the effort. A good, level and firm seedbed is desired. Wooden lawn rakes are very handy for the final grading operation.

Where lawns are to be started by vegetative planting, the soil should be prepared in the same manner.

8.6 Starter fertilizers

Starter fertilization is used to insure that enough readily available plant nutrients are present near the seedbed surface where grass seed germinates. Complete fertilizers are usually used. Nitrogen for grass seedlings is needed and therefore nitrogen alone as a starter fertilizer will do the job. Apply the starter fertilizer at a rate that will provide 1.0 lb. of actual nitrogen per 1,000 sq. ft. Table 8.2 indicates the amounts of fertilizer needed to provide nitrogen per 1,000 sq. ft. and per acre as starter fertilization. Starter fertilizers should be raked lightly into the soil surface (about one inch deep). By using only 0.5 lb N/1,000 sq. ft., seeds and starter fertilizer may be mixed with the soil as one operation.

Table 8.2. Starter inorganic fertilizers for seedbed preparation in establishing a lawn.

Fertilizer	Amount in pounds per	
	1,000 sq. ft.	acre
1. 10-10-10	10	440
2. 10-6-4	10	440
3. 8-6-4	12	530
4. 20-10-10	5	220
5. 20-20-20	5	220
6. 10-20-10	10	440
7. 33-0-0	3	130
8. 5-10-10	20	880

In cases where the topsoil of the seedbed is of good quality, rich with organic matter and when basic fertilizers were mixed in with higher rates of nitrogen, starter fertilization is not a critical factor in establishing a good lawn. In regions where soils are rich with phosphorus and potassium and where basic fertilization is not used, starter complete fertilizers should be applied.

Starter fertilization can be applied as early postemergent treatment when grass seedlings reach 1-2 inch height. Rate of application is 0.5 lb. N per 1,000 sq. ft. Due to the possibility of burning, higher rates should be avoided.

8.7 Seeding time

In establishing a lawn by seed or vegetatively, the best results can be expected when seeding or planting is done just prior to the most favorable conditions for the grass to grow. Once germination of grass seed starts it should be continued without interruption and therefore it is best to plant grass just ahead of the season that favors grass growth most. Grasses seeded at the proper time can get a good start and compete well weeds before an unfavorable season comes. Typical grasses of the northern cool region grow and develop best in the fall and early in the spring. Therefore, late August through September usually is the best season of the year to establish a lawn. Seedings too late in the fall are no good: seedlings do not develop before winter and often can be killed by low temperatures or by thawing and heaving in the spring. The second best season for lawn building is early spring before the middle of May in the northern regions of the United States. Seeding after mid-May is risky and should be avoided. Usually, spring seedings should be put in as soon as the soil is in workable condition. Early spring seeding takes advantage of cool temperatures and spring rains in the humid areas.

Because of climatic differences in the fall as well as in the spring the best dates for seeding will vary in the northern region of the United States. In the northern parts of this region the best dates for seeding will be earlier in the fall and later in the spring than in the more southern areas. Even within the limits of single states, hundreds of miles from north to south like New York, Missouri, or Illinois, slight variations in the best dates for seeding are present (   ). In some cases the date of seeding may need to be adjusted to a specific week problem, e.g., in the eastern part of Washington state the best time is late summer and early spring. In western Washington because of weeds, it is best to seed in the spring. Annual bluegrass, chickweed (*Stellaria* spp.) and pearlwort (*Sagina* spp.) will grow all winter while the grass seedlings are dormant if the lawn is fall seeded. Where enough water for irrigation is available time of seeding becomes a less important factor. It is important to get grass seedlings established before the advent of warm weather and the germination of summer weeds.

A satisfactory turf establishment in the northern cool region can be obtained by seeding even in July or August but newly seeded areas should be kept continuously moist without any interruption by irrigation. Due to the possibility of continuous hot weather conditions in the transition zone, summer seeding of northern grasses should be avoided. Seeding in the summer is less desirable because more frequent watering is required and the grass seedlings grow slowly during hot weather. In addition, if summer germinating weed seeds (e.g., crab-grass, barnyard grass, foxtails, fall panicum, common purslane, redroot pigweed, lambsquarters, etc.) are present in the soil their seedings strongly compete and may destroy the lawn before it can become established.

Under exceptional cases where because of wet soil conditions spring seedings are impossible, early winter seedings may be successful if low temperatures and continuous snow cover protect seeds from germination and desiccation before the spring. In case of overseedings for renovation of deteriorated turf, March-April or so called "frost seedings" can be successful. Seeds get into soil cracks, germinate and establish. To insure success, higher seeding rates should be used.

In the southern states warm season grasses are usually propagated vegetatively — common Bermuda, centipede, carpet grass, Bahia and *zoysia japonica* can be propagated also by seeds. At the present time seedings of common Bermuda, Bahia and centipede provide high quality lawns. The best time to seed is early in the spring during March, April and May. If soil can be kept moist seedings can be done until late August in most parts of the South. Generally, for southern grasses that require warm temperatures, planting is usually best in late spring or early summer before the warm season. Ryegrass, fescues, bluegrasses, and bents for winter over-seedings of southern main grasses are best to seed in September and October. These grasses planted in the South are usually winter annuals. Tall fescue, even in the deep South, is a perennial grass and if seeded as a main turf grass is best seeded in the fall.

For lasting good results use a recommended seed mixture and seeds of the best available quality (see Chapter 5).

8.8 Seeding

In establishing a turf grass area it is best to do broadcast seeding. It is most important to get seeds distributed over the whole area as uniformly as possible. Seeding can be done by using a mechanical drop-from-hopper spreader, cyclone-type rotary seeder or by hand. Regardless of the seeding method, divide the seed into two equal lots. The second lot should be seeded at right angles to the first, with each lot covering the entire lawn area. Turf grass seeds are small and small amounts are hard to distribute uniformly even when dividing them into two lots. To obtain a uniform distribution, mix the seed with small amounts of topsoil or sand. There are excellent tractor-pulled cultipacker type grass seeders. They are widely used for larger turf areas. Distribution of seed is uniform and the seedbed is also firmed by a corrugated roller. To seed steep slopes and hard to reach terrains, hydroseeders can be used. With a hydroseeder the waterseed suspension is spread on the area together with synthetic mulches. Seeds are left on the soil surface uncovered and continuous soil moisture or irrigation is needed for satisfactory establishment. The hydroseeder is normally used on hilly road-side banks and rocky areas, where cultipacker type seeders cannot be used.

Once distributed, grass seeds should be lightly covered. This can be done by hand raking or by dragging with a brush or mat in two directions. The teeth on the rake should be spaced far enough apart so that the soil flows through the rake and does not build up in front as it is pulled through the soil. Cover large seeds up to ⅜ inches deep and small seeds about ¼ inches deep. It is all right if some of the seeds are still observable (5-10%) after covering. Firm the seeded area with a light empty roller (30 lb.) or cultipacker. This promotes better germination as the seed easily obtains moisture from the soil. When rolling, soil should not be pushed by the roller or scuffed when turning.

New seedings should be kept moist until well established. Once seeds have begun to germinate they must not dry out or they will die. Avoid saturating the soil, excessive moisture is favorable for the development of ''damping off'' (a fungus disease). Light applications of water should be made several times daily, if necessary, to insure that the surface ½ inch of soil is moist at all times.

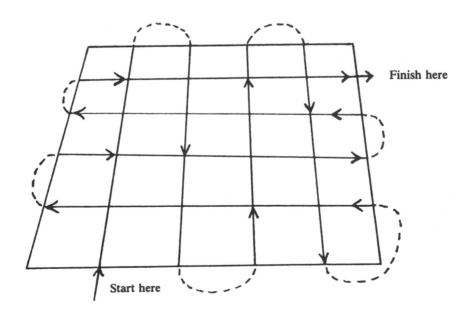

Fig. 8.3 Pattern for seeding of a lawn

In arid or semi-arid regions without irrigation; wheat grasses, buffalo grass or blue grama grass are used for low maintenance turf. Where liberal quantities of organic residues from previous crops are present, seeding is usually made with a seed drill. Annual cereals or Sudan grass also can be seeded during the season prior to planting turf grasses. These crops in the fall are cut leaving a stubble 5-8 inches tall. Grasses are seeded the following spring in this stubble with a seed drill having a farrow opener. The stubble normally retains sufficient moisture needed for turf grasses to establish.

Seedmats. Felt-like mats impregnated with grass seed are on the market to make grass seeding easier. Of course, seed distribution is very uniform. These mats are sometimes impregnated with fertilizers and growth stimulants. These mats also serve as a mulch. The seedbed should be prepared as usual. The mat is unrolled on a prepared seedbed. Theoretically it sounds well but they are not practical. Often the mat disintegrates, weeds sprout below the mat and may lift the mat. In short, they are not practical to use for larger areas on a large scale. They may be applicable on a very small scale for small areas needing a repair job.

8.9 Mulching

The best growth and establishment of turf grass seedings is often obtained by mulching, i.e. covering the seedbed after seeding. Mulching of newly planted areas will reduce erosion by preventing soil and water losses by run off, conserve moisture by reducing moisture loss by evaporation, prevent wasting and blowing of the seed, and permit watering in dry periods without danger of floating out the seed. Finally, mulching will protect soil from puddling and guard seedlings against extreme fluctuations of the weather. In the south, turf grasses such as Bermudas, zoysias, St. Augustine, and centipede, which must be propagated vegetatively using sprigs, plugs or stolons can be successfully established by using various mulches. Specialized machines are available with which sprigs, stolons and manufactured mulches can be applied in a one-step operation.

The use of mulches is especially valuable on slopes, terraces, sloping banks, in waterways or if the seeding is to be done at odd seasons of the year. Mulch must be loose enough to allow rain, air, and some light to reach the sprouting seeds. The most commonly used mulch materials are hay and straw. These materials should be clean and weed-free. At least one 70-80 pound bale of hay or straw mulch will be needed to cover a 1,000 sq. ft. area adequately. Usually 2-3 tons of straw is needed for mulch per acre. It should be spread 3-5 intermeshed straws deep. On steep slopes or windy sites straw or hay can be tied down by strings run between stakes driven into the soil. On sloping areas cheesecloth, open mesh sacking, burlap, used tobacco shade cloth are especially good as a mulch. They will help hold moisture and seeds in place. The covering with these cloth materials should extend from the top of the bottom of the slope and should be pinned down with nails or wire "hairpins" 4-6 inches long. They should be pressed completely into the soil so they will not interfere with mowing. Hay, straw, and the above mentioned cloth materials need not be removed. Grass will grow through the mulching materials, which may be left to rot. Peat moss and uncomposed sawdust are not satisfactory mulches. Polyethylene films to cover seedbeds are also available as mulches. The plastic should be removed shortly after the grass sprouts. It is costly and seems practical to use on small areas only.

Several manufactured fiber mulches are available for mulching lawns. These mulches can be applied like straw or hay by hand or in a single operation when seeding with special hydroplanting equipment. These mulches are most useful on steep roadside banks or rocky areas where conventional planting is difficult. Synthetic mulches should be applied as the label indicates.

8.10 First mowing

The first mowing of new turf grass seedings should be done when the tallest grasses are about 1 to 1½ inches taller than the normal mowing height. Kentucky bluegrass and red fescue sods should be cut at the height of 1½ to 2 inches and therefore the first cutting should be done when plants reach a height of 3-4 inches. It is necessary to remove clippings if they are excessive. Whenever new growth exceeds ⅓ above the cutting height, the lawn should be mown again. To allow grass to grow too high and then cut to height produces a physiological shock to grasses. This is more damaging than always cutting at ⅓ above the normal anticipated height.

Summary

Main points in establishing a lawn by seed:

1. Rough grading, proper slopes, drainage.

2. Mixing in 4-6 inches deep lime, basic fertilizers and needed additives to improve soil. It is time to enrich the soil with phosphorus.

3. Rolling with heavy roller or cultipacking to make seedbed firm.

4. Final grading, starter fertilization with 0.5 to 1 lb. of nitrogen per 1,000 sq. ft. Use complete fertilizer or nitrogen fertilizer alone.

5. Seeding and covering with soil.

6. Light rolling and keep soil moist until seedlings are rooted.

7. In some cases, mulching is advisable.

CHAPTER 9
VEGETATIVE TURF PROPAGATION

9.1 Introduction

For many types of grasses seed is not available or, if available, may not produce plants that are true to type. Such grasses are usually propagated vegetatively using plugs, sprigs or stolons. Grasses planted by vegetative methods include Bermuda, zoysia, St. Augustine, centipede, carpet grass, buffalo, creeping and velvet bent grasses. Centipede, carpet, buffalo and bents may also be seeded. Advantages of vegetative propagation are: a) turf will be identical to the parent sod and, b) a lawn can be established quickly. Disadvantages are: a) very expensive, and b) it is easier to introduce diseases, insects or noxious weeds.

Vegetative propagation of turf is used much more in the South than in the North. This is because preferred grasses for the South are usually not available as seed.

Whether we use plug, sprig or the stolonizing method of vegetative turf propagation, the seedbed should be well prepared. Grading, cleaning, drainage and good fertilization of the upper 4-6 inch seedbed layer should be done in the same manner as for seeding. Soil analysis should be done to determine liming and fertilization needs. Again, it is most important to incorporate enough phosphorus into the soil. Generally, practical rates of phosphorus for areas where Bermuda, zoysia or St. Augustine will be established should be 2-6 lb. P_2O_5 per 1,000 sq. ft. of seedbed. Nitrogen and potassium can be lower. It is best to use a complete fertilizer and, if needed, additional superphosphate or basic slag in regions close to the steel industry. Centipede grows well even under low soil fertility levels and incorporation of 1-3 lb. each of N, P_2O_5 and K_2O will be satisfactory. A complete starter fertilizer can be mixed in 1-2 inches deep before planting. For better feeders like Bermuda, up to 2 lb. of N may be used.

The best time for vegetative turf propagation will vary from place to place, but the best time to plant is in the spring after the last frost. If necessary, most dormant grass plugs and sprigs can be planted in the winter. Of course, warm-season grasses fare better in late spring or early summer.

9.2 Sodding

Sod can be defined as grass-covered earth (turf) tightly knit together by plant roots, rhizomes and stolons about an inch thick which can be used for turf vegetative establishment. Sodding is a fast and most satisfactory way to establish a good turf. One can establish sod turf any time as long as the soil is not frozen.

Sodding is the most expensive method in establishing turf but there are many situations where this method is preferred such as on steep slopes, terraces, and places where grass seedlings can not become well established because of traffic conditions, or when immediate turf is desired. By sodding usable turf is obtained in 2 weeks (when seeding 10-15 weeks is required).

Sod production

Common turf grass species used in sod production are K. bluegrass alone or with red fescue, Bermuda grass and St. Augustine grass. Many states have certification standards for commercial sod production and it is best to use true-to-type certified commercial sod.

A site for growing sod must be level with just enough slope to provide surface drainage. A deep sandy loam with some clay approaches the ideal soil for sod production. However, any soil that holds nutrients, accepts and holds water and produces a uniform sod roll which is acceptable for sod production. Light sandy soils do not hold sod together and should not be used for sod production. Of course, soil should be free of debris, stones, stumps, logs, hardpan layers, and other material which may interfere with tillage and sod cutting operations. Muck and peat soils offer stability of water supply and can be used for production. The sod can be cut more easily and uniformly on muck soils than on mineral soils. Also organic soil weighs less per unit than mineral soil and it is much easier to handle and transport to the customer. Natural drainage of much soils is poor. During fall or early spring organic soils may be soaked with water, become unstable and unaccessible to heavy tractors, trucks or other equipment. Also, muck soils may be exposed to wind erosions during the establishment period.

Mineral soils are definitely better for the sodding of athletic fields or golf greens and tees. On these situations, the type of play involved results in a cleavage plane or point of separation between sod and existing soil. Therefore, it is desirable to have the two soils as similar as possible.

Seedbed preparations, mixtures or single grass seeds, fertilizer program, seeding time and maintenance are the same as used in establishing a lawn by seeding. The goal in sod production is to produce a well knit sod in the shortest time possible. Root and rhizome production are important factors and therefore the fertilization program should be adjusted somewhat by decreasing the nitrogen and increasing the phosphorus and potassium supply. Irrigation during drought will quicken maturity. About one inch of water is suggested at each application. Irrigate weekly when rainfall is inadequate.

Sod is ready for harvest as soon as it has knitted sufficiently to permit handling without tearing. Bluegrass sod planted in mid-August and fertilized properly can sometimes be harvested as early as mid-June of the following year. It usually takes from a half year to two years to produce sod. K. bluegrass and Bermuda grass need the shortest time and zoysia grass, St. Augustine grass and red fescue need much longer time periods when bents or centipede grass are intermediate types.

Cutting

Mechanical sod cutters are available which cut the sod in thin layers with widths of 12, 18 or 24 inches. These are then cut into strips 4-6 ft. in length. The long strips are usually rolled for convenience in handling and laying. Kentucky bluegrass-red fescue sod is usually cut in strips about one sq. yd. in size and warm-season grasses are cut in units of 1 X 2 ft. The thickness of sod removed is an important factor in the productive life of the sod field as well as in the handling and laying of the sod. It is important to both the grower and the buyer that thin cut sod handles more easily, lays better and knits faster than thick cut sod. Sod establishes by producing new adventitious roots rather than by branching old cut roots. From thin sod, roots emerge faster. On the other hand, soil adhering to sod is a source of moisture and too thin sod will be less tolerant to drought. The poorer the sod density and strength the thicker the sod must be cut. Of course, sod species and soil type is also important. Bluegrass, Bermuda grass and zoysia grass sods should be cut at depths of 0.5-0.8 inches, red fescue at 0.7-1.0 inches, bent grass as low as 0.3-0.6 inches and St. Augustine grass, Bahia grass, centipede grass and ryegrasses at 0.8-1.3 inches thick.

Mechanical sod handling machines are available which can cut, roll, fold and convey sod pieces to the loading trucks. Cut sod should be laid out within 1-2 days. Sod injury occurs if temperatures rise to 100°F or higher. Southern grasses are more tolerant to higher temperatures. It is important to cut sod when the soil temperature is lowest and therefore early morning cutting is advisable. During shipping, ventilation and cooling is helpful. In recent years, some sod producers have vacuum cooled their produce to maintain quality during shipping. This is an expensive proposition.

Laying sod

To sod, prepare and fertilize the seedbed in the same manner as for seeding. Firm the seedbed with a roller after final hard raking. Sod should not be laid on dry soil. A soil should be moist to a depth of 6 inches but not saturated. Lay the sod pieces as you would lay brick and fit them together as tightly as possible. After laying the first strip, place a board on the sodded strip. Kneel on this board, and move it forward as the job progresses. This eliminates tramping on the prepared seedbed. Staggering the ends of the pieces of sod will prevent lines across the turf caused by slower establishment at the edges of the sod pieces. Make sure that the edges of the sod are in good contact but not overlapping. The newly laid sod should be rolled or tamped to press the sod firmly against the soil. It is advisable to topdress the surface of the newly sodded lawn with weed-free soil and work the topdressing into the cracks between sod pieces with a broom or the back of the wooden rake. On steep slopes the sod should be held in place by wooden pegs driven in at right angles to the slope. When strips of sod are used on steep slopes, the long dimension of the strip should be laid at right angles rather than up and down the slope, to prevent washing between the pieces of sod.

After sodding is completed, and the area is rolled a liberal irrigation should be applied and the lawn kept well watered until the grass is established. After the sod is established good management practices will be necessary to maintain a high quality turf.

9.3 Plugging

Plugging is vegetative propagation of turf by planting small blocks or plugs of sod at measured intervals. Round plugs of sod, usually 2.5 inches in diameter and about 2-3 inches in depth are used. Pluggers of various sizes and shapes are available. Cores of soil the same size as the sod plugs should be removed to insure good soil contact with the plug. Plugging, i.e., cutting plugs, and planting them, can be done manually or by special machines.

Strip sodding is the planting of sod strips 2-4 inches wide in rows 12 inches apart. Firm contact with surrounding soil is necessary. Strip sodding and especially plugging is used for patching bare spots on turf. It may also be used to plant a new, more adapted species or variety in an area where poor turf exists. This is an efficient way to introduce warm-season grasses into a cool-season grass lawn and vice versa. When plugging is used to change grass species the original stand can be inhibited by herbicides like MH-30 (Maleic hydrazide, 1-2-dihydro-3,6-pyridazinedione). Fertilization of old sod should be excluded but plugs should be well fertilized. This replacement can be done gradually. New, already established areas, can be used as a source for plugs. In this way, e.g., zoysia grass lawn can be established. Generally the plug method is most widely applied in practice for zoysia propagation. Also for propagation of St. Augustine, centipede, buffalo grass, Bermuda or even bent grasses. It is an expensive method, mortality is high and during establishment the area has an unsightly appearance.

Plugs are usually spaced at one foot intervals. Zoysia develops very slowly and it is advisable to set zoysia plugs into 6-12 inch centers. Dropping some fertilizer into the holes before putting the plug in is a good practice especially if introducing a new grass into old sod. The plugs should be dropped into a container of water before dropping them into the holes. They should be pressed firmly into the holes with the foot to insure good soil contact. It is essential that the plugs be kept moist for the first 2-3 weeks after planting to prevent the roots from drying out.

Planting sod plugs 2-3 inches in diameter into 12 inch centers, 30-50 sq. ft. of sod will be needed for a 1,000 sq. ft. area. Nurseries and garden centers sell plugs or chunks of sod in paper cups. These chunks are usually hand planted at spaced intervals in the prepared seedbed.

9.4 Sprigging

Sprigging — the planting of stolons, rhizomes or vegetative segments of plants in furrows or small holes.

Sprigs are stolons (shoots) or rhizomes that root when planted in the soil. They are obtained by shredding the sod into individual stems 4 to 8 inches long, depending on the type of grass. Zoysia sprigs usually contain 3-4 nodes. Thus sprigs are sections of individual stems and runners of grasses that are separated from sod. They are usually with few leaves and roots. A stiffer grass like zoysia is commonly propagated by sprigs. In recent years sprigs in polyethylene bags have appeared on the market. Zoysia packed and refrigerated will survive for many weeks. Six to ten sq. ft. of zoysia or Bermuda sod is needed to sprig 1,000 sq. ft. of lawn area.

In planting sprigs, the space interval should be governed by the rate of spread of the grass, how fast coverage is desired and the amount of planting material available. When sprigging Bermudas, St. Augustine or centipede, sprigs are placed 12 inches apart in 12 inch rows. Zoysias usually are placed 6 inches apart on 6 inch rows. Bermuda grasses spread faster and can make a complete cover under favorable conditions in a few weeks. Zoysias are slow growers and may need a year or two to build a tight turf. Zoysia should be more carefully planted. Usually one node of zoysia is inserted about an inch deep into the seedbed and the stem inclined with the leaves showing above the ground.

Sprigs may be planted by inserting them in holes made in the soil by an aerifying machine or by any round sharp tool or a slit made by a spade. They also may be planted in shallow, 3 inch deep furrows and covered 1 to 1.5 inches with soil. The sprigs must be pressed in firmly. Large plantings may be firmed by driving a small tractor wheel over the furrows or by a roller or cultipacker. Another method to plant sprigs over large lawns under more humid conditions is to spread or scatter the sprigs over the area to be planted, then pull a disk over the ground with the disk set straight. This presses the sprigs into the soil far enough so that they root readily when watered and fertilized properly. Topdressing is helpful. Tractor-drawn machines are available for sprigging large areas.

Plugs are more expensive and usually require more time to develop rhizome or stolon growth than do sprigs Plugs also require more time to build sod. This is because it takes time to bridge the gap between the soil of the plug and seedbed. Plugs give a greater assurance of survival than sprigs, since they already have roots established in a small chunk of soil.

Rapid spread of sods, plugs and sprigs occurs only when closely mown. Closer mowing encourages the spread of grass and reduces the competition of weeds and other grasses.

9.5 Stolonizing

Stolonizing refers to broadcasting shredded stolons or fragments of stoloniferous grasses like Bermuda grass or bents. In stolonizing, the grass sod is chopped into fine pieces that are spread like seed. Shredded stolons are spread over the area with mechanized equipment. Stolonizing is practicable only when large amounts of planting materials are available for planting large area. Large Bermuda grass, areas may be established by spreading shredded stolons with a manure spreader and disking lightly to firm them into the soil. This method requires about 100 bushels of shredded stolons per acre. Creeping and velvet bent grass can be stolonized by spreading shredded stolons at a rate of 4-10 bushels per 1,000 sq. ft.

Spread (seeded) stolons must be covered lightly by some means. They can be pushed into the soil by harrows or cultipackers or topdressed with good soil to a depth of ¼ inch and rolling to firm the stolons into the topdressing. Of course, the soil should be kept moist until the small sprigs are rooted.

9.6 Maintenance of southern grasses during establishing period

It is important to support southern grasses during the establishing period with nitrogen fertilizers. After planting, Bermuda grass usually recovers and starts to grow after a week or so. Zoysia requires about 3 weeks until it recovers and starts to grow. Fertilizer can speed up recovery and establishment. Both these grasses should be fertilized after recovery with 1 lb. per 1,000 sq. ft. of actual and available mineral nitrogen every 3-4 weeks through the growing season. Although zoysia is not as high in fertility needs as Bermuda, it is a very slow establishing grass and a good nitrogen fertilizer the first year can speed up establishment very much.

St. Augustine should be topdressed the first establishing year with 1 lb. of available nitrogen every 3-5 weeks. Carpet grass, centipede and Bahia should be topdressed with ½-1 lb. N per 1,000 sq. ft. every 3-5 weeks for faster establishing. Centipede is a low-fertility grass but responds well to nitrogen fertilization during the establishing period.

The soil should be kept moist all the time until grasses establish. Topdressing at regular intervals of areas established by stolonizing or sprigging will be needed. Herbicide and other pesticide applications for good maintenance are also needed.

9.7 Planting material

Vegetative grass material like sprigs, plugs or stolons are usually produced in special nurseries. Regardless of the propagation method used, the material should be bought from a reputable dealer, and it is advisable to use certified material. Nearly all southern states have certification of vegetative lawn grasses and certified nurseries.

Normally, a square yard of zoysia or Bermuda grass sod will yield 324 two inch plugs or about 1,000 or 2,000 sprigs. 324 plugs will cover 324 sq. ft. planting at 12-inch centers and 81 sq. ft. planting in 6-inch centers. 2,000 sprigs planted in 12-inch centers are enough for 2,000 sq. ft. area or if in 6-inch centers enough for a 500 sq. ft. area. A square yard of St. Augustine or centipede sod will yield about 500 to 750 sprigs, and thus will provide sprigs only for 500 to 750 sq. ft. planted at 12-inch intervals. The Table 9.1 presents some data concerning vegetative propagation of turf grasses.

Table 9.1 Vegetatively propagated grasses

Grass	Method	Plant material per 1,000 sq. ft.	Planting time
1. Bents, creeping & velvet	sprigs, seeds	10 sq. yd. sod, 10 bushel stolons or 0.5-1 lb. seed	fall
2. Bermuda	sprigs	1 sq. yd. sod or 1 bushel sprigs or 2-3 bushels stolons	spring, summer
3. Buffalo	sprigs, seed	3-5 sq. yd. sod or 0.5-2 lb. seed	spring
4. Carpet grass	sprigs, seed	1 sq. yd. sod or 3-5 lb. seed	spring, summer
5. Centipede	sprigs, seed	1 sq. yd. sod or 0.3-1 lb. seed	spring, summer
6. St. Augustine	sprigs	1.5-2 sq. yd. sod	spring, summer
7. Zoysia	sprigs	1.5 sq. yd. sod or 1 bushel sprigs, 3 sq. yd. sod when plugging is needed.	spring, summer

Summary

Turf can be vegetatively propagated by a) sodding, b) plugs, c) sprigs, and d) stolonizing.

1. Sodding has many advantages and its use is increasing rapidly. Sodding is a fast and most satisfactory way to get a turf any time when the ground is not frozen. Sodding is preferred on sloping areas and where immediate turf cover is needed.

   In sod production, soil preparation and maintenance are the same as when establishing a lawn by seeding.

2. Plugs or small blocks of sod are planted at measured intervals. Plugs are used mostly to repair bare spots of old sod and where there is a need to introduce a new grass species or variety. For the later case larger plugs should be used. In places where poor maintenance conditions exist plugs are better to use than sprigs.

3. Sprigs are sections of individual stems, or runners of grasses that are separated from sod. They usually have few leaves and roots and at least 3-4 nodes. Sprigging is the best method to establish turf vegetatively. Under proper conditions sprigs establish quicker and form a more uniform sod than plugs.

4. Stolonizing is chopping or shredding grass sod into pieces and then spreading them on a prepared seedbed like seed. It is used under first class maintenance and on large areas. It is widely used in establishing golf greens. It is fast but requires a lot of material and is therefore expensive.

5. Mostly southern warm-season grasses are vegetatively propagated. The best time to plant is in the spring when the soil warms up after the last frost. At that time soil has enough moisture and it is easier to get faster establishment. Plantings can be done between early spring and late summer. Control weeds, keep clean and start mowing as soon as shoots reach mowing height.

CHAPTER 10
MAINTENANCE FERTILIZATION

10.1 Introduction

In an established lawn we are concerned with maintaining adequate vegetative leaf growth. We expect uniform, dense and green foliage from a good turf.

For normal turf grass growth sufficient amounts of maintenance fertilizers should be applied uniformly and at the right time. Plant nutrients are needed most when grasses reach their maximum growth rate. Cool-season grasses like bluegrass and fescues need higher levels of plant nutrients in the early spring and in the fall when, on the other hand, warm-season grasses need it late in the spring and summer. Fertilization of cool-season grasses during a warm summer period does not help at all and N may be harmful to the grass and may also stimulate some weed growth (e.g., crabgrass). Seasonal growth cycles of cool-season grasses and some weeds are presented in the Figure 10.1 below.

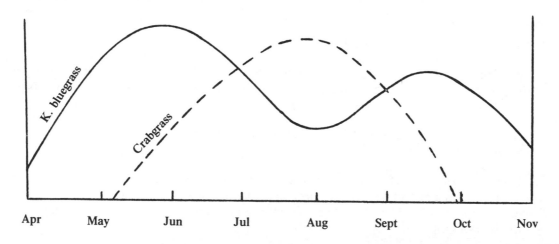

Figure 10.1 Growth cycle patterns of Kentucky bluegrass, a cool-season grass and crabgrass, a summer weedy grass in Northeastern region of United States.

Good lawn care and fertilization is the best method to control weeds. Schery (36) shows that fertilization of a broad-leaved weed population decreased density to 23 per sq. ft. as compared to 50 for unfertilized areas. Conversely, grasses increased to as much as 90% of the cover, compared to only 50% grass on the unfertilized portion.

Nitrogen is a major plant nutrient and is most important for vegetative plant growth. The chemical composition of turf grass clippings represents their nutritional needs. The ratio of major plant nutrients in turf grass clippings are approximately $N:P_2O_5:K_2O = 3:1:2$ (16). The nitrogen and potassium (K_2O) ratio for maintenance should be balanced at 2 to 1 for a continued healthy growth of grasses. Clippings left on the lawn will decay and plant nutrient elements will be returned. Because of solubility and leaching, potassium and nitrogen may be partly lost. Phosphorus is fixed in the soil and not lost. Taking all these factors into consideration we see that in turf maintenance the most important plant nutrient is nitrogen, second is potassium and the third is phosphorus. Of course, for normal grass growth secondary as well as micro nutrients should be supplied. For good maintenance of lawns proper fertilizer analysis can be in 3-1-2, 4-1-2, 2-1-1, or even 6-1-2 ratios. In practice, to be sure that all important plant nutrients are supplied, a complete fertilizer is recommended and should be applied at least once a year. Some examples of turf fertilizers are: 16-4-8, 12-4-8, 23-7-7, 18-4-9, 24-6-12, 10-3-7 and 15-5-10.

Fertilizers that contain slowly available organic or readily available inorganic nitrogen can be used to maintain lawns. Pure organics are usually low in plant nutrients. Added inorganics increase analysis. Synthetic ureaform is slowly available and it can be used alone as a nitrogen source or in mixtures with inorganic nitrogen sources. Organic nitrogen is more expensive per unit of actual nitrogen than inorganic nitrogen. The advantages are: a) organic releases nitrogen slowly and thus gives more uniform stimulation to grass growth over a longer period and b) it is possible to apply larger rates without injuring grasses. It is an advantage to use organic nitrogen fertilizers and also a convenience because we do not need to apply them as often as inorganics. Because of the greater safety and longer lasting effect of the insoluble forms, it is a common practice in making lawn fertilizers to combine an insoluble form with a soluble one. It is desirable that fertilizers for maintaining established lawns contain at least 50 percent of the nitrogen in the water insoluble form. Generally, mixed fertilizers which contain less than 50 percent of their nitrogen derived from natural organic sources or synthetic ureaform (UF) should not be considered slow-release or slow-available N fertilizers. In some cases when under low temperature conditions rapid plant response is needed and inorganic easily available nitrogen fertilizers should be applied.

10.2 Rates

Nutrient status and fertility requirements of a turf area can be determined by visual observations, tissue tests and soil analysis. Nutrient deficiency symptoms are easy to confuse with disease lesions or insect damage but in general, the color of the grass and the rate of growth is a good criterion for fertilization needs. If the plant is short of: N — pale, yellowing, older leaves dying; P — purplish tints on the leaves, dark green color, reddish; K — short stalks, leaves show yellow streaking, scorching on older leaves. For more detailed plant nutrient deficiency symptoms see the chapter on fertilizers. Soil analytical tests should be done to determine lime, potassium and phosphorus needs. Soil tests are especially important when lawns were neglected and in the past were not regularly fertilized and limed. Fertilizer rates, especially nitrogen, will depend upon length of season, grass species, maintenance intensity and other factors. Turf grass in California or Georgia with a long growing season will need more nitrogen than in New England, Ontario or Oregon-Washington areas with a much shorter growing season. Again, K. bluegrass, St. Augustine or ryegrass need a good supply of plant nutrients for good growth and competitiveness when red fescue or centipede are good competitors at low levels of fertility and poor competitors under intensive fertilization (26). Clear-cut differences in plant nutrient needs can also be observed between varieties of the same species, e.g., Merion K. bluegrass for normal growth needs about twice as much nitrogen than common K. bluegrass.

In shaded turf areas maintenance fertilization rates should be increased in some cases to meet the plant nutrient needs of trees as well as grasses. Nutrients are easily leached from sandy soils, and will be needed in great amounts than in heavy soils rich with organic matter. Maintenance intensity, irrigation, and whether clippings are returned or removed are also important factors in plant nutrient needs of a lawn. Madison indicates (27) that in many cases, when striving for increased density and color, a turf can be over fertilized with nitrogen. He suggests that the density of a turf is a better indicator of proper quality and adequate fertilization than color. Too high nitrogen rates may detrimentally affect normal grass growth and development. Northern cool-season grasses are rather susceptible to nitrogen fertilization during hot summer months.

Approximate nitrogen needs for maintenance of various turf grasses are presented in Table 10.1. Creeping bent grass, Merion K. bluegrass, Bermuda grass nitrogen needs are high and on the other hand buffalo grass, centipede, carpet grass, Bahia and red fescue needs are low or very low.

Table 10.1 Approximate nitrogen requirements

Grasses	Lb. per 1,000 sq. ft. per growing season
Cool-season grasses:	
1. Creeping bent grass	4-6
2. Merion K. bluegrass[a]	4-6
3. Colonial bent grass	3-5
4. Velvet bent grass	3-5
5. K. bluegrass, common[b]	3-4
6. Tall fescue	3-4
7. Ryegrasses	3-4
8. Rough bluegrass	2-4
9. Redtop	2-4
10. Canada bluegrass	2-3
11. Red fescues	2-3
Warm-season grasses:	
1. Bermuda grass	4-8
2. St. Augustine grass	3-5
3. Zoysia grass	3-5
4. Bahia grass	2-4
5. Carpet grass	2-3
6. Centipede grass	1-3
7. Buffalo grass	1-2

[a] Also Fylking, Pennstar, Nugget.
[b] Also Kenblue, Park, Delta, Newport.

10.3 Application

In fertilizer application the most important factor is uniform distribution. Drop hopper or centrifugal type distributors can be used. Wet grass should not be fertilized. To avoid grass burning soluble fast acting fertilizers should be washed into the soil by irrigation immediately after application. Foliar liquid fertilizers are usually applied to correct deficiencies of micronutrients.

10.4 Cool humid region

Cool-season grasses in the spring should be supplied with enough fertilizer to keep them vigorously growing but overfeeding should be avoided. The grasses should be able to prepare for the hot summer season. Proper fertilizer applications in the spring will prevent too lush growth of grass, reduce the incidence of disease, and lessen the amount of mowing. Furthermore, well fertilized grasses in the spring will grow vigorously, fill bare spots in the lawn faster, produce thick lawn which will compete with present weeds and prevent weed encroachment.

Cool-season grasses should not be fertilized immediately before or during the warm summer months. Between late May and the middle of August fertilization should be avoided. Fertilization will stimulate foliage growth and with increased respiration will result in root depletion. Top growth and respiration has priority over root development in the utilization of carbohydrates. Generally, root growth appears to be enhanced only when carbohydrates are accumulating. Fertilization with N stimulates respiration and top growth causing a net reduction of carbohydrate reserves. Excessive applications of nitrogen during the period when top growth is stimulated leads to thatch build up. Normally, carbohydrates of cool-season grasses increase during the fall and early winter. In the spring, top growth is stimulated and reserve carbohydrates are used. Seasonal root growth follows essentially the seasonal pattern of carbohydrate content. Several workers have shown that some root growth initiates during the fall with the greatest development occurring in early spring — evidently prior to the flush spring top growth. This indicates the need of good fertilization in the fall before winter. For best results about half of the amount of nitrogen should be applied in the fall. Too late and excessive nitrogen application may lead to winterkill due to poorly balanced fertilization. Nitrogen decreases root growth and favors top growth and results in more succulent toliage. Succulent tissue is more prone to low temperature injury. Evapotranspiration also increases and due to poor root systems the water supply is inadequate. Thus, grasses are weakened and less resistant to diseases. Fall applications of N should be carried out 30-35 days before winter dormance in the North where direct winterkill may be the case.

It is practical to fertilize lawns with complete fertilizers of 3-1-2 or 4-1-2 ratio all the time. In any case, for cool-season grasses, complete fertilizers should be used in the fall and for warm-season grasses complete fertilizers should be used in spring applications.

Mixtures of cool-season grasses like Kentucky bluegrass and red fescues should receive 2-4 pounds of actual nitrogen per 1,000 sq. ft. per growing season for normal growth. Red fescues are low-fertility grasses and if they are dominant 2-3 lb. should be enough and if K. bluegrass is dominant or along 3-4 lb. is suggested. Merion Kentucky bluegrass is a high-fertility grass and requires 4-6 lbs. of actual nitrogen per growing season. Tall fescue turf should receive somewhat lower amounts of fertilizer as Merion K. bluegrass (Table 10.1). It is best to use fertilizers with at least 50% of actual nitrogen in slow available natural organic or synthetic (ureaform) form. When applying inorganic nitrogen fertilizer it should not be applied at once with more than 1 lb. of actual nitrogen per 1,000 sq. ft. Never apply fertilizer, especially an inorganic fertilizer when the grass leaves are wet. Nitrogen and potassium will burn the plants. Prevent burning by washing the applied fertilizer from the grass leaves immediately.

For specific local recommendations consult your county agricultural agent or state agricultural experiment station. For the northeast and generally for the average conditions of northern cool region the following guide might be used (Table 10.2).

Table 10.2 Lawn fertilization in northern cool humid region

Number of applications	When to apply	
	Northeast	Southern parts of region
2	April & early September	March & early September
3	April, late August & September	March, Sept. & Oct. or early November
4	April, May, late August and September	March, September, October & November

The annual amount of fertilizers should be divided into two, three or even more applications when inorganic soluble forms of nitrogen are used. Twice a year maintenance lawn fertilization should be considered as average and normal. Exact timing will vary from state to state. Heavier nitrogen applications in the spring will increase the need of mowing and in many cases heavier fall applications should be used. On the other hand in northern regions heavy fall applications may increase incidence of snowmold. In the transition zone area where snowmold is not a problem one spring and two fall applications will be good for root-rhizome development and turf density. Summer applications of N-containing fertilizers are not suggested. Recently, excellent crabgrass preemergent herbicides are available and 0.5 lb. N/1,000 sq. ft. as a summer application in conjunction with irrigation may be helpful in improving turf color.

In southern part of cool humid regions where Bermuda and zoysia are used, the first application (complete fertilizer) should be done when grasses start to break dormancy in the spring. Then it should be followed by 2-3 summer applications when the grass is growing actively. The last application should be made in August or early in September. Excessive late fall applications may be detrimental.

10.5 Warm humid region

Warm-season grasses are more variable in their nitrogen requirements than cool-season grasses (Table 10.1). The heaviest feeder is Bermuda grass, followed by zoysias, St. Augustine, Bahia, carpet grass and centipede. Depending on the growing season Bermuda grass needs 4-8 lb. of nitrogen per 1,000 sq. ft. area each year. Zoysia and St. Augustine does not require as much fertilizer as Bermuda grass, 3-5 lb. of N/1,000 sq. ft. is enough. Two to 3 lb. N for Bahia, carpet grass and 1-3 lb. N/1,000 sq. ft. for centipede grass will be enough in most cases. Bermuda and zoysia in the northern part of the southern warm region (e.g., transition zone) will need less fertilization than in the deep South because of the shorter growing season.

Of course, nutritional balance should be maintained among the major elements. Normally, 1-2 complete fertilizations are needed during the growing season. The root system develops during the fall or early spring time and grasses should be supplied with all the plant nutrients needed. Complete fertilization should be applied in March-April and also in September-October, 4-5 weeks before grasses become dormant. Overstimulation of warm-season grasses in late fall should be avoided because of possible susceptibility to frost. Also late liberal fertilization will encourage some weeds when turf grasses are dormant. In addition to a complete fertilizer an additional nitrogen fertilizer should be applied every 30 to 60 days during the growing season. Bahia, carpet grass and centipede, (the low fertility grasses), usually need only 2 applications of fertilizers per year for satisfactory growth.

For fertilization of southern grasses typical lawn fertilizers like 16-4-8, 15-5-10, 20-5-10, 16-8-8 and 10-5-5 or even regular farm fertilizers, like 10-10-10 and 8-8-8 can be used. It is best to use, (especially in the spring and fall), a complete fertilizer of analysis 3-1-2 or 4-1-2 ratio. Special lawn fertilizers can be applied from early spring until mid-September every 4-6 weeks to supply needed nitrogen for the specific grass. In applying a complete fertilizer early in the spring on dormant grass the rate can be high enough to apply up to 2 lb. actual available nitrogen per 1,000 sq. ft. The last complete fertilization in the fall should not supply more than 1 lb. of actual nitrogen per 1,000 sq. ft. When non-soluble nitrogen is used the needed maintenance fertilizer amounts can be supplied in 2 or 3 applications during the growing season, e.g., in April-May, June-July and September-October.

10.6 Semiarid and arid regions

Semiarid and arid regions include 3, 4a and 4b turf grass adaptation areas (Fig. 4.1). Soil as well as climatical conditions may differ extremely in various parts of this region. Requirements of turf grasses for plant nutrients will also vary widely. In some soils and in some areas even an excess of major plant nutrients may exist (16). Also, minor plant nutrients may be a problem: (a) they may be in toxic amounts or (b) they may be unavailable because of high pH due to an excess of salts in the soil. County agents and experiment station people should be consulted on local conditions and problems. In many cases acidifying fertilizers or acidified irrigation water will be helpful in supplying needed plant nutrients for turf grasses of this region.

In areas with a short growing season 1-2 lb. N per 1,000 sq. ft. will be enough but when Bermuda grass or bent grass is used for golf greens under irrigation and intensive management conditions 6-10 lb. of N per 1,000 sq. ft. will be needed. In timing the supply of plant nutrients it is important to fertilize shortly before the growing season starts. It will be best to fertilize cool-season grasses for summer turf early in the spring. For fall and spring growth cool-season grasses, in winter wheat areas, should be fertilized in late summer and again late in winter or early spring. Winter cover grasses should be supplied with N late in the fall and again at the beginning of the growing season.

Warm-season grasses should be fertilized in the spring at the beginning of the growing season. Blooming lilacs and forsythias are a good indication that the season for Bermuda grass and zoysia starts. Over-fertilization with N will contribute to thatch buildup. Therefore, the nitrogen supply should be adjusted to needs. Buffalo grass is not tolerant to shade and is a poor competitor with weeds.

Heavy fertilization can add to salt concentrations in this region's soils. Organic low-salt-index fertilizers are favored in arid and semiarid regions.

10.7 Maintenance liming

For most turf grasses with the exception of centipede grass and carpet grass, soil acidity-alkalinity should be kept at pH 6.0-7.0. Fescues and zoysia grass will tolerate a lower pH than Kentucky bluegrass. Lime is needed for most grasses when the pH drops below 6.0. Carpet grass and centipede grass should be limed if the pH is below 5.0. Soil should be tested for acidity every 3 to 5 years and ground limestone applied as needed. As a rule, light sandy soils usually require 50-75 lb/1,000 sq. ft. of lime every 3 or 4 years, and heavy clay soils require around 100 lb. ground limestone every 5 to 6 years. Overliming can be as detrimental to good turf as not supplying enough of it. As a rule of thumb, applications of 50 lb. every three years will be satisfactory.

Summary

1. In turf maintenance the most important plant nutrient is nitrogen.

   In keeping plant nutrients in balance and supplying all plant nutrients needed, cool-season grasses as well as warm-season grasses should receive at least one or two applications of complete fertilizers during the growing season. The best time for cool-season grasses is fall, and early spring is the best time for warm-season grasses.

2. A slowly available nitrogen source in a maintenance fertilizer is preferred. It gives a more uniform stimulation to grass growth over a longer period and it is possible to apply larger rates without injuring grasses. Fertilizers which contain less than 50% of their nitrogen derived from natural organic sources or ureaform should not be considered slow available N fertilizers.

   Inorganic nitrogen fertilizers should not be applied at one time at rates higher than 1 lb. of actual N per 1,000 sq. ft.

3. For cool-season grasses late summer or early fall maintenance fertilization is most important. They also need a good fertilization in the spring. They should not be fertilized during hot summer months.

Southern warm-season grasses grow most vigorously during the warm spring-summer season and at that time they should be supplied with maintenance fertilizers.

Northern cool-season grasses should receive needed plant nutrients with 1-2 applications in late summer-fall and 1-2 applications in the spring. Southern warm-season grasses should receive needed plant nutrients well distributed every 3-6 weeks from early spring to the middle of September.

4. For most northern or southern turf grass soil acidity should be kept at pH 6.5. Carpet grass and centipede lawns should receive lime only if pH is below 5.0. Soil should be tested for acidity every 3-5 years and ground limestone applied as needed. Late fall or winter are the best times to apply needed lime.

CHAPTER 11
WATERING LAWNS

11.1 Introduction

Water is very important in plant growth and well being. Water is necessary for germination, cellular development, tissue growth, photosynthesis and temperature control. It acts both as a solvent and as a carrier of plant food materials. Nutrients dissolved in the soil are taken in through the roots and then carried to all parts of the grass plant in water. The food manufactured in leaves is also distributed throughout the plant body by water. Water transpired by the leaves serves as a temperature regulator for the plant. The amount of water within the cells of the grass leaves plays a role in counteracting the effects of traffic. For all these functions, very large quantities of water are required for normal grass growth and development. Usually 500 to 600 pounds of water are needed (about 75 gallons) to produce one pound of dry matter in plants. Grass itself is over 80% or more water. During a drought, plant nutrient uptake is decreased and normal growth and development is impaired. Thus, water is (a) needed for seed germination; (b) part of the composition of the plant; (c) needed for photosynthesis and is the hydrogen source in carbohydrates; (d) a solvent and transporting agent for plant nutrients; and (e) a temperature stabilizer.

11.2 Water absorption. Transpiration:

Water mainly enters the plant through the roots. The root hair zone is most active in water absorption. Water supply, soil temperature, transpiration rate, extent and effectiveness of the root system all effect water absorption. Some water absorption may even occur by dead roots. Water can be absorbed by leaves, especially by young, actively growing ones. Water condenses on leaves in the form of dew during the night or early hours and can supplement soil water needs to some extent. Some desert species can exist entirely upon dew water. Under water stress, *syringing,* i.e., light watering — or showering, of the grass will create conditions for absorption of water by the foliage.

Absorbed water is distributed in plants through xylem tissue and the majority of it is transpired to the atmosphere. Only about 2% of the absorbed water is utilized by plants for physiological and metabolic processes. Grass leaf stomata play the most important role in water transpiration and as much as 90% of water is lost into the atmosphere through stomata. Stomata are small groups of cells on the leaf surface which allow water to be evaporated to the atmosphere. Turf grasses use about 0.2 inches of water per day. This includes water used by the plant itself plus transpiration water along with water soil evaporation. *Evapotranspiration* includes water lost by transpiration and evaporation. Internal water deficit or stress occurs when plants transpire more than they absorb, i.e., when water use exceeds supply. Of course water stress affects grass growth, development and physiological processes. Under such conditions grass roots are usually larger, longer and deeper and the shoot-root ratio decreases. Plant leaf folding, rolling and becoming flaccid due to the loss of turgidity is called *wilt.* Just before wilt, grass leaves usually turn a gray-blueish green in color. Wind and high temperatures increase transpiration and evaporation and thus contribute to wilt. Of course, syringing will help to prevent wilting. Various antitranspirants are being investigated to decrease transpiration and thus prevent wilting. Although some methods and procedures are interesting, at present their practicability in turf management is questioned.

An excessive water condition in the soil usually produces grass of yellowish-green color. This is probably caused by a deficiency of nitrogen due to leaching. Excessive water may reduce iron availability and thus could cause iron deficiency symptoms in grasses. More importantly, excessive water causes an oxygen deficit in the soil. This condition is extremely detrimental to turf grass growth and development.

11.3 Plant-moisture relationships

Various turf grasses used for lawn establishment differ in water requirements and drought resistance. Fescues have a rather low wilting tendency whereas bent grass and ryegrass wilt much more quickly. The wilting tendency is medium in K. bluegrass and Canada bluegrass. The tendency to wilt of Bermuda grass and zoysia grass is low, Bahia grass is intermediate and carpet grass is high. It is interesting to note that usually the grass with the strongest root system wilts last and those with the weakest roots wilt first. Drought is caused by prolonged water stress. Lack of water occurs during the dry hot summer months, especially on sandy light soils and arid or semiarid climatical conditions. During drought grasses protect themselves from desiccation by going into dormancy. Shoots and foliage die but crown, rhizome or stolon buds survive and their meristematic tissues serve to start new growth when moisture is available. Well fed grasses resist drought better. In most cases lawns suffer from starvation than from lack of water. Drought is a natural occurrence of grasses and they usually withstand seasons of desiccation. The purpose of watering a lawn during the summer months is to maintain an attractive green appearance. It is a mistake to expect watering to improve the appearance of a turf which is in poor condition due to lack of fertility, improper mowing, or infestations of weeds or diseases.

Grasses differ in tolerance or resistance to drought (14, 16, 27)

(a) *Drought tolerant* grasses:

1. Bermuda grass — deep rooted and able to store water in roots for later use.
2. Buffalo grass — able to store water in roots; becomes dormant during drought period.
3. Zoysia grass — curling leaves during drought period.
4. Bahia grass — deep rooted.
5. Wheat grasses —
6. Fescues — red fescues: curling leaves during drought period and become dormant. Tall fescue has a good root system.

(b) *Intermediate:*

1. Kentucky bluegrass
2. Canada bluegrass
3. Redtop
4. Colonial bent grass
5. Ryegrasses
6. St. Augustine grass
7. Centipede grass

(c) *Moisture loving* grasses:

1. Creeping and velvet bents
2. Rough bluegrass
3. Carpet grass
4. Annual bluegrass — shallow root system

Winter desiccation may be a problem in areas where lack of a snow cover occurs in addition to low precipitation. Desiccation may also occur where transpiration is rapid but because of frozen ground and a poor root system, water is not available for absorption. When winter desiccation occurs in small degree, grasses usually regain normal growth and appearance. Topdressing, mulches and irrigation may be helpful in preventing winter desiccation.

Water availability can decrease when high salt concentrations are present in soil solutions. Osmotic pressure increases and water availability to grass roots goes down. Fertilizers vary in their ability to increase salt concentrations in the soil. Salt indexes of various fertilizers are presented in Chapter 7 (Tables 7.1, 7.2, 7.4).

Plant-moisture relationships are important in water management in turf. With too much water, water loving species will increase — bents, rough bluegrass, annual bluegrass. Annual bluegrass is a noxious weed in lawns and rough bluegrass is tolerated in shady moist areas only. On the other hand, clover and other legumes often show considerable drought resistance because of the extended root system and the fixation of nitrogen. Trees strongly compete with grasses for water. Under trees suitable grasses should be seeded and watered adequately. Trees exhaust the water in the soil profile. Extra irrigation is needed to replace water in shaded areas.

11.4 Soil-water relationships

a. Infiltration and retention

The quantity of water needed for turf grasses depends on the kind of soils. Two important properties of soils affecting their water management are: (a) the infiltration rate or capacity of soil to absorb water and (b) the ability of soil to store water or so-called water-holding capacity. Movement of water downward in the soil is called soil-water percolation. These properties are closely related to the number and size of pores in the soils. An average productive soil will contain about 50% pore space. Pores range in size from fine capillary pores to large aeration pores. Much of the available water retained in the soils is held in the capillary pores. The larger aeration pores drain rapidly and have an important effect on infiltration (absorption) rates, water movement, drainage, and aeration in the soil. Soils differ greatly in their ratio of large to small pores due to differences in soil texture, structure, organic matter, and management. Coarse soils have large infiltration rates; water enters fast. Contrary to this infiltration rate is low in fine textured soils where large pore volume is small. Organic matter increases infiltration rates in both coarse textured and fine textured soils. Percolation is also rather good in coarse sandy soils and poor in heavy clay soils where soil particles and pores are small and water retention is good.

(a) Coarse soils — may store from about 0.5 to 1.5 inches of useable water for each one-foot depth of soil.

(b) Medium textured soils — may store from 1.5 to 2.5 inches of useable water per one-foot depth of soils.

(c) Heavy soils — may store up to 3.0 inches per foot of soil depth.

These soil-water relationships are shown in Figure 11.1 below (52).

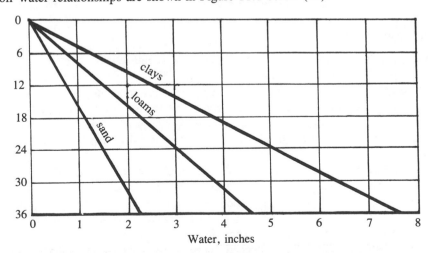

Figure 11.1 Inches of water held by the soil or depth to which a given amount of water will wet the soil.

When the soil surface is dry and gravitational forces minimal, water may start to flow up to the soil surface, to the root zone.

The infiltration rate of a soil is determined largely by the amount of larger pores in its surface and is greatly influenced by management. To maintain a high capacity of water falling or applied on the soil, the surface should be kept as open and porous as possible. Compaction by heavy traffic or use can reduce the porosity and infiltration rate drastically. A compacted soil should be aerated and loosened to increase water intake. Mulches can be used on newly-seeded areas to prevent raindrop impact from sealing the surface. The infiltration rate of soil determines how fast water can be applied without causing run off. Various wetting agents are often suggested for use in order to get better water infiltration. Their use, as yet, is not too practical.

Energy with which water is held in soil is called *soil moisture tension*. Fine-textured soils high in clay hold large amounts of water but much of it is held too tightly to be used by plants. Coarser sandy soils, on the other hand, have too few fine pores, retain too little water, and are often droughty. Silt loam soils with a good balance of sand, silt and clay usually have the highest available water-holding capacity. Organic matter increases a soil's water-holding capacity. The available water-holding capacity of a soil determines how often water must be applied to maintain good plant growth. Sandy soils hold less water than clays and water drains through faster, so watering needs to be done more often. Loams are intermediate between sands and clays. Water loss due to evaporation and transpiration is also an important factor in turf grass water management. Mulch applied on a seeded area will decrease evaporation considerably.

b. Soil moisture content

Moist soil appears darker and thus by noting color change of the soil with depth, the depth to which water has penetrated can be estimated. Visual symptoms, such as wilting which is observed as a bluish cast to the grass, are also clues that moisture stress (i.e., lack of available water) is present in the soil. Simple visual hand tests can be used to get a rough estimate of soil moisture conditions. A medium-textured silt loam soil contains an adequate amount of moisture if it can be squeezed into a ball and retain its shape until pressed gently. If the soil feels dry and hard and can't be formed into a ball, it should be watered.

There are several methods to determine soil moisture content. The standard method is to oven dry field samples and determine the difference between wet and dry weights. Tensiometers, commonly used for irrigation control, measure the water tension in the soil as water moves in and out of porous cups buried in the soil and give direct readings of soil moisture content. Electrical resistance blocks of several types are also available for determining moisture changes through the growing season.

11.5 When and how much?

In order to maintain satisfactory top growth there must be adequate soil water in the turf grass root zone at all times. If soil dryness persists, the grass color turns slightly bluish, then under continuing dry conditions turns brown. At this point grasses begin to suffer. Under water stress grass turgidity is low and grass does not bounce back to normal position as fast as under normal conditions. After walking, footprints can be observed on turf under water stress, i.e., turgidity is low and grass does not bounce back fast enough. This indicates irrigation need. Visual investigation of the 6-8 inch topsoil layer may also give some practical clues.

Under favorable conditions grasses usually have roots to a depth of 1-4 ft. (16). Bermuda grass, Bahia grass and tall fescue are deep rooted grasses and withstand drought periods well. Depending on soil moisture and fertility, their roots often go beyond 4 ft. depth. New grass seedlings are shallow rooted and require frequent light waterings. Established grass seedings should be irrigated less frequently and with enough water to replenish the entire root zone to a depth of 6-8 inches. It is important to soak soil enough so that surface and subsurface water would be in contact. This is needed for normal grass growth. Soil moisture should be contained at a uniform level throughout the profile.

For thatched turf it is better to irrigate lightly but more frequently. Putting green bent grass turf with shallow root systems need more frequent irrigation. *Syringing*, i.e., applications of shower-like light amounts of water, are normally used not for irrigation purposes but (a) to cool turf, (b) to remove frost, and (c) to prevent wilt by reducing transpiration. Inadequate watering, especially during the dormant season may even weaken grasses. Watering just to break dormancy may add to the exhaustion of plants. Continuous good watering during the dormant season is all right. Most grasses require 1 inch or more weekly. On light sandy soil this may require 0.5 inch applied twice weekly. A heavy soil may need a slow application of 1 inch every 8-10 days. Frequent too light applications of water encourage shallow root growth and should be avoided on established turf grass areas. Most medium-textured soils require at least 1-2 inches to wet soil 12 inches deep (Figure 11.1). It is important to measure the amount of water applied to be sure to apply adequate amounts to wet soil deep enough. The rate of application can be measured with empty cans distributed on the ground surface on a lawn. The rate of application should not be greater than the soil is able to absorb. Infiltration rates which can be used as guidelines are (26).

Sands	0.5-1.0 in/hr.
Sandy loam	0.3-0.5 in/hr.
Loam	0.2-0.4 in/hr.

Many sprinklers can apply water at the rate of 0.5 to 2 inches per hour.

Some problems can affect water management in turf areas. Layers of coarse sand, gravel or debris just under the soil surface can cause wilting of the grass. Also, thatch accumulation may act as a water-proof barrier. Thatch and layers of gravel, sand or debris should be removed. Frequent irrigation of such an area can be used as a temporary remedy only.

11.6 Water application

Water supply should be available before installing any irrigation system. This is especially important for larger turf areas such as golf courses or athletic fields. It is most practical if lake, pond, river or well water is available for irrigation purposes. It is impossible to depend on a public community water supply. The quality of water for irrigation should be good. Water with too high concentrations of some compounds, objectionable odors or too high levels of soluble salts should not be used. Water containing less that 650 ppm (1) of dissolved salts is all right to use.

Irrigation systems. It is most important that uniform applications and cheap, practical irrigation systems be used. Irrigation engineering is a highly specialized field. Systems designed to apply the right amount of water at the right time can be automatically regulated with a good margin of safety. Irrigation systems are rather expensive propositions and in most cases professional help in designing and installing is needed.

Overhead surface irrigation with sprinklers is the most commonly used. It may be (a) pop-up buried sprinklers, (b) sprinklers attached to recessed valves, or (c) moveable sprinklers attached to hoses. Turf type, size and money involved should be considered in selecting the proper system. For small home lawn areas spinklers attached to hoses are used. Where water pressure is low on small level areas perforated hoses can be used.

Water distribution lines from the source of water to the distribution area can be installed below the ground or portable lines can be used. The latter are widely used on sod farms.

Flooding may be applicable as an irrigation system in exceptional cases and where the turf area is level. In larger areas where larger money investments are possible, such as in sod production on swampy muck soils, subsurface irrigation may be the answer in watering turf. The water table can be controlled by open ditches, flood gates and pumping stations. Water through capillary system from underneath reaches the turf grass root zone.

11.7 Day and time of application:

Actually, the best time to water a lawn is when the grass needs it. The time of day makes little difference. There is less evaporation when water is applied in the evening but grass that is wet all night runs the great risk of becoming diseased. There may be some advantages to watering a lawn in the morning — low temperature, high humidity and absence of winds reduce water losses due to evaporation. Diseases have no advantage of spreading. Midday may be a practical time to irrigate in case of possible disease pathogens. On the other hand midday applications on athletic fields are unacceptable usually because of sports activities. Conclusion — do as it is convenient and practical.

Summary

1. Water is important in grass seed germination, plant growth and well being. Turf grasses differ in water requirements. The quantity of water needed for turf grasses also depends on the kind of soils. Capacity of a soil to absorb water (infiltration rate) and ability to store it (water-holding capacity) are two important properties of soils affecting turf grass water management. Sandy soils require frequent watering in small amounts. Heavy clay soils require infrequent watering in larger amounts.

2. The best time to water turf is just before wilting signs appear, i.e., when internal water stress is apparent. Slight water stress between waterings tends to develop deep grass roots. The deeper rooted the grass, the less it is necessary to water. When irrigating, the soil should be soaked with water 5 inches deep or more. Light watering (syringing) at frequent intervals, when contact between surface and subsurface water is not reached, causes shallow grass roots.

3. Irrigation water should not be applied faster than it can be absorbed by the soil.

CHAPTER 12
MOWING

12.1 Introduction

Turf grasses have a low lying and compact growing point and thus is well protected from injury by mowing. They are able to regrow fast. Earlier, before mechanical mowers were available, turf grass areas were cut only 3-4 times a year. Such a practice is still followed in some European parks and even some home lawns. Turf grass areas can be grouped into (a) high or intensive maintenance areas and (b) medium to low maintenance areas. To the first group belong lawns, golf courses, athletic fields, parks. These areas need good care and frequent cutting. On the other hand low maintenance turf, such as airfields, play areas, highway rights-of-way, stream banks, shore areas, roughs of golf courses and industrial turf need little maintenance and few mowings during the growing season.

The main objective of mowing is to keep grass even and attractive. A newly mown lawn is attractive, whether it is clipped short or long. Uniformity is important for appearance. In athletic fields and sports turf the main objective of cutting is to have the correct height for play. Some turf grasses are inclined to produce seedheads readily. This affects uniformity of the turf area considerably and should be mowed. Such grasses are: Bahia grass, carpet grass, St. Augustine grass and Bermuda grass.

12.2 Mowing heights

Turf grasses vary considerably in their tolerance to height of cut and therefore height of mowing should be adjusted to the physiological and morphological characteristics of various grasses. Grass should endure mowing and should be able to continue normal growth and development. Creeping bent grass spreads by stolons, does well under close short cutting and should be mown below 0.5 inch. This grass is naturally tolerant to the close cutting height. Creeping bent mown too high builds thatch and creates turf problems. More upright growing grasses like chewing red fescue should be mown higher because they are not tolerant to close cutting. Canada bluegrass has elevated apical meristems and it is not tolerant to close cutting. It should be cut above 2.5 inches in order to survive and continue to form a proper sward. Besides grass (natural) tolerance to cutting, the function of use also plays a role in deciding cutting height, e.g., sports turf, golf course turf, greens, fairways. Bent grass on putting greens will be cut closer than on a lawn or fairway.

It is important to not remove too much of the leaf area at one time. Never more than 0.3-0.4 of the surface should be removed at one mowing. In general, when a grass is about 0.5-1.0 inch above standard height in a lawn, it should be mown. By allowing grass to grow tall the lower blades are shaded and when the tall growth is removed, the exposed lower blades are *scalded* by the sun. Therefore, frequent, regular mowing is essential for a good lawn. The shorter a turf is mown, the more often it must be mown to avoid scalding. Fine-leaved grasses may be mown much closer than those having coarse leaf texture. Fine-leaved Bermuda grass or velvet bent grass cut to a height as low as 0.5 inch or even 0.3 inch still has considerable leaf area remaining. Tall fescue or St. Augustine grass, large-leaved grasses, cut at 0.5 inch would practically be defoliated. Again, creeping stoloniferous grasses, such as zoysia grass, creeping bent grass or Bermuda grass, can be cut closer than upright growing ones. Also, creeping grasses can be mown shorter not only because of photosynthetic area but mostly for best appearance and slower accumulation of thatch. The secret of preventing excess thatch build-up in zoysia grass is frequent mowing.

Table 12.1 Recommended mowing heights for lawns and similar areas

Grasses	Mowing height in inches
Cool-season grasses	
1. Creeping and velvet bent grass	0.25-0.5
2. Colonial bent grass	0.5 -1.0
3. K. bluegrass	1.0 -2.0
4. Red fescues	1.0 -2.0
5. Ryegrasses	1.0 -2.0
6. Tall fescue	1.5 -3.0
7. Fairway wheat grass	1.5 -3.0
8. Canada bluegrass	2.5 -4.0
Warm-season grasses	
1. Bermuda grass	0.5 -1.0
2. Zoysia grass	0.5 -1.0
3. Buffalo grass	1.0 -2.0
4. Carpet grass	1.0 -2.0
5. Centipede grass	1.0 -2.0
6. Bahia grass	1.5 -3.0
7. St. Augustine grass	1.5 -3.0

The height of mowing is measured on a solid surface (floor, sidewalk) to the edge of the bedknife on reel-type mowers or the cutting edge on other types of mowers. Before purchasing a mower, one should be certain that it can be adjusted to the height range required for the grass in question. It is advisable to have a lawn mower that can be adjusted from 0.5 inch to 3 inches so that one may change to improved types of grasses and mow at the recommended height.

12.3 How clipping affects grasses

Mowing does not benefit grass since it removes part of the leaf area which is important for photosynthesis, i.e., manufactures food for growth and other life processes. Also, cut leaf tops are injured and the possibility for grass disease infection increases. To reduce the damage caused by mowing, it should be done frequently — to remove as little of the green area of each leaf as possible. It is poor practice to allow grass to grow too tall and then cut down to the normal height at one time. To decrease shock it is better to gradually return to the normal height over a period of several weeks. Cutting northern grasses excessively at one time is damaging, especially during warm summer season. A brown, stubby turf appearance after close cutting and removing leaves is called *scalping*. Infrequent mowing, thatch and most of all turf areas that are not level cause scalping.

Growth hormones present in the apex of plants inhibit lateral bud growth and tillering. This physiological phenomenon is called *apical dominance*. By clipping grasses, apical dominance is destroyed and stimulation of lateral buds and grass tillering is induced. As a result of this budding, tillering of grasses increases. Grass becomes finer, sod thicker, more dense, and more attractive. Tillering is stimulated by clipping only if the stem apex and its inhibitory effects on lateral buds are removed. Clipping of only leaves will not promote tillering. Due to clipping the crown grass population density increases but total yield of clippings decreases, grass is weakened, grass root growth is disturbed, food reserves in roots are poorer, and roots weakened and shallower. Cutting stimulates top growth at the expense of root growth. After defoliation shoot regrowth has priority in utilizing carbohydrate reserves and the shoot: root ratio increases. Although cutting stimulates rhizome multiplication and sod formation, their growth and development is decreased. Numerous research data show that there is a reduction in root growth of a given species as a result of decreasing heights of grass cut. Close and intensively clipped grass needs better care and a better maintenance program. Mowing too high is also not good because of thatch formation problems, especially with stoloniferous grasses like creeping bent grass, Bermuda grass or zoysias. In shaded areas photosynthesis is not as active as in sunny areas and therefore grasses should be cut somewhat higher.

Grasses vary in tolerance to defoliation, e.g., rough bluegrass or red fescues are much less tolerant than perennial ryegrass, a typical pasture grass (27). Warm-season grasses are generally more tolerant to defoliation than northern cool-season grasses. Also, some grasses are easy to cut and with others it is difficult to get a clean cut. Ryegrass and zoysia have fibrous leaves high in silica content and are, therefore, difficult to mow. On the other hand, bent grasses, K. bluegrass or Bermuda grass are easy to mow.

12.4 Seasonal consideration

Established lawns should be mown early in the spring as soon as the grass greens and begins to grow. It should be mown as often as needed to prevent scalding and scalping of the grass.

Grass grows in cycles. Cool-season grasses grow faster in the spring and in the fall. Golden rule — mow when needed. K. bluegrass and red fescue should be cut when about 1 inch above cutting height. Bents or Bermuda grass should be cut when about 0.5 inch above cutting height.

Too close mowing in hot weather will weaken cool-season grasses. This could be explained by increased respiration, increased use of plant nutrient reserves and weakened photosynthesis due to the defoliations. It is advisable to increase cutting height of cool-season grasses during the warm dry summer months. Keeping the grass long prevents many weed seeds (e.g., crabgrass) from germination, helps smother weed seedlings, keeps grass healthier and the lawn more attractive. Irrigation and other maintenance practices (fertilization) may affect the need for clipping considerably. Grass itself will provide some criterion as to need to adjust mowing practices: if in July-August clippings decrease because of heat, reduction in mowing frequency and raising height will help grass to survive. In spring and fall grass grows faster, produces more clippings. It should be mown more often and at normal height. Bermuda and other warm-season grasses are favored by summer temperatures. Clipping height can be lowered during a warm period and then raised in the fall to promote winter hardiness. In general, warm-season grasses should be mown higher and less frequently during cooler weather conditions in fall or spring.

Before winter, under normal conditions, in the regions of adaptation turf grasses should be clipped at normal height. Bermuda grass in the northern areas of its region overwinters better if allowed to grow into winter a little on the long side.

12.5 Clippings

Clippings can be removed or left on the sod. Of course, plant nutrients are removed with the clippings and should be substituted for by increased maintenance fertilization. Schery (35) showed that on a well tended lawn 2.8 lb. of nitrogen, 2.3 lb. of potassium (K_2O) and about 1 lb. of phosphorus (P_2O_5) can be recovered from clippings per 1,000 sq. ft. of lawn per year. According to Holt (16) clippings contain 3-5% N, 0.5% P and 2.0% K. Wood's[1] research results indicate that the amount of nutrients returned to the grass in clippings is substantial. They increase as the fertility level of the clipping source increased. He concludes that clippings are a valuable source of nutrients and should be considered in a fertilization program.

When lawns are mown frequently only a little top growth is removed each time. Clippings may be left on the lawn. Young, tender, short clippings decompose fast. In cases where the lawn inclines to develop thatch,

---

[1] Wood, H.P. 1968. The role of clippings in the maintenance of a Kentucky bluegrass turf. Master's Thesis. University of Massachusetts.

clippings should be removed. Zoysia grass clippings decay very slowly and it would be better to remove them to help prevent thatch formation. It is bad practice to let grass grow high and then clip it back. This is a physiological shock to the grasses and necessitates removal of the clippings to prevent smothering of the grass and build up of thatch and diseases.

It is advisable to mow a lawn in different directions. Some planning is needed. It is better to throw clippings on unmowed lawn when using a rotary mower because they will get chopped up and pulverized better or a reel mower that throws grass clippings to the front can be used.

12.6 Arid and semiarid regions

In this region grasses are usually under high temperatures and drought stress and defoliation under these conditions may result in dormancy or death to grasses. With the exception of buffalo grass most other grasses do not benefit from mowing. Buffalo grass benefits due to the removing of shade producing companion plants. In the northern section and at higher altitudes, K. bluegrass and red fescue tolerate normal cutting height. At higher temperatures these grasses should be cut at 2-3 inch height in order to survive. Buffalo grass, tall fescue or tall growing Bermuda grass do not tolerate mowing below 1 inch. In order to develop satisfactory root systems and survive, tall fescue, K. bluegrass, ryegrass, wheat grasses are best mowed at a 3 inch height. The best stands of these grasses are obtained when they are mown at the end of the season after seedhead formation. In mixtures of warm and cool-season grasses close, frequent mowing during the hot season favors warm-season grasses and less frequent and higher mowing (especially during winter) favors cool-season grasses.

12.7 Mowers

Grass cutting is the most time consuming part of a lawn maintenance program. Good mowing practices are perhaps the most important single factor in appearance and attractiveness of a lawn.

A good mower should be: (a) maneuverable, (b) easily adjustable, (c) sturdy, and (d) of adequate horsepower. There are all kinds of mowers and each year manufacturers improve them. Two basic types of mowers are most widely used — the *rotary* and the *reel* lawn mower. Mowing units are of various sizes and the mower should be selected according to the needs to do the job efficiently.

The rotary mower has a horizontally mowing, high-speed blade which cuts grass by impact. They are mechanically simpler, less expensive and require less skill to operate and maintain than the reel mower. The reel mower has fixed blades, part of a turning cylinder (reel) which moves down and back against a stationary bedknife at the base of the mower.

The reel mower, if sharp, does a better job. It travels usually on two wheels and adjusts to the lawn surface much better than the rotary mower which usually travels on four wheels. Experiments show better turf results when mown by a reel mower, when everything else is equal. These mowers are well suited for mowing extensive areas where the surface is smooth and where close cutting and dense turf should be maintained. This type of mower is limited to cut relatively short grass. It does not cut taller grass. In short, the reel mower is best for fine turf areas and should be standard for such a turf.

The rotary mower is more versatile, easy to adjust to a 2 or 3 inch mowing height and does not jam on small twigs and chops clippings well. Generally, the rotary mowers are more adaptable to rough conditions and to areas where control of the grass, rather than appearance, is the major objective. This mower is preferred in mowing grasses which readily form seedheads, such as Bahia grass, St. Augustine grass or carpet grass. For the average lawn, a rotary mower is more practical to use. For formal or better lawns the reel type mower should be used. Very often a home owner finds it advantageous to own both a reel and a rotary mower.

Rotary mowers are much more dangerous both to the user and to anybody near-by than reel mowers. Reel mowers require less power than rotary ones. Needless to say, mowers should be sharp and kept clean.

A gasoline motor for a lawn mower is more practical than an electric one. Electric motors are all right but the cord makes it inconvenient to do the job. Battery operated electric mowers are available and do a good job. The wheels usually operate on bearings and are easy to push. A rotary mower larger than 20 inches should be self-propelled. Most reel-type power lawn mowers are self-propelled. Self-propelled mowers have adjustable speeds.

Vertical and *sickle bar* mowers are sometimes used in low maintenance turf areas. In a vertical mower cutting blades or knives operate in a vertical plane. It is used in stony areas or on turf with irregular contours. Sickle bar mowers are used where high cutting is applied, e.g., roadside banks, slopes, or terraces.

12.8 Chemical mowing

Hormone type growth regulators might be used to inhibit grass growth and thus decrease the number of mowings. Maleic hydrazide (MH) (1,2-dihydropyridazine-3,6-dione) can be used to a limited extent on roads, turnpikes and ditchbanks where mowing is difficult. This chemical inhibits leaf and stem growth and also impairs flowering. Normal rates of maleic hydrazide are suggested — 4 lb. per acre of actual herbicide. It is not practical on home lawns. At higher rates discoloration, thinning of turf were observed. Root and rhizome growth also may be impaired. Most of all, various grasses respond differently to this growth inhibitor and result in uneven, unattractive lawns.

Most experimental and commercial growth retardants show some degree of phytotoxicity to turf grasses. They are more useful on rough turf grass areas (highway, roadbanks) than on home lawns or similar areas.

Summary

1. The main purpose of mowing lawns is to get them uniform and attractive. Never remove more than ⅓ to ½ of the leaf area at one mowing.

2. Mowing stimulates bud development and tillering of grasses and the sod becomes thicker and denser. Mowing weakens roots; they are shallower and reduction in root growth occurs. Close clipped grass needs better care because of its poor root system.

3. A rotary mower is better adaptable to rough conditions. For the average or poor lawn a rotary mower is recommended. The reel mower does a better job than a rotary mower. For formal or better lawns the reel type mower should be used.

4. Grass growth inhibitors like maleic hydrazide are not practical to use on home lawns. Various grasses respond differently to this growth inhibitor and result in uneven, unattractive lawns.

CHAPTER 13
TURF PROBLEMS, RENOVATION

13.1 Shade

About 20% of lawn turf is grown under partial shade. A 50% or more reduction of light is not uncommon. Shading effects turf by: a) reduced light intensity, b) extremes of temperatures are moderated, c) wind movement is restricted, d) relative humidity is increased, e) intensity and duration of dews are increased and, most important, f) turf has to compete with tree roots for water and plant nutrients. Very often grass grows well in shade between buildings where no competition for water or plant nutrients are present.

If shading is extreme, it may be necessary to eliminate some of the shade or grasses by using other plants for ground cover, such as, periwinkle (*Vinca minor* L.) and pachysandra (*Pachysandra terminalis* Sieb. & Zucc.). Also, removing unnecessary trees should be the first step in shady lawns. If the shading is not too extreme, adapted grasses can be used for shade areas, such as red fescues, rough bluegrass in northern cool regions or St. Augustine and zoysia in the south. In the transition zone the best grass for shaded areas will be tall fescue alone or in mixtures with red fescue. To get these grasses to establish, the best time to seed is in the late summer or early fall. This will give enough time for seedlings to establish before the leaves fall. Also, frost seeding in March may be of help in northern regions.

Shady lawns should be adequately fertilized. Give at least 2 lb. of nitrogen per year per 1,000 sq. ft. Too excessive nitrogen fertilization is not advisable because grasses may be too succulent and more susceptible to diseases. Trees should be supplied with plant nutrients by deep fertilization. Soil reaction should be favorable to grasses. The shady lawn is better if mown slightly higher and excessive watering avoided. It is important to water deeply and infrequently. In order to decrease shading it is helpful to prune lower tree limbs to heights of 10 feet, thin crowns and prune the shallow roots to reduce competition. For root pruning a special tractor-mounted blade or small ditching machine can be used. They cut roots one foot or so deep around the trees. Leaves and other debris should be removed from lawns as often as needed. Use of fungicides in shaded turf areas is helpful and usually needed.

13.2 Steep slopes

Lime or fertilizers applied on a sloping lawn are often washed away. On slopes with southern exposure high temperatures may destroy the turf. Where possible warm-season grasses should be used.

Rates of fertilizers and lime should be lighter but applied more often. Frequent watering keeps slopes with southern exposure cool. Spiking of the slope will reduce the washing of fertilizers, lime and run-off water. A number of machines are available to do the spiking.

For extreme slopes it is more practical to use retaining walls or ground cover plants other than turf grasses.

13.3 Moss and algae

Lack of fertility is the most common cause of moss in a lawn. Also, poor drainage, soil acidity, improper watering, too much shade and soil compaction may be causes for moss occurrence in a lawn.

If moss gets established, remove it by raking and treat the areas with ammonium sulfate or copper sulfate. Apply concentrated amounts of ammonium sulfate when the moss is damp. Do not wash the material into the soil. Apply copper sulfate at a rate of 150 grams per 4 gallons of water per 1,000 sq. ft. Correct factors which caused moss to invade.

Algae are green plants adapted to wet soil conditions. At wet spots turf deteriorates, bare spots appear, light reaches soil and thus conditions are created for algae to invade. Poor drainage and low fertility encourage invasion. These factors should be corrected before control means are applied. Copper sulfate at a rate of 15 grams per 4 gallons of water or 2-5 lb. of hydrated lime ($Ca(OH)_2$) per 1,000 sq. ft. can be used to control algae in turf.

13.4 Soil compaction

Soils too wet and generally of poor physical condition or subjected to trampling, heavy wear and compactive forces, may form an impervious layer at the surface which prevents water infiltration, nutrient penetration, and gaseous exchange between the soil and the atmosphere. Under these conditions turf grasses tend to thin out and often are replaced by weeds, such as prostrated knotweed, goose grass and clover which flourish on compacted soils. Fine textured, especially heavy clay soils, incline more readily to compaction than coarse textured soils. Therefore, in turf where compaction possibilities are great, coarse textured soils should be preferred. Usually compaction occurs on the upper 2-3 inches of soil surface. In compacted soil the particles are pressed or packed together and fewer large pores exist. The air and water relationships may vary drastically, depending on the severity of the compaction. Compacted and water logged soil conditions are most important in impairing normal root growth in turf.

In average lawns soil compaction usually is not as much a problem. In sports turf soil compaction and turf grass wear are foremost problems.

Aerification, also called coring or hole punching, is making holes or slits (scarification) in turf with the purpose of improving physical soil conditions for plants to grow. Such a cultivation aerifies compacted soil, increases water infiltration and percolation and plant nutrient mobility. Conditions for soil microorganisms increase the plant nutrient availability improves. Severed roots, rhizomes, stolons are stimulated to produce new shoots and thus increase sod density. Aerification and increased microbe activity contribute to the decomposition of thatch. Aerification procedures such as hole punching, slicing or spiking, open the soil surface for better water-fertilizer movement into the root zone of turf. On lawns aerification is most valuable on paths, walks and other areas where there is a heavy foot traffic. Lawns exposed to heavy traffic may require aeration at least twice during the season. Spring and early fall are the best times to aerate in northern cool regions. For southern warm-season grasses late spring and summer aeration will be best. Of course, soil conditions should be favorable. Too wet soil should not be treated. Aerifying may be done every month if needed as long as soil is not frozen or too wet. If done properly, aeration does not harm the lawn or roughen the turf.

Aerifying is done by power or hand-driven machines that usually remove cores of soil 0.25-1 inch across and about 3-4 inches deep. The holes in the turf are usually made 4-6 inches apart. This kind of aerification should be done on well moistened soil; tines usually do not penetrate the needed depth on compacted dry soil. Cores can be collected and removed. Crushing and raking cores into the soil is particularly helpful where thatch has begun to accumulate. There are also machines which make slits, grooves or perforations in turf. All these methods are done for loosening the soil surface in compacted turf or to destroy thatch and improve soil conditions for turf grasses. Lawn and garden supply centers usually have lawn aeration equipment available on a rental basis.

In practice aerification work is often followed up by topdressing.

13.5 Rolling

The objectives of rolling established lawns are as follows:

a. To firm the ground around grass roots after freezing and thawing of winter have heaved the soil and left the surface loose and uneven, and thus to avoid the drying out of grass crowns.

b. To level the surface and thus facilitate uniform mowing in contrast to scalping on an uneven surface.

c. Rolling may increase the capillary system of a loose soil surface and thus help to bring moisture up to grass roots. For this job a heavier roller should be used. Of course, an excessively heavy roller may contribute to compaction of the soil. Heavy soils should not be rolled when they are wet. Rolling will be most beneficial if the soil is slightly moist, not wet.

13.6 Thatch

Thatch is a tightly intermingled layer of living and dead stems, leaves and roots of grasses, which develops between the layer of green vegetation and the soil surface. Thatch is a layer of partially decomposed turf grass leaf shoots, vascular strands of stems, nodes, crowns, stems and roots. Generally, it consists of grass parts high in lignin content. Most thatch accumulation results from stems since they contain more woody material and do not decompose as fast as clippings. Thatch is a layer above the ground, i.e., above the soil but below the visible grass leaves. It produces a mat or cushion effect. The mat between the soil and underneath the grass crowns may become so dense that a water-tight isolation layer is formed.

Thatch accumulates when dead grass organic matter production exceeds the rate of decomposition. Good conditions for organic matter accumulation and poor conditions for its decomposition create thatch. One-sided liberal fertilization with nitrogen plus irrigation prolong the growing season and may contribute to the thatch problem. Of course, lack of nitrogen for microorganisms, cool weather and generally poor conditions for decomposition of organic matter contribute in forming thatch. High mowing, acid compacted soil, will also contribute to the accumulation of organic matter and thatch formation. Vigorous grass species like Merion K. bluegrass and Bermuda grass are more inclined to form thatch. Fibrous species and varieties containing high lignin content decompose more slowly and a thatch problem may often occur (zoysias, red fescues). Thatching is very common with St. Augustine and bent grasses. Stoloniferous grasses can form a heavy thatch and grasses without stolons form thatch mostly from clippings which decay leaving threads of thick-walled fiber cells which contribute to thatch formation. Some grasses may form over one inch of a thatch layer per growing season.

A thin layer of thatch could be tolerated because it decreases (a) water evaporation, (b) temperature fluctuations in the turf, and (c) its presence creates a mat which in sports turf provides needed cushion (resilience) for play. Adverse effects of thatch usually outweigh the benefits. Thatch is an isolation layer and usually decreases the vigor of turf grasses by restricting the movement of water, air, fertilizers and pesticides into the soil. Grass roots are somewhat elevated, shallower and less tolerant to temperature and drought stresses. In some cases thatch can be so thick that roots and rhizomes of grasses fail to enter the soil below. Disease attacks may be accentuated by thatch. Thatch in dense growing grasses like fine leaf Bermudas could result in scalping due to the shallow area of green leaves defoliated by clipping.

Preventive thatch control is of prime importance and good turf management practices are the best preventive means. Fertilization and irrigation should be proper to create a well balanced condition for grasses to grow. One-sided fertilization with nitrogen plus irrigation usually create conditions for organic matter to accumulate and thus build thatch. Frequent, light nitrogen fertilization, proper pH, good drainage and good conditions for microorganisms are important in decomposition of organic plant matter without excessive accumulation. Thatch accumulation may be reduced by close cutting and removing the clippings.

Thatch accumulation of 0.5 inch or more should be controlled. Mechanical thatching is rather effective by applying vertical mowing (cutting) — thinning — aerification and raking. To create better conditions for microorganisms and decomposition of organic matter mechanical thatching should be combined with liming and balanced fertilization. Besides vertical cutting, topdressing is the best means for controlling thatch. The best results are usually obtained when vertical cutting and thinning is done during the period when the grass grows best; spring or fall in cool regions and spring or summer in the south.

13.7 Topdressing

Topdressing a lawn or turf area refers to the practice of spreading a thin layer of soil, compost or humus materials over its surface. It is effective and used in controlling thatch. It may also serve in leveling turf surfaces or covering seeds in renovation or stolons or rhizomes in vegetative turf propagation. Presently, topdressing is a common golf course maintenance operation.

Soil for topdressing should be homogenous, clean and free of pests and similar in texture to the turf soil where it will be used. If needed soil fumigation and sterilization should be applied. For topdressing usually 0.5-1.5 cubic yards of soil per 1,000 sq. ft. are used. This amount of soil covers approximately 0.2-0.5 inches deep. Soil should be worked into the turf. Brushes, rakes or special drag mats are used to work topdressing soil into turf. *Matting* — working topdressing or other materials into a turf grass area with rakes, drag mats, brushes and other similar tools. In controlling thatch topdressing could be applied at 3-6 week intervals as many times as needed. If thatch is thicker than 1 inch burying by topdressing may not be practical: it may not decompose. Thatch should first be verticut, thinned, removed and then topdressed.

13.8 Vertical mowing

Vertical mowing (verticutting) is cutting by blades or tines, which move perpendicular to the soil surface. Specifically designed to thin turf, to control turf *grain* (pattern of turf grass growth and distribution horizontally), and aid in controlling and eliminating thatch. Vertical mowing is cutting and slicing the turf vertically. It works like a mechanical rake: blades or tines cut vertically into the turf. It is effective and used in removing thatch or preparing turf for renovation or overseeding. When operating, tines or blades cut the old thatch and bring up the dead material which should be removed immediately. Of course, verticutting should be coordinated with liming, fertilization and irrigation. Large mechanical units usually do the job in one operation. With smaller machines the area should be worked at least twice in opposite directions giving a vigorous combing. If a vertical mower is not available, cutting close with a regular mower, collecting clippings and hand raking may be helpful, especially with cool-season turf grasses. After dethatching, the bare spots and light created may cause weed seeds which are present in the ground to germinate. In southern areas annual bluegrass and in northern regions crabgrass create problems. Verticutting combined with herbicide and pesticide treatment may be needed.

Vertical mowing should be employed only when grasses are growing vigorously. Late summer or early spring are the best seasons for dethatching cool-season grasses, while late spring and summer are best for thatch removal from warm-season grasses.

13.9 Renovation

Renovation is a term with varied meanings. *Complete renovation* or re-establishment (reconstruction) will be needed in deteriorated lawns or any turf areas where sods are too poor to save. It will be necessary to reconstruct weedy lawns or lawns with structural faults, such as poor drainage or soil that is too heavy or too light in texture. Sod should be destroyed by using chemicals, plowing, disking, improving soil and re-establishing turf by using procedures previously outlined (Chapters 8 and 9).

Renovation or partial renovation may be defined as a process for restoring a poor quality turf into good condition without completely tilling or removing present sod. In this kind of renovation the turf surface is disturbed without killing the old sod grasses; in this way the seedbed is prepared. New turf grasses are then seeded to improve the deteriorated sod.

Causes of old sod deterioration can be varied: due to the selection of the wrong grasses, poor soil conditions, low fertility, poor management practices, drainage, weeds, and other pests. Usually, in any deterio-rated lawn various weed species invade and contribute to further deterioration. Here it is most important before renovation to determine the cause or causes of lawn deterioration and then to carry out a corrective program, or it will require renovation again within a few years.

If less that 40 to 50% of the lawn is composed of desirable grass species, it is best to plow, rototill or cultivate, and reconstruct the lawn. This may be needed when some noxious lawn weeds invade, such as nimblewill (*Muhlenbergia* spp.) or bents. Chemicals may be used to kill old sod weedy plants (See Chapters 8 and 15). For the latest developments consult your county agent or state agricultural experiment station. Recon-struction or complete renovation is also necessary when lawns are improperly drained.

If more than 50% of the lawn consists of desirable grasses, it is possible to renovate, i.e., replant without eliminating the old sod. Grasses that spread rapidly such as Bermuda, centipede or St. Augustine can be renovated even if the percentage of desirable grasses is somewhat lower than 50 percent.

Faults that can usually be corrected by renovating an existing lawn include low fertility, surface compac-tion, too much shade, too many undesirable grasses and general neglect. Compaction from constant hard use can be remedied by applying an aerifier. Paved walks where foot traffic is heaviest will help protect the lawn. Severe pruning of trees with low branches causing heavy shade is desirable.

In the cool humid region late summer or early fall is the best time for renovation. In most cases fall seedings should be preferred because competition by weeds is not as great as with spring seedings. In southern humid regions the best renovation time is late spring or early summer. There the weeds are present and compete all the time and their control is needed.

Steps in renovation of deteriorated lawn

1. Eradicate weedy plants by using suitable herbicides. It is most important to use herbicides which will not leave in the soil residues that are injurious to grass seedlings or present grasses. Herbicides should not leave residues or they should be applied far enough in advance so that they will decom-pose before renovation (See Chapters 8 and 15).

2. Have soil tested for lime and fertilizer needs.

3. Mow area closely and remove dead vegetation and thatch by vigorous raking with steel rakes, so that new seeding can come into contact with the soil. For larger areas renovation by mechanical machines can be used. Don't plant seed on thatch. Motorized vertical mowers or slicers are avail-able for renovation. Thatch or debris brought to the surface should be removed.

4. Lime and fertilize by using fertilizers such as those used in the construction of a lawn (basic fertilization).

TURF PROBLEMS, RENOVATION   131

5. Rake fertilizers and lime into the soil. On large areas a power spiker or aerifier can be used. It mixes fertilizers and lime into the soil and makes a good seedbed for grass seedings.

6. Seed proper mixture of grasses. Use the same seeding rate as in establishing a new lawn. Specialized renovation machines provide grooving or slicing operations combined with insertion of seeds in slits. In renovating golf greens stolons can be inserted in slits or in holes made be aerification.

7. Rake area lightly to cover seeds and firm soil around seeds by rolling. Due to the fact that old sod soil is usually firm, a heavier or a lighter roller can be used. Topdressing, especially after vegetative planting, is helpful.

8. Keep surface moist and mow old sod grass closely until new seedlings establish.

13.10 Overseeding

In the winter warm-season common lawn grasses are dormant. The ground is not covered with snow and climatic conditions are mild enough for various cool-season cultural plants, wild plants or weeds to encroach and grow. Of course, these natural invaders usually do not produce a uniform green cover, contaminate lawn ground with weed seeds and create more troubles for the future. The home owner can do two things: (a) control invader plants and weeds by using herbicides and keep dormant brown or dyed green lawn until the next spring or, (b) overseed his permanent warm-season grass sward for the winter with cool-season grasses. Even perennial cool-season grasses of the North usually turn out to be short-lived plants in the South but do provide green cover for the winter season in the southern regions of the United States.

Grasses for overseeding are: K. bluegrass, rough bluegrass, red fescues, tall fescue, ryegrasses, bents, redtop — at approximately double the rate for lawns and tenfold rate for golf course greens as it is used for northern cool regions in establishing turf (Table 5.1). The most widely used is annual ryegrass for overseeding because of price and fast establishment. More heat, drought and disease (Pythium cottony blight) tolerant ryegrass varieties are more suitable for overseeding southern grass sods in winter. Redtop and bents are often used also. These grasses mix well, especially with Bermudas. Bents that live through the summer are less apparent than ryegrasses. Bents need more water and are more susceptible to diseases and insects than Bermuda grass. Bents are slow in establishing and this is probably the greatest drawback. Mixtures of red fescues, bluegrasses and bents offer some promise (27), especially for golf greens. Red fescue is good for early start and stiffness and bents for late transition. In the transition zone annual ryegrass, tall fescue or K. bluegrass can be used to overseed Bermuda grass turf. Tall fescue is all right for lawns or golf course roughs only.

In the transition zone mixtures of warm and cool-season grasses promise good turf the year round. Mixing is accomplished by seeding cool-season grass into established warm-season sod in September. Where the cool-season grass is established, the warm-season grass may be introduced as plugs in May or June (as the growth of the cool-season grasses slows with higher temperatures). These mixtures should be managed to maintain the mixture. Height of mowing, fertilizing and watering should favor the weaker grass while maintaining a satisfactory appearance to the lawn. Short mowing favors warm-season grasses; tall mowing, cool-season grasses. Fertilizing in March and September favors cool-season grasses; in June and July, warm-season grasses.

Matching the texture and color of grasses used in a mixture is desirable to avoid a spotty appearance, e.g., U-3 Bermudas can be mixed with bluegrasses or bents. In Kansas (22) Meyer Zoysia and Merion K. bluegrass are accepted and considered the best mixture available. Under those conditions these two grasses are most complimentary in texture, color and growth habits.

Seedbed. When using overseeding, first a good seedbed should be prepared by mowing the base southern grass as close as possible, raking, liming according to needs, and fertilizing. Raking can be done with an iron rake or special renovators. The surface should be roughed up well. After roughing up, the exposed runners should be cut off by another mowing. Aerification 3 to 4 weeks before overseeding, vertical mowing, spiking if possible, are helpful in the preparation of a seedbed. If the soil surface is not even, one should spread some soil on top to bring low spots up to grade.

In case where Bermuda, zoysias or other southern grasses have developed thatch, the seedbed preparation for overseeding northern cool-season grasses should be more thorough. Renovating machines are helpful. Thorough dethatching with special machines on the other hand may weaken southern grass sod too much and they will be slow in establishing the next spring. Crabgrass and other weeds may encroach when, in the spring or early summer, winter grasses will be eliminated or weakened due to too warm weather conditions. Therefore, it is advisable not to use renovating machines every year but every third year or so.

Seeding and care. The date for overseeding will vary from the northern part of the southern region to the very South from mid-September to mid-December. After seeding the area to insure seed contact with the soil, it should be raked. If the sod was not opened by aerifying, spiking or slicing the base sod, the topdressing should be about ⅛ to ¼ inch deep, with soil or compost recommended. Topdressing a lawn or turf area refers to the practice of spreading soil, compost or humus material over its surface.

For fast germination soil should always be kept moist. Under good moisture conditions seeds will germinate in 5 to 12 days. If disease problems occur, fungicides should be used. Grass seedlings should be well supplied with nitrogen by applying 1 lb. of N every 30 to 60 days. In general, nitrogen should be applied as much as needed for green color and good growth. Mowing should be kept at 1½ to 2 inch heights until mid-March or so. High height of mowing favors northern grasses and close height favors southern grasses. Therefore, about March the mowing height should be lowered and fertilization with nitrogen should be stopped, until permanent base grasses are actively growing.

In overseeding, transition periods in the fall and in the spring are important. We expect a good stand of cool-season grasses at the time southern grasses get dormant in the fall and conversely cool-season grasses should get dormant when southern grasses start to grow in the spring. This is difficult to get; often winter overseeded grasses persist and create unsightly, mottled effect on turf. Killing tops of southern grasses in the fall and northern grasses in the spring with glyphosate, paraquat or cacodylic acid may be helpful (15).

13.11 Colorants

Dormant brown grass is far less unattractive where there are no green weeds to interfere with the uniformity of the sward. Clovers and summer annuals like annual bluegrass may invade southern dormant turf in winter and make it spotted, mottled and unsightly. To improve the appearance of dormant, brown turf overseeding, artificial heating or colorants can be used. As turf colorants green dyes and plastic coating pigments are available. Dyes are less persistent than plastic coating pigments. To maintain a desired depth of color, usually repeated applications are needed. The use of colorants is in its infancy and is mostly applied to televised athletic fields. Also, it could be used as a temporary measure where disease, insect or mechanical damage has occurred to turf. Dyeing should be done on dormant, close cut and clean turf. To protect from desiccation colored dormant turf should be irrigated. The longevity of the colorants depends highly on weather conditions. Rainfall and sunshine are two factors which usually cause the greatest deterioration of color. The practicability of colorants for lawn use is questioned: (a) usually repeated applications are needed, (b) it is unnatural, and (c) it may dye walks, foundations, shoes, etc.

CHAPTER 14
LAWN WEEDS

14.1 What is a weed?

A weed is a plant growing where it is not desired, i.e., a weed is a plant out of place. In practice, we understand a weed as a wild, not intentionally sown or planted plant which grows between cultural plants and is harmful because of competition for light, moisture and plant nutrients. In recent years after the Second World War with the development of agricultural chemicals and urbanization, the concept of weeds was broadened and covers all unwanted plants. Formerly, weeds were pests in farmers' crops but now-a-days we have aquatic weeds, weeds of irrigation ditches, nurseries, lawns, roadsides, ornamentals, woods, parks, golf courses, etc.

14.2 Weed classification

From a biological point of view weeds may be a) *parasite* (heterotrophic) or b) *green plants* (autotrophic). Parasitical weeds like dodders (*Cuscuta* spp.) or witchweed (*striga* spp.) send suckers into the stem or roots of the host plant and in such a way obtain nutrients from them. Dodders cause the greatest damage to legumes, whereas witchweed is mainly a parasite of corn.

Autotrophic, green plant weeds obtain their plant nutrients through their roots and assimilate carbohydrates with the help of chlorophyll through the green foliage. Green plant weeds are grouped into three major types on the basis of their life cycle: a) annuals, b) biennials, and c) perennials.

Annuals complete their life cycle in less than 12 months. They reproduce by seeds. Seed production is abundant. Once the area is infested, they spread rapidly.

Summer annuals germinate in the spring, produce seeds, and die in the fall. Their seeds lie dormant until the next spring. Redroot pigweed, lambsquarters, ragweed, smartweed, crabgrasses, foxtail, and barnyard grass belong here.

Winter annuals germinate in the fall or winter, produce their seed in the spring or early summer and then die. Usually, plants live less than 12 months. Seeds stay dormant during the summer, germinate in the fall, produce growth and go into dormancy in winter. In the spring they resume growth. Downy brome, shepherd's purse and common chickweed belong here. In northern regions of the United States these weeds are winter annuals but in the transition or southern regions these plants can germinate in the spring or summer and produce seed the same growing season and thus may be considered as summer annuals.

Biennials produce leafy growth from the seed during the first growing season. They are dormant during the winter and in the second season develop stalks with flowers and seeds. Plants live more than 12 months but less than 36 months. This group is easily confused with the winter annuals. Wild carrot, burdock, white sweet clover and common mullein are examples.

Usually biennials possess a fleshy tap root where plant food reserves are stored.

Perennials live more than 2 years and can persist indefinitely. Generally, the classification according to length of life is not always too clear because climatic factors may play a role. Many weeds that are annuals or biennials in severe climatic regions may act as biennials or even perennials in milder climates.

14.3 Reproduction of weeds

Annual, biennial and perennial weeds usually reproduce by seeds. Most perennial weeds also reproduce vegetatively. With many perennial weeds vegetative propagation plays a more important role than reproduction by seeds.

Dandelion, plantains and curly dock reproduce by seeds as well as by roots or crowns, when chopped or fragmented by tillage or other implements.

Wild garlic and wild onion reproduce by seeds, bulbs and bulblets. A bulb is a very short stem with fleshy leaf base closely pressed together. Bulbs are normally produced below the ground. Bulblets are usually produced above ground and are referred to as aerial bulblets ("onion sets").

So-called creeping perennials usually reproduce by rhizomes, stolons, roots and tubers.

Rhizomes (rootstocks) are underground stems identified by their nodes. New shoots develop from the buds at nodes. If chopped, each piece which possesses a node may produce a shoot. Quack grass, common yarrow and hedge bindweed are examples.

Stolons are like rhizomes except that they grow horizontal and are termed above ground stems. Ground ivy and mouse-ear chickweed are examples.

Roots of field bindweed, Canada thistle, common milkweed, Carolina horsenettle, red sorrel and leafy spurge serve for spreading of these weeds. Roots are able to produce adventitious buds which produce new shoots and independent plants.

Tubers are enlarged rhizomes for additional food storage. They develop new shoots. Yellow nutsedge (nut grass) and Jerusalem artichoke are examples.

14.4 Dissemination of weeds

Spreading by seeds

Weeds spread by seeds and vegetatively. The number of seeds produced by weeds varies widely among species and within a species. Soil fertility, climatic conditions, available space, etc., play an important role in seed production. Stevens (39) found approximately the following number of weed seeds per plant:

for 101 annuals	21,000 seeds
for 19 biennials	27,000 seeds
for 61 perennials	17,000 seeds

As we see there are no great differences between various groups of weeds in the production of seeds.

The number of weed seeds in the soil can reach millions per acre. Brenchley and Warington (2) found in Rothamsted (England) heavy clay 2.4 mil. viable seeds of prostrated knotweed and 92.4 mil. viable poppy *(Papaver rhoeas)* seeds per acre.

In dissemination of weed seeds in our lawns a) turf grass seed, b) winds, c) water, d) animals and man himself are important factors. Contaminated turf grass seed is a major factor in the spreading of noxious lawn weeds. This problem has been already discussed (See 5.4).

Some weed seeds are equipped with parachute-like structures which make the seed float in the wind and in that way they can be carried far away. Dandelion, Canada thistle and milkweed are examples. Tumble pigweed and old witchgrass plants may break off near the soil and roll for miles in the wind, scattering their seed.

Irrigation water can also be an important factor in weed spreading. Some weed seeds float for days and may be carried great distances away without losing viability. Weeds can be stored in water for 3 or more years without losing viability, e.g., pigweed seeds after 33 months storage in water still sprouted (9%). Quack grass seeds germinated (50%) after storage in water for 21 months (3).

Many seeds have adapted hooks, barbs, or twisted awns to cling to animals or to man's clothing. Sandburs, beggar-ticks and burdocks are examples. Many weed seeds can pass through the digestive tracts of animals without losing viability. Harmon and Keim (17) research results are presented in Table 14.1.

Seed dormancy is an important factor in weed seed dissemination. Dormancy is delayed germination of seeds. Also, dormancy may be defined as a resting stage of a seed. Under suitable conditions seeds may stay dormant for many years and then germinate and infest your lawn, garden or field. Weeds usually produce seeds with varying periods of dormancy and often germination takes place throughout the growing season. Beal (1879) started weed seed germination tests. These tests indicate that some seeds were able to stay for more than 50 years without losing viability (7).

Table 14.1 Seed viability after passing digestion tracts of various animals

Animal	Whole seeds passed digestion tracts	Based upon total number of seeds fed. % viable seeds
Calves	23.1%	9.6%
Hogs	24.1%	8.8%
Horses	12.9%	8.7%
Sheep	10.7%	6.4%
Chicken	0.3%	0.2%

Table 14.2 Viability of some buried seeds in Beals' test

Weed	Germination % after years in storage			
	40 years	50 years	60 years	70 years
Curly dock (*Rumex crispus*)	18	52	4	8
Moth mullein (*Verbascum blattaria*)	0	62	68	72

Stored seeds stay viable longer under dry, cool and low oxygen conditons.

Vegetative reproduction

Weeds which spread vegetatively are most persistent. Weeds that spread vegetatively are usually perennial. Also, some annual weeds can spread vegetatively, e.g., crabgrass by rooting of above ground stems.

Perennial weed roots and rhizomes may sometimes penetrate soil as deep as 17 ft. Often the weight of quack grass rhizomes exceeds the weight of the foliage of this weed and may reach up to 4-5 tons in yield. The same is also true of other perennials. In Minnesota yellow nutsedge yielded 9 tons of fresh weight tubers per acre (45). One tuber in one year produced 1,900 plants and 6,900 tubers to a 10 inch depth in a patch 7 ft. in diameter.

14.5 Common turf weeds

Even under good management conditions weeds invade our lawns. Most persistent weeds are those which have their growing points close to the surface of the ground and thus are not injured by frequent close mowings. Here belong a) plants which have a very short stem or crown with a rosette of leaves close to the ground, and b) those which make a mat of rhizomes or stolons. As such, plants considered as typical turf weeds can be mentioned: dandelions, plantains, prostrate knotweed, ground ivy, spotted spurge, heal-all, crabgrass, quack grass, annual bluegrass and many others.

Data of important turf weeds (51) in the United States and Canada (Fig. 14.1) are presented in Table 14.3. Numbers indicate how many states-provinces listed a specific weed as important in the region. In parenthesis, data are expressed in percentages, taking the total number of states-provinces in the region as 100. In this list only weeds included which in at least two states-provinces were listed.

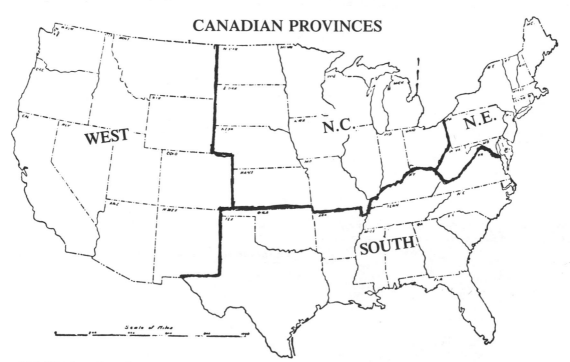

Figure 14.1 Weed regions of the United States and adjacent Canadian provinces.
   N.E. — Northeastern region with Ontario, Quebec and Maritime provinces;
   N.C. — North Central region with west Ontario, Manitoba and Saskatchewan;
   Western region with Alberta and British Columbia; South region

Table 14.3 Most important turf weeds in various regions of United States and adjacent
Canadian provinces

Terms: a-annual; wa-winter annual; ba-biennial; p-perennial; s-seed; rhiz.-rhizomes; stol.-stolons

Species	Life form	Repro-duction	Number of states, provinces listed as important weed in				Total (average)
			North-east	North Central	South	West	
MONOCOTYLEDONOUS:							
1. Bent grasses - Agrostis spp.	p	s, stol, rhiz	7 (44)[a]	7 (50)	0	5 (38)	19 (34)
2. Bermuda grass - Cynodon dactylon (L.) Pers	p	s, rhiz, stol	1 (6)	1 (7)	3 (23)	1 (8)	6 (11)
3. Bluegrass, annual - Poa Annua L.	a	s	9 (56)	8 (57)	11 (85)	9 (69)	37 (66)
4. Brome, downy - Bromus tectorum L.	a, wa	s	1 (6)	2 (14)	1 (8)	0	4 (7)
5. Crabgrasses - Digitaria spp.	a	s, rooting stems	13 (81)	9 (64)	13 (100)	8 (62)	43 (77)
6. Dallis grass - Paspalum dilatatum Poir.	p	s, rhiz	1 (6)	0	6 (46)	1 (8)	8 (14)
7. Fescue, tall - Festuca arundincea Schreb.	p	s	5 (31)	5 (36)	0	4 (31)	14 (25)
8. Foxtails - Setaria spp.	a	s	0	3 (21)	1 (8)	0	4 (7)
9. Garlic, wild - Allium vineale L.	p	bulbs, bulblets, s	1 (6)	0	6 (46)	0	7 (12)
10. Goose grass - Eleusine indica (L.) Gaertn.	a	a	4 (25)	2 (14)	8 (62)	0	14 (25)
11. Johnson grass - Sorghum halepense (L.) Pers	p	s, rhiz	1 (6)	0	1 (8)	1 (8)	3 (5)
12. Nimblewill - Muhlen-bergia schreberi J.F. Gmel.	p	s, rooting stems	2 (12)	5 (36)	1 (8)	1 (8)	9 (16)
13. Nutsedge, purple - Cyperus rotundus L.	p	tubers, s	0	0	4 (31)	1 (8)	5 (9)
14. Nutsedge, yellow - Cyperus esculentus L.	p	tubers, s	5 (31)	6 (43)	6 (46)	0	17 (30)
15. Orchard grass - Dactylis glomerata L.	p	s	1 (6)	0	0	2 (15)	3 (5)
16. Quack grass - Agropyron repens (L.) Beauv.	p	s, rhiz	5 (31)	9 (64)	0	6 (46)	20 (36)
17. Sandbur - Cenchrus spp.	a	s	0	1 (7)	1 (8)	0	2 (4)

Table 14.3 (continued)

Species	Life form	Repro- duction	Number of states, provinces listed as important weed in				Total (average)
			North- east	North Central	South	West	
18. Velvet grass - *Holcus lanatus & H. mollis* L.	p	s, rhiz	1 (6)	0	0	6 (46)	7 (12)
DICOTYLEDONOUS							
19. Bellflower, creeping - *Campanula rapuncu- loides* L.	p	s, roots	0	2 (14)	0	2 (15)	4 (17)
20. Burclover - *Medicago hispida* Gaerth.	a	s	0	0	1 (8)	2 (15)	3 (5)
21. Buttercups - *Ranunculus* spp.	p	s, stol	2 (12)[a]	0	1 (8)	2 (15)	5 (9)
22. Chickweed, common - *Stellaria media* (L.) Cyrill.	a, wa	s, rooting stems	9 (56)	12 (86)	10 (77)	5 (38)	36 (64)
23. Chickweed, mouse-ear - *Cerastium vulgatum* L.	p	s, stol	10 (62)	5 (36)	1 (8)	6 (46)	22 (39)
24. Cinquefoil - *Potentilla* spp.	p, ba	s, stol	3 (19)	1 (7)	0	0	4 (7)
25. Clover, white - *Trifolium repens* L.	p	s, stol	5 (31)	5 (36)	5 (38)	6 (46)	21 (38)
26. Dandelion - *Taraxacum officinale* L.	p	s, roots	13 (81)	12 (86)	7 (54)	10 (77)	42 (75)
27. Dichondra - *Dichondra repens* Forst	p	s, creeping stems	0	0	2 (15)	0	2 (4)
28. Hawkbit, fall - *Leontodon autum- nalis* L.	p	s, rhiz	2 (12)	0	0	0	2 (4)
29. Hawkweed - *Hieracium* spp.	p	s, rhiz	5 (31)	0	0	0	5 (9)
30. Heal-all - *Prunella vulgaris* L.	p	s, rhiz	2 (12)	0	0	0	2 (4)
31. Henbit - *Lamium amplexicaule* L.	wa, ba	s, rooting stems	0	2 (14)	11 (85)	0	13 (23)
32. Ivy, ground - *Glechoma hederacea* L.	p	s, stol	9 (56)	7 (50)	0	1 (8)	17 (30)
33. Knotweed, prostrate - *Polygonum aviculare* L.	a	s	10 (62)	11 (79)	5 (38)	6 (46)	32 (57)

Table 14.3 (continued)

Species	Life form	Repro- duction	Number of states, provinces listed as important weed in				Total (average)
			North- east	North Central	South	West	
34. Kochia - *Kochia scoparia* (L.) Schrad.	a	s	0	1 (7)	0	2 (15)	3 (5)
35. Medic, black - *Medicago lupulina* L.	a, wa	s	1 (6)	2 (14)	2 (15)	3 (23)	8 (14)
36. Pearlwort - *Sagina procumbens* L.	a, p	s	2 (12)	0	0	1 (8)	3 (5)
37. Plantain - *Plantago* spp.	p	s, roots	12 (75)	9 (64)	5 (38)	7 (54)	33 (59)
38. Plantain, buckhorn - *Plantago lanceolata* L.	p	s, roots	4 (25)	1 (7)	3 (23)	1 (8)	9 (16)
39. Sorrel, red - *Rumex acetosella* L.	p	s, roots	3 (19)	0	1 (8)	1 (8)	5 (9)
40. Speedwell - *Veronica* spp.	a, wa p	s	6 (38)	2 (14)	1 (8)	3 (23)	12 (21)
41. Speedwell, creeping - *Veronica filiformis* Sm.	p	s, stol	1 (6)	0	0	2 (15)	3 (5)
42. Spurge, prostrate - *Euphorbia supina* Ref.	a	s	3 (19)	3 (21)	5 (38)	2 (15)	13 (23)
43. Spurge, spotted - *Euphorbia maculata* L.	a	s	5 (31)	1 (7)	2 (15)	1 (8)	9 (16)
44. Starwort, little - *Stellaria graminea* L.	p	s, stol	3 (19)	0	0	0	3 (5)
45. Woodsorrel - *Oxalis* spp.	p	s	3 (19)	1 (17)	3 (23)	1 (8)	8 (14)
46. Yarrow, common - *Achillea millefolium* L.	p	s, rhiz	5 (31)	1 (7)	1 (8)	3 (23)	10 (18)

ᵃ Numbers in parenthesis indicate percent of states-provinces in the region listing the weed as important.

The most important turf weeds, as indicated by their frequency of listing (Table 14.3) include crabgrass (43 states-provinces), dandelion (42 states-provinces), annual bluegrass (37 states-provinces), and common chickweed (36 states-provinces), followed by plantains and prostrated knotweed. From the monocotyledonous group, the most troublesome are annual bluegrass, nutsedges and perennial grasses such as bent grass, Bermuda grass, tall fescue, nimblewill, quack grass and velvet grass. Perennial grasses cannot generally be controlled selectively in lawns or any turf areas. Worse, most are difficult to eradicate conveniently by any means.

Typical weeds of northern cool regions often occur in the south. These most common weeds of the north are usually not dominating in the south and they are seldom disastrous there, e.g., quack grass prefer the north, wild onion the transition zone between north and south and kochia or Russian thistle is most troublesome in dry plains. On the other hand some weeds may be quite troublesome in all climatical regions. Annual bluegrass, crabgrass, common chickweed, dandelion, prostrate knotweed, plantain and white clover are rather common turf weeds in all states. Bermuda grass, Dallis grass, purple nutsedge, wild garlic, goose grass and henbit are typical weeds of the southern region. On the other hand, bent grasses, tall fescue, quack grass or ground ivy, are not important in the south.

14.6 Vegetative characteristics of common weedy lawn grasses*

Weedy grasses are the most difficult to identify in a turf area. Because of continuous cutting they are always kept in a vegetative stage of growth and are therefore like the seeded lawn grasses. Presented below in concise form are vegetative characteristics of most common weedy grasses found in turf areas.

1. Barnyard grass (*Echinochloa crusgalli* [L.] Beauv.)

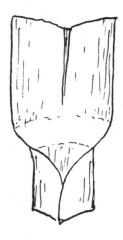

A coarse annual bunch grass exhibiting considerable variation in morphological characteristics. It is a common weed of cultivated soils, poorly drained fields, new lawn seedings and waste places.

Leaves rolled in bud-shoot. *Sheath* somewhat flattened, mostly smooth, split with hyaline margins. *Blades* 8-15mm wide, pale green, glabrous, keeled, not ridged. *Ligule* absent. *Auricles* absent. *Collar* broad, conspicuous. *Inflorescence* — a compact panicle with short, densely flowered, spike-like branches. Distinct characteristics: no ligule, coarse grass.

2. Bluegrass, annual (*Poa annua* L.)

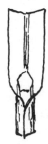

Annual bluegrass is one of the most troublesome weedy grasses in turf especially in golf courses. It is common in the north as well as in the southern regions (Table 14.3). In the northern cool region it is usually annual when in the south it is a winter annual plant. Some strains of this weedy grass produce creeping and rooting stems and act like a perennial, persistant plant.

Leaves are folded in the bud-shoot. *Sheath* distinctly flattened, somewhat keeled, smooth and split with overlapping hyaline margins. *Blades* 2-4mm wide, short, and somewhat tapering to boat-shaped but subacute tips, not glossy. The upper surface of the leaf blade is not ridged but has the characteristic midrib: two distinct light lines along midrib. *Ligule* 1-3mm long, membranous, white, rounded to acute. *Auricles* absent. *Collar* distinct, glabrous, divided. *Inflorescence* — a small, open, few branched panicle. It is able to produce seed stalks even under close turf mowing. Distinct characteristics: blades not glossy, somewhat tapering, rather long (1-3mm), white ligule.

---

* Grass drawings enlarged approximately x 3

3. Brome, downy (*Bromus tectorum* L.)

An erect, tufted annual or winter annual, somewhat purplish tinged, found in waste places, new turf seedings and alfalfa fields.

Leaves rolled in bud-shoot. *Sheath* round, closed (split above), softly pubescent, pale green and often purple tinged. *Blades* 5-10mm wide, pubescent. *Ligule* membraneous, coarsely toothed, 1.5-3mm long. *Auricles* absent. *Collar* divided, hairy. *Inflorescence* — dense, soft, drooping, often purple panicle. Distinct characteristics: sheath closed, soft pubescent.

4. Chess, soft (*Bromus mollis* L.)

A common, wide-spread, erect annual weed in fields, new lawns and waste places.

Leaves rolled in bud-shoots. *Sheaths* round, closed (split above), densely soft white hairy. *Blades* 5-9mm wide, hairy throughout. *Ligule* membraneous 1-2mm long, rounded and toothed. *Auricles* absent. *Collar* narrow, divided, hairy. *Inflorescence* — an erect, contracted, crowded panicle. Distinct characteristics: sheath closed, pubescent.

5. Crabgrass, large (*Digitaria sanguinalis* L. Scop.)

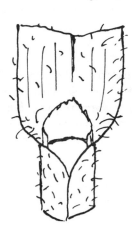

Most common annual noxious weed in lawns and cultivated fields. Purplish in fall, turns brown after first hard frost.

Leaves rolled in bud-shoot. *Sheaths* round to somewhat flattened, long hairy, split. *Blade* keeled below, 5-15mm wide, hairy above and below. *Ligule* rounded, may be toothed, 1-4mm long. *Auricles* absent. *Collar* broad, mostly divided by midrib, sparsely hairy. *Inflorescence* — 3-12 digitate spike-like branches. Reproduce by seeds and rooting lower nodes.

6. Crabgrass, smooth (*Digitaria ischaemum* [Schreb.] Muhl.)

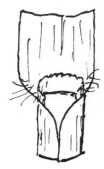

Common in lawns, fields and waste places. Without hairs, shoots somewhat purplish and smaller in size than large crabgrass.

Leaves rolled in bud-shoots. *Sheaths* compressed split, basal ones may be sparsely hairy. *Blades* smooth with few hairs near base, 5-10mm wide, dull green or purplish tinged. *Ligule* 1.5-3mm, slightly undulate. *Auricles* absent. *Collar* distinct with few hairs at margin. *Inflorescence* — 2-6 digitate spike-like branches.

7. Dallis grass (*Paspalum dilatatum* Poir)

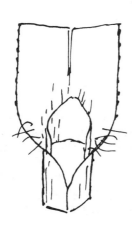

A coarse textured, leafy perennial pasture grass for southern regions. It is erect, ascending or slightly spreading from a decumbent base bunch grass. It is an objectionable weed in turf grass areas. Dallis grass is somewhat similar to crabgrass except its straight stiff stems radiate from center in a "star" pattern.

Leaves rolled in bud-shoot. *Sheaths* distinctly flattened, smooth, split with overlapping hyaline margins. *Blades* are 7-15mm wide, smooth above and mostly long hairy behind ligule, smooth keeled below, tapering to rounded narrow base, margins smooth to scabrous. *Ligule* membraneous, 2-5mm, rounded to acute. *Auricles* absent. *Collar* narrow to broad, glabrous, often hairy on margins. *Inflorescence* — 3-5 onesided, spike-like branches arising at different levels on top of stems. Flat, round to oval seeds. Seeds covered with fine silky hairs. Seeds arranged in two compact rows.

```
10 MILLI-1    2    3    4    5    6    7    8    9    10
METERS                CENTIMETERS
```

8. Foxtails, green (*Setaria viridis* [L.] Beauv.)

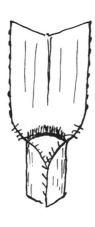

A coarse annual, semi-erect and branching from the base, common weed of waste places, new lawn seedings, cultivated fields. Common throughout the cooler parts of the United States. Heavy in the Midwest.

Leaves rolled in bud-shoot. *Sheath* round to slightly compressed, split with overlapping margins hairy (at least outer one). *Blades* light green, 5-12mm wide, narrow at the base, tapering to a fine point, margins serrulate scabrous. *Ligule* fringe of hairs 1-2mm long, fused at base with longer hairs at the edges of collar margins. *Auricles* absent. *Collar* pubescent along the margins. *Inflorescence* — spike-like panicle, bristly and broader than yellow foxtail.

Green foxtail distinguishable from yellow foxtail by ciliate margins of the sheath and absence of twisted hairs at the base of the blade. The ligule is longer and the sheath is not compressed.

9. Foxtail, yellow (*Setaria lutescens* (Weigel) Hubb. *S. glauca* [L.] Beauv.)

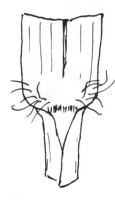

A semi-erect fibrous-rooted annual of waste places, cultivated ground, new turf seedings or over-grazed pastures. Heavy in Midwest of United States.

Leaves rolled in flattened bud-shoot. *Sheath* compressed, sharply keeled split, distinctly veined. *Blades* v-shaped toward base, 7-12mm wide with twisted hairs near the base, light green in color. *Ligule* a fringe of hairs fused at base, about 1mm long. *Auricles* absent. *Collar* narrow, continuous, hairy on margins. *Inflorescence* — spike-like panicle, yellow, erect.

Distinguished from green foxtail by twisted hairs at the base of blades and by absence of cilia on the flattened sheath.

10. Giant foxtail (*Setaria faberi* Herrm.)

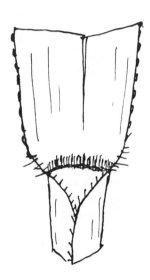

Annual reproducing by seed coarse weedy grass, prevalent in midwest and mid-Atlantic areas in the eastern part. Common throughout all but the northernmost and southernmost states. Most common in Illinois, Missouri and adjacent southern states.

Leaves rolled in bud-shoot. *Sheaths* round, smooth with overlapping hyaline margins. *Blade* 10-20mm wide, rough above, margins rough and hyaline, softly pubescent beneath to becoming glabrous, keeled below. *Ligule* fringe of hairs, 2-3mm long. *Auricles* absent. *Collar* broad, hairy. *Inflorescence* — bristly, cylindrical, nodding spike-like panicle.

11. Goose grass (*Eleusine indica* [L.] Gaertn.)

Flatstemmed with prostrate growth annual bunch grass. It forms distinct rosette, whitish in center. It occurs throughout all the United States except northern Maine and parts of the north central and northwestern areas of the U.S. As turf weed most noxious in the southern region (Table 14.3).

Leaves folded in bud-shoot. *Sheath* flattened hairy at top, split with overlapping margins. *Blades* sparsely long hairy near base above, smooth and keeled below 4-9mm wide. *Ligule* membraneous, up to 1mm long, truncate, sometimes short ciliate. *Auricles* absent. *Collar* broad, hairy on margins. *Inflorescence* — 2-10 flat spikes at or near summit.

12. Johnson grass (*Sorghum halepense* [L.] Pers.)

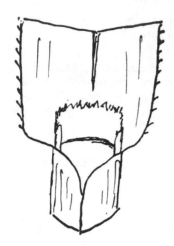

Perennial reproducing by large rhizomes and seeds. Cultivated as forage grass. Common throughout southern half of U.S. extending as far as up to New England, Michigan, Nebraska, Wyoming and reaching Oregon on the west coast.

Leaves rolled in the bud-shoot. *Sheath* round, smooth, split with hyaline margins. *Blade* 20-35mm wide, smooth above and below, midrib whitish above prominent below, margins rough and hyaline. *Ligule* 3-5mm long, abrupt, rounded, ciliate. *Auricles* absent. *Collar* broad, may be divided and hairy. *Inflorescence* — large, loose, erect panicle.

13. Kikuyu grass (*Pennisetum clandestinum* Hochst. ex Chiov.)

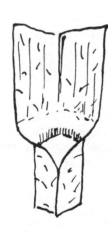

Introduced from Africa, low growing, coarse, warm-season perennial grass. Spreading by seeds, rhizomes and stolons. Adapted to higher elevations in most tropics. Introduced to southern California, Arizona and Florida. Hurt by leafspot in Florida. In areas of adaptation, suitable for erosion control and general purpose turf. Propagated vegetatively by sprigs and chopped stems. Aggressive, vigorous thatch forming grass and can become a troublesome weed in turf and cropland. It is a major turf problem in coastal California.

Leaves folded in the bud-shoot. *Sheaths* compressed, flat, strongly veined, covered with fine hairs. *Blades* flat or folded, sparsely hairy, tapering. *Ligule* fringe of hairs. *Auricles* absent. *Collar* medium with fine hairs. *Inflorescence* — flowering stems are topped with 2-4 flowers which bloom on short side shoots. Fertile and male-sterile strains recognized.

14. Nimblewill (*Muhlenbergia schreberi* J. F. Gmelin)

Perennial, shade-tolerant weedy grass common throughout most of the eastern and central areas of the United States. It grows in dense patches and spreads by seeds. Stems usually decumbent at the base, often rooting at the lower nodes but not forming definite creeping stolons. Stems are very slender with distinct nodes.

Leaves rolled in bud-shoot. *Sheaths* somewhat flattened, split with overlapping hyaline margins. *Blades* 3-6mm wide, short hairy near base. *Ligule* 0.4-0.8mm long, membraneous, truncate, entire or lacerate. *Auricles* absent. *Collar* medium, hairy on the margins. *Inflorescence* — slender, compressed panicle.

15. Orchard grass (*Dactylis glomerata* L.) see p. 28.

16. Panicum, fall (*Panicum dichotomiflorum* Michx.)

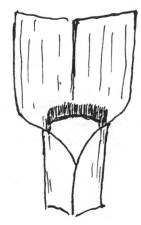

A coarse common annual weed. Culms ascending or spreading. Infestations are increasing in recent years.

Leaves rolled in bud-shoot. *Sheath* round, smooth, split with overlapping hyaline margins. *Blade* 10-20mm wide, smooth above or sparsely hairy near base; dull above, smooth and glossy below, margins soft to rough. *Ligule* a fringe of hair, 2-3mm long, usually fused at base. *Auricles* absent. *Collar* continuous broad. *Inflorescence* — widely spreading terminal and axillary panicles.

17. Quack grass (*Agropyron repens* [L.] Beauv.)

Quack grass is a coarse textured most troublesome perennial weed in the northern areas of the United States and adjacent Canada. It spreads by shallow rhizomes and seeds.

Leaves rolled in the bud-shoot. *Sheaths* round, split with overlapping hyaline margins; lower usually pubescent. Young plants and spring growth are usually more pubescent that older plants or growth produced later in the season. *Blades* 6-12mm wide, tapering to sharp point. *Ligule* membraneous, truncate to rounded, 0.5-1mm long, may be toothed or ciliate. *Auricles* claw-like, slender, clasping the stem. *Collar* medium, sometimes minutely hairy. *Inflorescence* — long narrow spike with spikelets placed side to rachis.

18. Sandbur (*Cenchrus pauciflorus*)

Annual, branching grassy weed of open sand ground. Found throughout the United States but most troublesome in warmer areas. Grows best in dry, sandy soils.

Leaves rolled in bud-shoot. *Sheath* distinctly flattened, smooth with a tuft of hairs at throat, split with overlapping hyaline margins, sparse hairs on the edges. *Blade* 3-6mm wide, rough above. *Ligule* a fringe of hairs, 0.6-1mm long. *Auricles* absent. *Collar* narrow to broad, often hairy on margins. *Inflorescence* — a nearly round, hairy bur with sharp spines.

19. Velvet grass (*Holcus lanatus* L.)

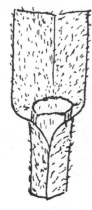

Coarse textured, grayish-green, velvety perennial bunch grass. Grows throughout the northern states, most troublesome in the Pacific Northwest.

Leaves rolled in the bud-shoot. *Sheaths* flattened, velvety, split, pinkish tinted below. *Blade* 5-10mm wide, velvety hairy above and below. *Ligule* membraneous, rounded, 2-3mm long. *Auricles* absent. *Collar* — divided hairy. *Inflorescence* — long, contracted panicle.

20. Velvet grass, German (*Holcus Mollis* L.)

Perennial velvety weedy grass with slender rhizomes. Spreading along Atlantic coast from Massachusetts through New Jersey and Pacific coast from Washington state through northern California (   ).

21. Witch grass (*Panicum capillare* L.)

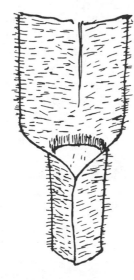

A coarse and very hairy branching annual weedy grass, widespread across the United States.

Leaves rolled in bud-shoot. *Sheaths* round, long hairy (papillose-hispid), split with overlapping hyaline margins, usually tinted reddish. *Blade* 8-15mm wide, hispid on both sides, veined below. *Ligule* a fringe of hairs 1-2mm long, fused at base. *Auricles* absent. *Collar* broad hairy. *Inflorescence* — terminal, densely flowered panicle, about half entire height of plant breaking away and rolling before wind following maturity.

Summary

1. A weed is a plant out of place, i.e. a plant growing where it is not desired.

2. Weeds may be classified (grouped) into three major types on the basis of their life cycle: a) annuals, b) biennials and c) perennials.

Annuals complete their life cycle in less than 12 months. Redroot pigweed, lambsquarters, ragweed, crabgrass, foxtails, and barnyard grass belong here.

Biennials live more than 12 months but less than 36 months. During the first growing season they produce leafy growth from the seed. They are dormant during the winter, and in the second season develop stalks with flowers and seeds. Wild carrot, burdock, white sweet clover, common mullein are examples.

Perennial weeds live more than 2 years and can persist indefinitely. Ground ivy, plantains, dandelion, quack grass and nimblewill are examples.

3. Annual, biennial and perennial weeds are reproduced by seeds. Most of the perennial weeds also reproduce vegetatively by rhizomes (quack grass, common yarrow), stolons (ground ivy, mouse-ear chickweed), tubers (nutsedge), roots (field, bindweed, red sorrel, common milkweed), crowns and taproot (dandelion, plantains, curly dock).

4. Factors for weed persistence are: a) prolific seed production, b) seed dormancy, c) effective means in seed dispersal and d) spreading by vegetative parts. Most persistent weeds in turf areas are those which have their growing points close to the surface of the ground and thus are not injured by frequent close cutting. Weeds producing leaf rosettes and weeds spreading by rhizomes and stolons are the most persistent lawn weeds.

5. The following can be mentioned as troublesome weeds of lawns and other turf areas:

Monocots

1. Bent grasses
2. Bermuda grass
3. Bluegrass, annual
4. Crabgrass
5. Dallis grass
6. Fescue, tall
7. Garlic, wild
8. Goose grass
9. Nimblewill
10. Nutsedge, yellow
11. Nutsedge, purple
12. Quack grass
13. Sandbur

Dicots

1. Chickweed, common
2. Chickweed, mouse-ear
3. Clover, white
4. Dandelion
5. Ivy, ground
6. Knotweed, prostrate
7. Plantains, broadleaf, blackseed
8. Plantain, buckhorn
9. Sorrel, red
10. Speedwells
11. Spurges, spotted, prostrate
12. Woodsorrel
13. Yarrow, common

Crabgrasses and annual bluegrass are most prevalent weedy grasses. Also they are common in all regions of the United States and Canada. Goose grass, nutsedges, wild garlic and Dallis grass are more prevalent and troublesome in southern regions, while quack grass, bent grass, nimblewill or velvet grass are more troublesome in northern parts of the country. Perennial grasses such as bent grasses, Bermuda grass, tall fescue, quack grass or nimblewill are difficult to control in turf selectively and belong to the most troublesome turf weeds.

Dandelion, plantains, chickweeds, prostrate knotweed and white clover are common broadleaf weeds and well distributed throughout the United States and adjacent Canadian provinces. Henbit is more prevalent and troublesome in the southern region of the United States.

CHAPTER 15
LAWN WEED CONTROL

15.1 Introduction

From early biblical times, when thorns and thistles were sent to plague Adam and Eve (Genesis 3:18) and when Man accused his enemy of sowing darnel *(Lolium temulentum)* in his crops (Matthew 13:25) to the present day, weeds have posed a significant challenge in man's struggle to control them.

Weed control is as old as agriculture itself. Weeding by hand, howing, tillage, and cultivation were the first methods in weed control. Even today these methods are important and accepted as classical methods in weed control. Revolution in weed control and generally in weed science came about immediately after the Second World War, when hormone type organic chemicals were developed and applied as herbicides. The United States and Great Britain are pioneers in the development of these modern chemical weed control methods.

15.2 Preventive weed control

The control of weeds is a continuing problem that requires constant attention. Temperature, day length, soil moisture and other factors determine the time of year and extent of germination of a given weed species. Some weeds appear in early spring while others have their peak level of germination in summer or fall. If conditions are favorable during the period of peak germination, a lawn weed may be unusually abundant in a given year. This is the reason that certain weeds appear in large numbers one season and are in little evidence the next year.

Competition is an important factor in seed germination and plant survival. One of the best weed deterrents is a dense stand of turf grass.

Preventive means in turf weed control are of first importance. One of the best forms of weed control is proper grass establishment and maintenance. Some main points are discussed below.

a) *Proper seedbed* preparation before seeding. Topsoil is often contaminated with various weed seeds which germinate with seeded turf grasses and thus compete with establishing lawn seedings. Many complaints are from people who wrongly think that seed used in establishing lawns was contaminated with weed seeds. Annuals, especially broad-leaved weeds, usually do not withstand normal turf maintenance practices, e.g., continuous mowing, and disappear. Noxious weed seeds, rhizomes, stolons, tubers or other vegetative propagation organs should be destroyed before seeding a lawn. Pre-plant weed control is costly, but often justified. Applied herbicidal compounds become decomposed in the soil, allowing planting of the lawn or turf area at a later date. In some cases test plantings on a small area are advised before seeding the entire area to determine whether the herbicide has yet been dissipated to a nontoxic level, making it safe to plant the grass species. Time required for breakdown in the soil depends primarily on temperature and soil microbial activity.

Establishment of new lawns, or rebuilding of old lawn or turf areas may be facilitated by preceeding treatments with herbicides or soil fumigants (cf. page 94). Soil fumigation for weed control is an expensive proposition. However, the nature of certain weeds, particularly perennial grasses like nutsedge, quack grass, tall fescue, Bermuda grass, orchard grass, requires this approach since there are currently no satisfactory control measures to be recommended for established lawns. Other beneficial results from soil fumigation include control of nematodes, fungus diseases and insect pests.

b) Seeding well *adapted grass seed-species* and at the right time are also important preventive factors in keeping lawns clean from weeds. Fall or early spring (in northern cool regions) and spring and early summer (in southern regions) generally are the best times for grass plantings. Because of prevalence of some specific weeds, special consideration may be needed, e.g., in the northern region where winter annual weeds are common (chickweed, shepherds purse) early spring seedings may be more advantageous than usually preferred fall seeding dates.

c) *Good management practices* such as fertilization, cutting, irrigation are also important factors in keeping lawns clean of weeds. These questions were already discussed in previous chapters.

d) *Vigilance* of lawn owner or supervision is probably the most important preventive means in keeping your lawn out of weed troubles. The battle should be started at the very beginning of infestation. Few dandelion plants, or small patches of ground ivy, nimblewill or speedwell recognized early are easy to eradicate while large patches of these weeds are often impossible to control without costly renovation of the whole lawn. Keep your eyes open and watch your lawn weed situation all the time.

15.3 Mechanical methods

Hand weeding by pulling and hoeing are the oldest methods. These methods are effective and efficient but now-a-days are not economical. These methods are still widely used and can be effectively applied in home lawn weed control. At the very beginning of infestation, hand weeding can be the most effective and practical method to get rid of invaders. Weed patches close to tree trunks or between shrubs can often be controlled by hand weeding only. The best time to control is after a soaking rain. Weeds with tap roots are best to eradicate by cutting below the crowns. Even the toughest perennial weeds are possible to eradicate.

Since there are no satisfactory herbicides to selectively control perennial weedy grasses and a few other lawn weeds, digging or removal with a hand-or motorpowered sod cutter is often suggested. In order for these control methods to be effective, as much as possible of the tops, rhizomes, stolons, crowns and roots of the plants must be removed.

Generally, the main purpose of tillage is weed control. Tillage as a means of weed control can be effectively applied in seedbed preparation before seeding a lawn. Soil is usually infested with weed seeds. It is important to clean, and destroy them. The best method is to encourage weed seeds to germinate and then to destroy seedlings by cultivation. Cultivation brings some new weeds close to the surface where they germinate faster and later on can be destroyed by subsequent cultivations.

In annual, biennial and perennial mechanical weed control it is important to prevent seed production and to destroy weed seeds present in the soil. Biennial and especially perennial weed persistence to a large extent belongs to the vegetative propagation means. Therefore with these two groups of weeds it is important to exhaust and to destroy vegetative propagation organs (roots, rhizomes, stolons, tubers, etc.)

Vegetative organ plant nutrient reserves are high early in the spring when growth first starts and decrease gradually with the lowest point at the early bloom stage of growth. Clipping or plowing under at the early bloom stage weakens plants the most. Continuous cultivation of regrowth every three weeks or so, without allowing assimilation of carbohydrates and thus restoring plant nutrient reserves in vegetative organs, can exhaust plants to death.

In summarizing weed control, principles by tillage are as follows:

1) Annual weeds   — a) reduce competition
                                             b) prevent seed production
                                             c) clean fields by encouraging seeds to germinate and then destroy seedlings
2) Perennial and biennial weeds —
                                             a) reduce competition
                                             b) prevent seed production
                                             c) destroy seed present in soil by encouraging them to germinate and then destroy seedlings.
                                             d) exhaust roots, especially crowns and other vegetative propagation organs

15.4 Chemical weed control

Herbicides are chemicals which kill or reduce plant growth. At present they are an excellent tool in a lawn management program. Herbicides are available for killing most of the weeds that infest lawns. If properly used, they do not damage the desirable plants. They differ in selectivity, e.g., one herbicide may remove weeds without injuring the lawn grasses while another herbicide may temporarily or even permanently injure the seedbed grasses. Herbicidal selectivity is relative, not absolute.

Some herbicides work best when applied through the soil and thus are absorbed by plant roots (DCPA, atrazine). Others are most effective when applied to the foliage, like amitrol, dalapon or 2,4-D. On the other hand, dicamba is common turf weed herbicide with which both root and leaf uptake are important.

Contact herbicides injure or kill by direct contact while systemic herbicides are usually absorbed by plants, and translocated to the other plant parts where they induce a toxic response. Plant tissues touched by the contact herbicide (oil, cacodylic acid, dinoseb) are killed. Dicamba, 2,4-D, DSMA are examples of systemic herbicides. They are absorbed through foliage or roots, translocated and move in vascular tissues: phloem and xylem. Xylem is composed of dead cells and the herbicide moves by mass flow with the transpiration stream. Phloem is a living tissue. Too high concentration of a herbicide may kill living cells of phloem and thus impair movement-translocation to the vulnerable points of action. This may explain cases where lower rates are more effective than higher ones.

Generally, young vigorously growing plant seedlings are more susceptible to herbicidal treatments than those more advanced in development or mature specimens. Dormant Bermuda or zoysia in winter sprayed with nonselective paraquat may be unaffected when winter weeds can be killed. Also, environmental factors such as relative humidity, temperature, light or nutritional status, may influence plant response to herbicides. Soil colloids and organic matter may absorb soil-applied herbicides and thus make them unavailable to kill plants. This explains why heavier soils or soils with high organic matter content need higher herbicide rates as compared with light sandy soils.

Herbicides are manufactured in different forms or *formulations* — as wettable powders, as liquids or as granules. Liquids and powders can be added to water and applied as a spray to the lawn. One can apply granulated herbicides with a lawn spreader or by hand. If one used wettable powders in water, frequent agitation is needed to keep the chemical evenly distributed.

15.5 Precautions

The label on the container will specify the amount, the time and the crops in using a certain herbicide. Be sure that herbicides are properly labeled. Always read the label before using any herbicide and follow the directions on the label as to the necessary precautions and rates to use.

Some herbicides are hazardous to man and animals. Use them only when needed and handle them with care.

Keep herbicides in closed, labeled containers in a dry place. Keep herbicide formulations containing 2,4-D separate from other pesticides and fertilizers.

Dispose of empty herbicide containers at an approved sanitary landfill dump, or bury them at least 18 inches deep in a level isolated place where they will not contaminate water supplies.

15.6 Glossary of some terms used in chemical weed control

Acid equivalent — The amount of active ingredient present in a herbicide formulation expressed in terms of the parent acid.

Active ingredient — That portion of the formulation that is responsible for the herbicidal activity. The remainder of the formulation will be carrier, emulsifier or other non-active ingredients.

Carrier — The liquid or solid material added to a chemical compound to facilitate its storage, shipment or use in the field by means of increasing the bulk.

Compatible — Two compounds are said to be compatible when they can be mixed without affecting each other's properties.

Contact herbicide — A herbicide that kills by contact with plant tissue rather than as a result of translocation.

Directed application — An application of herbicide to a restricted area such as a row, bed or at the base of plants.

Emulsifying agent — A material which facilitates the suspending of one liquid in another.

Emulsion — A mixture in which one liquid is suspended in another liquid; e.g., oil in water.

Herbicide — A chemical used for killing plants.

Postemergence treatment — Any treatment made after the crop plants emerge.

Preemergence treatment — A treatment made after a crop is planted but before it emerges.

Preplanting treatment — Any treatment made before the crop is planted.

Selective herbicide — One which has more toxic action on one plant than on the other. By this we mean weeds may be controlled without damage to the crop.

Soil sterilant — A material which renders the soil incapable of supporting plant growth. Sterilization may be temporary (2-4 months) or relatively permanent (2-5 years).

Spray drift — The movement of airborne spray particles from the spray nozzle outside the intended contact area.

Surfactant — A material which when used in pesticide formulations imparts emulsifiability, spreading, wetting, dispersability or other surface-modifying properties.

Suspension — A liquid or gas in which very fine solid particles are dispersed, but not dissolved.

Synergism — Cooperative action of different agencies (e.g., herbicides) such that the total effect is greater than the sum of the two effects working independently.

Systemic herbicide — A compound which is translocated readily within the plant and has an effect throughout the entire plant system.

Vapor draft — The movement of herbicidal vapors from the area of application to adjacent area.

15.7 Common chemical names of lawn herbicides*

1. Amitrole (ATA) — 3-amino-1,2,4-triazole
2. AMS (Ammate) — ammonium sulfamate
3. Arsonates — see, DSMA, MAMA, MSMA, CMA
4. Atrazine — 2 chloro-4-ethylamino-6-isopropyl-amino-s-trazine
5. Benefin (Balan) — N-butyl-n-ethyl-a,a,a-trifluoro-2,6-dinitro-p-toluidine (Elanco)
6. Bensulide (Betasan) — N-(beta-*o*,o-diisopropyl-dithio-phosphorethyl)
7. Bentazon (Basagran) — 3-isopropyl-(H-2,1,3-benothiadiazin-4-(3H)-one 2, 2-dioxide

8. Bromoxynil — 3,5-dibromo-4-hydroxybenzonitrile
9. Cacodylic acid — dimethylarsinic acid
10. Calcium cyanamide — CaCH$_2$
11. CMA — calcium acid methanearsonate
12. 2,4-D — 2,4-dichlorophenoxyacetic acid
13. DCPA (dacthal) — dimethyl 2,3,5,6-tetrachloroterephtalate
14. Dalapon (Dowpon) — 2,2-dichloropropionic acid
15. Dicamba (Banvel) — 3,6-dichloro-*o*-anisic acid
16. Dichlorprop (2,4-DP) — 2-(2,4-dichlorophenoxy) propionic acid
17. Diphenamid — N,N-dimethyl-2,2-diphenylacetamide
18. Diuron — 3-(3,4-dichlorophenyl)-1,1-dimethylurea
19. DSMA — disodium methanearsonate
20. Endothal — 7-oxabicyclo(2,2,1)heptane-2,3-dicarboxylic acid
21. Glyphosate (Roundup) — N-(phosphonomethyl) glycine
22. MAMA — monoammonium methanearsonate
23. MCPA — [(4-chloro-*o*-tolyl)oxy] acetic acid
24. Mecoprop (MCPP) — 2-(methyl-4-chlorophenoxy) propionic acid
25. Metham (SMDC, VAPAM) — Na-N-methyldithiocarbamate
26. Methyl bromide — methyl bromide
27. MSMA — monosodium acid methanearsonate
28. Oxadiazon (Ronstar) — 2-tert-butyl-4-(2,4-dichloro-5-isopropoxyphenil)-Δ^2-1,3,4-oxadiazolin-5-one
29. Paraquat — 1,1-dimethyl-4,4-bipyridinium dichloride
30. Prometon — 2,4-bis(isoprophlamino)-6-methoxy-*s*-triazine
31. Siduron (Tupersan) — 1-(2-methylcyclo-hexyl)-3-phenylurea
32. Simazine — 2-chloro-4,6-bis(ethylamino)-s-triazine
33. Stoddard solvent (Naptha) — selective weed-killing oil
34. Terbutol (Azak) — 2,6-di-tert-butyl-p-tolyl-methylcarbamate
35. Vorlex — methyl isothiocyanate with chlorinated hydro carbon

15.8 Grassy weeds

By far the grassy weeds are the most troublesome weeds in turf areas. Crabgrasses and annual bluegrass are on top of the list (Table 14.3). Two species, large crabgrass and smooth crabgrass are commonly found in turf grass areas. In recent years, many excellent chemicals have been put on the market to control crabgrasses and other annual weedy grasses in turf. Perennial weedy grasses are much more difficult to selectively control from seeded turf grasses because both groups are perennial plants and usually respond similarly to the chemical treatments.

Annual grassy weeds

Preemergence treatments. Bensulide, benefin, DCPA, oxadiazon, siduron, terbutol, and several other materials have consistently given good results in annual weedy grass control in turf. All these chemicals should be applied as directed on the label. Preemergent materials should be applied 10-14 days before weed seed germination. A rule of thumb is to apply the herbicide before lilacs bloom during forsythia bloom, or the early blooming magnolia petals fall.

Most materials for preemergent crabgrass and other annual weedy grass control should be applied only to well-established lawns. Chemicals which prevent crabgrass from appearing also may affect desirable grass seed.

---

* Where trade names are used for identification, no product endorsement is implied nor is discrimination intended.

Among northern lawn grasses, Kentucky bluegrass is most tolerant of preemergent chemicals. Bent grasses and fine-leaved fescues (red fescue) may be severely thinned by some of these materials. After treating a lawn with preemergent chemicals, reseeding should be delayed for 3-4 months following their application. Siduron has a unique selectivity for crabgrass and similar annual weeds without injury to K. bluegrass, fescues and most other turf grasses.

Postemergence treatments. Several materials have successful postemergent control of many of the annual weedy grasses in established turf. Arsonates (DSMA, MSMA, MAMA, CMA) may be used to control young and more advanced crabgrass and other annual weedy grasses. These arsonates are available in both liquid and dry forms. Of course, various turf grasses differ in tolerance to these arsonates as postemergent treatments. Discoloration of turf may occur especially in fescues and bent grasses. Some warm-season grasses are even susceptible to these chemicals (see 15.10).

Small, young fast growing weed seedlings are easiest to kill and therefore postemergent arsonate applications should begin when grasses are quite young, in the 2-3 leaf stage. Because of successive germinations of grassy weed seeds, it is best to apply 2-3 or more times at 7 to 14 day intervals for control throughout the season.

Herbicides can be combined to get a broader spectrum of turf weed control, e.g., DSMA and DCPA (dacthal). The first one is a postemergent annual weedy grass killer and the second one is a preemergent grass killer. Both applied late in spring or early in summer can do a good job keeping crabgrass and other annual weedy grasses out of turf. Mixtures of arsonates and 2,4-D may kill emerged crabgrass and some emerged broad-leaved turf weeds.

Perennial grassy weeds

Perennial grasses like bents, Bermuda grass, nimblewill, orchard grass, quack grass, tall fescue, timothy or velvet grass are difficult to eradicate from a turf area. Quack grass, nimblewill or velvet grass are common perennial grassy weeds. Some of the above mentioned perennial grasses are valuable in hay production as forage grasses, but act as noxious weeds in turf, e.g., orchard grass, timothy, and common Bermuda grass. Tall fescue, Bermuda grass or bents in some turf areas may be considered valuable grasses, but in other turf areas are undesirable tough weeds. Bermuda grass is often a serious weed in lawns in the transition zone.

Mechanical means. At present there is no herbicide which will selectively remove these perennial grasses from our lawns without hurting or killing good turf grasses. Small patches or individual plants of perennial grasses having no rhizomes (tall fescue, orchard grass, timothy, velvet grass) are possible to eradicate by cutting under the crowns and removing each plant or patch. Bare patches can be reseeded or have sodded. Bermuda grass, quack grass, nimblewill or German velvet grass have rhizomes or stolons and it is difficult to eradicate by this method, since even a small piece of plant left in the soil is enough to reinfest the area. Weed bent grasses are usually of the stoloniferous type, shallow rooted and in some cases can be eliminated by cutting them out of a lawn. A sod cutter set to cut at one-inch depth can be used. In some places where tall fescue is abundant, it would be practical to overseed (see 13.10) the area with this coarse grass. Thick stands of tall fescue kept mown at over 2 inches of height produces a satisfactory heavy duty turf grass.

Spot treatment. To eradicate small patches, some herbicides can be used for spot treatment. For this purpose dalapon, amitrole or glyphosate can be used. In some cases small brush or soaked sponge can be used to apply the chemical individually to each plant. It can be applied as spot treatments on patches. It will kill or injure all grasses sprayed. Amitrole will injure even broad-leaved plants. Again, where quack grass, nimblewill or bent grass present a problem, spot treatments with herbicides seldom will eradicate these vegetatively spreading weeds. Spot treatments with glyphosate will, however, be efficient.

Reconstruction. Sometimes it is advisable to kill all grasses and reconstruct (reestablish) a new lawn by using a complete renovation. In this case the first and most important job will be to kill old vegetation, especially the weedy perennial grasses. For this purpose dalapon, amitrole, cacodylic acid, paraquat, and glyphosate can be helpful. It is important to use effective herbicides and with short soil residual effects. Grasses are susceptible to dalapon and amitrole and their residue does not affect the soil for a long period. These herbicides leave a toxic residue in the soil for about 3-6 weeks. In northern regions dalapon should be applied in the spring or early summer to allow the herbicide to disappear from the soil for early September turf grass seedings. Amitrole can be applied as late as 3 weeks before grass seedings. The most practical method is to apply a mixture of these two chemicals especially where broad-leaved weeds also are a problem. Glyphosate has a very short residual time in the soil (seed 3-7 days after application).

Nutsedges spread by tubers, seeds and rhizomes and they are the most difficult to eradicate. Soil heavily infested with nutsedges, quack grass and Bermuda grass often will need soil sterilization by fumigation to get rid of these lawn pests. Methyl bromide is one of the most effective means for soil sterilization. Methyl bromide is a deadly poison and extreme caution is needed when applying. Use of professional help is suggested. Metham, and methylisothiocynate (Vorlex), may also effectively be used. All these chemicals should be applied as the label indicates. Lawns treated with any of these chemicals must be reseeded, i.e., reestablished.

A summary of chemical weed control in turf is presented in Table 15.1.

15.9 Broad-leaved weeds

Control of most weeds is best accomplished when applying herbicides during the periods when turf grasses are growing well. In the northern region, fall treatments are most satisfactory; lawn grasses fill in bare spots after fall treatment but crabgrass is more likely to fill in after spring treatment. Also, one should remember that young, fast growing weed seedlings are more susceptible to herbicides and lower rates are adequate to kill them.

Possible uses of herbicides in broad-leaved weed control are presented in Table 15.1. Most common turf broad-leaved weeds can be eradicated by postemergent applications of 2,4-D, dichlorprop, mecoprop or dicamba. Dandelions, plantains and some other less common lawn dicotyledonous weeds are readily controlled by 2,4-D. Chickweeds, clovers, and prostrate knotweed are less susceptible to 2,4-D and usually mecoprop or dicamba is used. Higher rates of 2,4-D applied during hot weather conditions may cause some discoloration of bent grasses. Creeping bent grass is undesirable in Kentucky bluegrass and red fescue turf. It tends to form patches and smother bluegrass. 2,4-D may be helpful in restricting growth of bents by using rates higher than those used for dandelion control. Mecoprop is rather safe to use on bent grass turf. Dicamba is an effective killer of broad-leaved turf weeds which are more difficult to control, such as red sorrel, common yarrow, clovers or some other weeds which earlier were considered resistant to herbicides. Bluegrass as well as bent grass is not susceptible to this chemical. Dicamba is a potent herbicide and should be used exactly as the label indicates. This chemical is injurious to trees and shrubs and should be used only outside the dripline of those decorative and shade plants.

Mixtures of 2,4-D with dicamba, mecoprop or dichlorprop can effectively kill a wide range of broad-leaved weeds in turf. A single application is usually adequate. These combinations are often formulated and marketed as "broad-spectrum" lawn herbicides.

On new lawns, 2,4-D or mecoprop herbicides for broad-leaved weed control should not be applied until 4-6 weeks after grass seedlings emerge. After the second or third mowing, if the broad-leaf weed problem is acute, 2,4-D, mecoprop could be applied. Bromoxynil and dicamba can be used to control broad-leaf weed seedlings in newly seeded turf. Thus, siduron can be used for grassy annual weed control in new turf seedings, and bromoxynil for broad-leaf weed seedling control. Use bromoxynil when weeds are in the 2-4 leaf stage. Of course, use as the label indicates.

Table 15.1 Lawn weeds and their control with herbicides[a]

Terms: a-annual; wa-winter annual; ba-biennial; p-perennial; s-seeds; rhiz-rhizomes; stol-stolons; Pre-preemergence; Post-postemergence; Ns-nonselective

Species	Life form	Reproduction	Control
MONOCOTYLEDONOUS			
1. Bahia grass-*Paspalum notatum* Fluge	p	s, rhiz	Post: arsonates (e.g., in Bermuda) Ns: dalapon, glyphosate
2. Barnyard grass-*Echinochloa crusgalli* (L.) Beauv.	a	s	Pre: benefin, bensulide, DCPA, terbutol, siduron; Post: arsonates
3. Bents-*Agrostis* spp.	p	s, stol	Ns: dalapon, amitrole, sterilization; higher rates of 2,4-D
4. Bermuda grass-*Cynodon dactylon* (L.) Pers.	p	stol, rhiz, s	Ns: dalapon, glyphosate, amitrole; reconstruction
5. Bluegrass, annual-*Poa annua*	a	s	Pre: benefin, bensulide, DCPA, terbutol
6. Carpet grass-*Axonopus affinis* Chase	p	stol, s	Post: arsonates; Ns: dalapon
7. Crabgrass, large-*Digitaria sanguinalis* (L.) Scop.	a	s, rooting stems	Pre: benefin, bensulide, DCPA, terbutol, oxadiazon, siduron, trifluralin in Bermuda; atrazine in St. Augustine; Post: arsonates; repeat
8. Crabgrass, smooth-*Digitaria ischaemum* (Schreb.) Muhl.	a	s, rooting stems	(Same as for Crabgrass, large)
9. Crowfoot grass-*Dactyloctenium aegyptium* (L.) Richter	a	s, rooting stems	Pre: benefin, bensulide, DCPA, etc. Post: arsonates; repeat
10. Dallis grass-*Paspalum dilatatum* Poir	p	s, rhiz	Post: arsonates; repeat
11. Fescue, tall-*Festuca arundinacea* Schreb.	p	s	Ns: dalapon, glyphosate, amitrole; reconstruction
12. Foxtail, green-*Setaria viridis* (L.) Beauv.	a	s	Pre: benefin, bensulide, DCPA, etc. Post: arsonates; repeat
13. Foxtail, yellow-*Setaria lutescens* (Weigel) Hubb.	a	s	Pre: benefin, bensulide, DCPA, etc. Post: arsonates, repeat
14. Garlic, wild-*Allium vineale* L.	p	bulbs, s	Post: 2,4-D, dicamba; as spot treatment on St. Augustine, centipede, carpet grass
15. Goose grass-*Eleusine indica* (L.) Gaertn.	a	s	Pre: benefin, bensulide, DCPA, etc. Post: arsonates; repeat

[a]1. For specific local recommendations consult your county agent or Experiment Station in your state.

2. Apply as label indicates.

3. Where trade names are used for identification, no product endorsement is implied nor is discrimination intended.

Table 15.1 (continued)

Species	Life form	Repro-duction	Control
16. Nimblewill-*Muhlen-bergia schreberi* J. F. Gmel.	p	s, rooting stems	Ns: dalapon, amitrole; reconstruction Post: arsonate + 2,4-D mix applied 3 times, 10 days apart.
17. Nutsedge, purple-*Cyperus rotundus* L.	p	tubers, s	Post: bentazon (Basagran), arsonates, 2,4-D; repeat
18. Nutsedge, yellow-*Cyperus esculentus* L.	p	tubers, s	Post: bentazon (Basagran), arsonates, 2,4-D; repeat
19. Onion, wild-*Allium canadense* L.	p	bulbs, b	Post: 2,4-D; dicamba; as spot treatment on St. Augustine, centipede or carpet grass
20. Orchard grass-*Dactylis glomerata* L.	p	s	Ns: dalapon, glyphosate, amitrole; reconstruction
21. Panicum, fall-*Panicum dichotomiflorum* Michx.	a	s, rooting stems	Pre: benefin, bensulide, DCPA, etc. Post: arsonates; repeat
22. Quack grass-*Agropyron repens* (L) Beauv.	p	rhiz, s	Ns: glyphosate, dalapon, amitrole; reconstruction
23. Sandbur-*Cenchrus* spp.	a	s	Post: arsonates; repeat. Do not use on St. Augustine
24. Star-of-Bethlehem-*Orni-thogalum umbellatum* L.	p	bulbs, s	Post: dicamba, 2,4-D
25. Stink grass-*Eragrostis cilianensis* (All.) Lutati	a	s	Post: arsonates; repeat. Ns: dalapon
26. Timothy-*Phleum pratense* L.	p	s	Ns: glyphosate, dalapon, amitrole; reconstruction
27. Velvet grass-*Holcus lanatus* L.	p	s	Ns: glyphosate, dalapon, amitrole; reconstruction
28. Velvet grass, German-*Holcus mollis* L.	p	s, rhiz	Ns: glyphosate, dalapon, amitrole; reconstruction

DICOTYLEDONOUS

Species	Life form	Repro-duction	Control
29. Bedstraw, smooth-*Galium mollugo* L.	p	s, rhiz	Post: dicamba; repeat
30. Bellflower, creeping-*Campanula rapunculoides* L.	p	s, roots	Post: dicamba; glyphosate, reconstruction
31. Betony, Florida-*Stachys floridana* Shuttlew	p	s, tubers	Post: dicamba
32. Bindweed, field-*Convol-vulus arvensis* L.	p	s, roots	Post: 2,4-D, dicamba; repeat

Table 15.1 (continued)

Species	Life form	Repro-duction	Control
33. Bindweed, hedge- *Convolvulus sepium* L.	p	s, rhiz	Post: 2,4-D, dicamba; repeat
34. Burdock-*Arctium* spp.	ba	s	Post: 2,4-D; repeat
35. Buttercup, creeping- *Ranunculus repens* L.	p	s, stol	Post: 2,4-D, dicamba, mecoprop, MCPA
36. Carpetweed-*Mollugo-verticillata* L.	s	s	Post: dicamba, 2,4-D, mecoprop
37. Carrot, wild-*Daucus carota* L.	ba	s, roots	Post: dicamba, 2,4-D
38. Catsear, spotted- *Hypochaeris radicata* L.	p	s, roots	Post: 2,4-D
39. Chickweed-*Stellaria media* (L.) Cyrillo	a, wa	s, rooting stems	Post: dicamba, mecoprop; arsonates Pre: DCPA
40. Chickweed, mousear- *Cerastium valgatum* L.	p	s, stol	endothal, paraquat and glyphosate on dormant turf in south
41. Chicory-*Cichorium intybus* L.	p	s, roots	Post: 2,4-D, dicamba
42. Cinquefoil, common- *Potentilla canaden-sis* L.	p	s, stol	Post: dicamba, 2,4-D, mecoprop; mixtures
43. Cinquefoil, rough- *Potentilla norvegica* L.	a, wa, ba	s	
44. Cinquefoil, sulfur- *Potentilla recta* L.	p	s	
45. Clover, low hop-*Tri-folium procumbens* L.	a	s	Post: mecoprop, dicamba; endothal & paraquat on dormant turf in south
46. Clover, strawberry- *Trifolium Fragiferum* L.	p	s, stol	
47. Clover, white-*Trifo-lium repens* L.	p	s, stol	
48. Daisy, English-*Bellis perennis* L.	p	s, roots	Post: dicamba, mecoprop; mixtures
49. Dandelion, common- *Taraxacum officinale* Weber	p	s, roots	Post: 2,4-D, mecoprop
50. Deadnettle, red- *Lamium purpureum* L.	wa, ba	s	Post: dicamba

Table 15.1 (continued)

Species	Life form	Repro- duction	Control
51. Dichondra-*Dichondra repens* Forst	p	s, stol	Post: 2,4-D, dicamba
52. Dock, curly-*Rumex crispus* L.	p	s, roots	Post: dicamba, 2,4-D; repeat
53. Dog fennel-*Eupatorium capillifolium* (Lam) Small	p	s	Post: dicamba
54. Filaree, redstem- *Erodium cicutarium* (L.) L'Her.	a, ba	s	Post: dicamba, 2,4-D
55. Hawkbit, fall-*Leonto- don autumnalis* L.	p	s, rhiz	Post: 2,4-D
56. Hawkweed, orange- *Hieracium auran- tiacum* L.	p	s, rhiz	Post: dicamba, mecoprop, 2,4-D or mixtures
57. Hawkweed, yellow- *Hieracium pratense* Tausch.	p	s, rhiz	
58. Heal all-*Prunella vulgaris* L.	p	s, rhiz	Post: dicamba, 2,4-D, MCPA or mixtures
59. Henbit-*Lamium amplexi- caule* L.	wa, ba	s, rooting stems	Post: mecoprop, dicamba, MCPA
60. Ivy, ground-*Glechoma hederacea* L.	p	s, stol	Post: dicamba, mecoprop; repeat
61. Ivy, poison-*Rhus radicans* L.	p	s, rhiz woody	Post: amitrole, AMS, mecoprop
62. Knapweed, spotted- *Centaurea maculosa* Lam	ba	s	Post: dicamba, 2,4-D
63. Knawel-*Scleranthus annuus* L.	a, wa	s	Post: dicamba, mecoprop, 2,4-D or mixtures
64. Knotweed, Japanese- *Polygonum cuspidatum* Sieb & Zuce	p	s, rhiz	Post: dicamba, AMS, picloram; repeat
65. Knotweed, prostrate- *Polygonum aviculare* L.	a	s	Post: dicamba, mecoprop; Pre: DCPA
66. Kochia-*Kochia sco- paria* (L.) Schrade.	a	s	Post: 2,4-D
67. Lambsquarter-*Cheno- podium* spp.	a	s	Post: 2,4-D

Table 15.1 (continued)

Species	Life form	Reproduction	Control
68. Lespedeza-*Lespedeza* sp	a	s	Post: dicamba, mecoprop
69. Mallow, common-*Malva neglecta* Wallr.	a, ba	s	Post: dicamba
70. Medic, black-*Medicago lupulina* L.	a, wa	s	Post: dicamba, mecoprop
71. Moneywort-*Lysimachia numularia* L.	p	s, stol	Post: 2,4-D
72. Mugwort-*Artemisia vulgaris* L.	p	s, rhiz	Post: dicamba
73. Mustard, wild-*Brassica kaber* (DC) L.C. Wheeler	a	s	Post: 2,4-D, dicamba
74. Ox-eye-dairy-*Chrysanthemum leucanthemum* L.	p	s, rhiz	Post: dicamba, mecoprop
75. Pearlwort, birdseye-*Sagina procumbens* L.	a, p	s	Post: dicamba, mecoprop
76. Pennywort, lawn-*Hydrocotyle sibthorpioides* Lam.	p	s	Post: dicamba, 2,4-D
77. Pepperweed, field-*Lepidium campestre* (L.) R. Br.	wa, ba	s	Post: 2,4-D, dicamba
78. Pepperweed, Virginia-*Lepidium virginicum* L.	a, wa, ba	s	
79. Pigweed, redroot-*Amaranthus retroflexus* L.	a	s	Post: 2,4-D, mecoprop, dicamba
80. Plantain, blackseed-*Plantago rugelii* Done	p	s, roots	Post: 2,4-D, mecoprop, dicamba
81. Plantain, Broad-leaf-*Plantago major* L.	p	s, roots	Post: 2,4-D, mecoprop, dicamba
82. Plantain, buckhorn-*Plantago lanceolata* L.	p	s, roots	Post: 2,4-D, mecoprop, dicamba
83. Poorjoe (Buttonweed)-*Diodia teres* Walt.	a	s	Post: 2,4-D
84. Puncturevine-*Tribulus terrestris* L.	p	s	Post: 2,4-D; repeat
85. Purslane, common-*Portulaca oleracea* L.	a	s	Post: dicamba, mecoprop, 2,4-D

Table 15.1 (continued)

Species	Life form	Repro-duction	Control
86. Ragweed, common-*Ambrosia artemisii-folia* L.	a	s	Post: 2,4-D, mecoprop, dicamba
87. Rocket, yellow-*Bar-barea vulgaris* R. Por.	wa, p	s, roots	Post: 2,4-D, dicamba
88. Sandwort, thymeleaf-*Arenaria serpylli-folia* L.	a	s	Post: 2,4-D & dicamba; 2,4-D
89. Shepherds purse-*Cap sella bursa pastoris* L. Medic	a, wa	s	Post: 2,4-D, mecoprop, dicamba
90. Smartweeds-*Poly-gonum* spp.	a	s	Post: dicamba
91. Sorrel, red-*Rumex acetosella* L.	p	s, roots	Post: dicamba
92. Sowthistle, perennial-*Sonchus arvensis* L.	p	s, rhiz	Post; dicamba, 2,4-D
93. Speedwell, birdseye-*Veronica persica* Poir	a, wa	s	Post: dicamba & 2,4-D; endothal; repeat Pre: DCPA
94. Speedwell, corn-*Veronica Arvensis* L.	a, wa	s	
95. Speedwell, creeping-*Veronica filiformis* Sm.	p	s, stol	Post: dicamba & 2,4-D; endothal; repeat Pre: DCPA
96. Speedwell, purslane-*Veronica peregrina* L.	a, wa	s	
97. Speedwell, thymeleaf-*Veronica serphylli folia* L.	p	s	
98. Spurge, groundfig-*Euphorbia chamaesyce* L.			Post: mecoprop, dicamba, 2,4-D
99. Spurge, prostrate-*Euphorbia supina* Raf.	a	s	Pre: DCPA
100. Spurge, spotted-*Euphor-bia maculata* L.	a	s	
101. Starwort, little-*Stellaria graminea* L.	p	s, stol	Post: dicamba
102. Stonecrop, mossy-*Sedum acre* L.	p	s, stol	Post: 2,4-D ester; repeat
103. Strawberry, *Fragaria* sp.	p	s, stol	Post: dicamba

Table 15.1 (continued)

Species	Life form	Repro- duction	Control
104. Thistle, Canada - *Cirsium arvense* (L.) Scop.	p	s, roots	Post: dicamba, 2,4-D; repeat
105. Vervain, prostrate - *Verbena bracteata* Lag. & Rodr.	a, p	s	Post: 2,4-D; repeat
106. Violets - *Viola* sp.			Post: dicamba, glyphosate - renovation
107. Woodsorrel, yellow - *Oxalis stricta* L.	p	s	Post: dicamba, mecoprop, 2,4-D
108. Yarrow, common - *Achillea millefolium* L.	p	s, rhiz	Post: dicamba, mecoprop, 2,4-D; repeat

[a]1. For specific local recommendations consult your county agent or Experiment Station in your state.
2. Apply as label indicates.
3. Where trade names are used for identification, no product endorsement is implied nor is discrimination intended.

For latest news in grassy weed as well as broad-leaved weed control in lawns consult your county agent, regional agricultural workers or Experiment Stations in your state.

15.10 Weed control in warm climate lawns.

Established southern turf grasses are tolerant to benefin, bensulide, DCPA and terbutol (Table 15.2) treatments. These chemicals applied before weed emergence in the spring can control crabgrass, goose grass, foxtails and other grasses. For annual bluegrass, these herbicides should be applied in September or October, before bluegrass sprouts. DCPA is also rather effective against the germinating of some broad-leaf weeds. Late fall applications can be made only if the area is not planned for overseeding.

Table 15.2 Southern lawn grass tolerances to herbicides

	Preemergence		Postemergence		
				2,4-D	
Grasses	Benefin bensulide, DCPA, terbutol	Atrazine	Arsonates	Dicamba	Dalapon
Bahia	t	s	s	t	s
Bermuda	t	s-i	t	t	s
Centipede	t	s-1	s-i	s-i[b]	s
St. Augustine	t	t	s	s	s
Zoysia	t	s-i	s-i	t	s

a) t = tolerant; s = sensitive; s-i — intermediately tolerant, some injury may occur
b) tolerant when dormant

Paraquat, endothal, cacodylic acid or glyphosate can be used in winter on dormant Bermuda or zoysia turf to control cool-season grasses and broad-leaved weeds such as: annual bluegrass, clovers, chickweeds, henbit, woodsorrel, shepherds purse, or fescue grass (*Bromus willldenowii* Kunth). Overseeding after using paraquat, glyphosate or cacodylic acid can convert a Bermuda turf to ryegrass in the fall and conversely can be effective in converting ryegrass to Bermuda turf in the spring.

St. Augustine and centipede are rather tolerant to atrazine and on established turf 2 lb/A rates can successfully be used to control germinating annual grasses or broad-leaved weeds. Zoysia and common Bermuda grass tolerate only low rates of atrazine. Atrazine can be used successfully in sod production.

Already germinated weedy grasses like crabgrass, Dallis grass, goose grass, sandbur, stink grass, can be controlled by postemergence treatments with arsonates, like MSMA, DSMA, MAMA, and CMA in Bermuda and zoysia turf areas. Repeated applications are usually needed. St. Augustine, centipede, carpet grass and Bahia are susceptible to these arsenicals and should not be treated.

Nutsedge can be controlled by increased rates of arsonates. Applications should be made every month. In two years these applications usually eliminate nutsedge in established zoysia and Bermuda grass turf. Nutsedge can also be controlled with 2 or more summer applications of bentazon (basagran) ½-1.0 lb Ai/acre.

2,4-D and dicamba are highly important herbicides which control broad-leaved weeds in zoysia, Bermuda, Bahia and buffalo turf grasses. St. Augustine, centipede and carpet grass are susceptible to these chemicals and only lower rates (50%) can be used in broad-leaved weed control. Mecoprop is also an effective herbicide in broad-leaved weed control in the south. It should not be used for St. Augustine or centipede turf grasses.

In establishing dichondra lawns repeated preemergence applications of diphenamid will control varieties of annual grasses and broad-leaved weeds. Irrigation after application of this chemical will improve control.

A summary of chemical weed control in turf is presented in Table 15.1.

15.11 Complete vegetation control

In turf culture often complete vegetation control is needed, e.g., when preparing a seedbed for lawn construction, when renovating deteriorated turf or keeping driveways, parking areas, patios or walks free of vegetation. There are modern chemicals on the market which can be used to kill vegetation. In preparing a seedbed, soil should be treated with chemicals which do not leave residues in the soil for a long time. Complete eradication of plants for an extended period is needed on driveways or parking lots. In this case one should use chemicals with long residual effects. On the other hand, soil fumigants usually decompose and disappear quickly without leaving any residues in the soil. Fumigation will kill most weeds, weed seeds and other soil pests. All these chemicals should be applied exactly as the label indicates. A list of chemicals which kill vegetation is presented in Table 15.3.

15.12 Herbicide mixtures with fertilizers

There are fertilizers on the market with herbicides added for weed control in turf areas. Of course, mixed chemicals should be compatible. Practicability of these mixtures is questioned. First of all one has to pay for a chemical he may not need at all. Secondly, the time for weed control is often not the same as the time for fertilization. The same can be said about fertilizer mixtures with fungicides and insecticides.

Table 15.3 Some chemicals for complete vegetation control

Chemical and rate[a]	Remarks
A. Soil Sterilization-fumigation	
1. Methyl bromide	Used in preparing seedbed prior to seeding lawns,
2. Metham (VAPAM)	Follow label exactly. Materials dangerous unless
3. Methyl-isothiocyanate (Vorlex)	properly handled. Seeding must be delayed after
	treatment as indicated by labels.
B. Short-term residues	
1. Glyphosate (Roundup) 2-4 lb/A a.i.	Visible effects within 7-10 days. Best results on unmown turf.
2. Dalapon & amitrole 10 + 2 lb/A a.i.[a]	Useful especially for perennial grass control. Seeding may be done 4-6 weeks after treatments.
3. Cacodylic acid 20-40 lb/A	Follow label directions.
4. Paraquat 1-2 lb/A	Apply in 100 gal. of water per acre. Can reseed immediately.
C. Long-term residues	
1. Amizine (amitrole + simazine) 3 + 9 lb/A	Use where vegetation is established.
2. AMS (Ammate) 60-100 lb/A	Apply as drenching spray. Repeat if necessary. Least hazardous to adjacent plants.
3. Simazine (Princep) 10-20 lb/A	Apply before plants emerge for best results.
4. Prometon (Pramitol) 20-60 lb/A	Several formulation available.

15.13 Herbicide application equipment

Liquid formulations of herbicides on a lawn can be applied by a compressed air knapsack or pump-type sprayer. The product is added to water in the sprayer, mixed and sprayed onto a measured area. Also, it can be used in a bottle-type sprayer, attached to the end of a garden hose. This method of application with a garden hose is not as accurate as other applications but it is inexpensive and rapid.

A gravity flow sprayer for liquid materials has been developed. The herbicidal material is added to water in the tank and the sprayer ("meter-mixer") is pushed over the lawn like a lawn fertilizer spreader. It uniformly applies without marking areas to be treated as long as the proper amount of herbicide is added to the tank.

For small areas, a sprinkling can or a gallon jug equipped with a sprinkler nozzle can be used. Cane-type applicators are available for treating individual weeds with 2,4-D. 2,4-D is also available impregnated on wax bars which are pulled over the weed-infested area.

A lawn fertilizer spreader can be used for applying granulated herbicides. The spreader should be calibrated to deliver the herbicide at the recommended rate. Herbicides should be applied uniformly so that no area is skipped and none are treated twice.

15.14 Cleaning sprayers

Clean your sprayer after each use.

It is extremely difficult to completely remove hormone-type herbicides such as 2,4-D from a sprayer. If a herbicide sprayer must be used for other purposes, thorough cleaning is a must because even minute amounts of residue may deform or otherwise damage sensitive plants. It is almost impossible to remove 2,4-D and similar materials from a wooden tank.

The following method can be applied to remove 2,4-D and other hormone-type herbicides from metal spray equipment:

1. Drain and rinse all parts with water and then with detergent soap.
2. Repeat rinse process using one cup of household ammonia to 4 gallons of water.
3. Fill sprayer, boom and all lines with above mentioned ammoniated water and allow to soak for 24 to 36 hours.
4. For oil soluble compounds, flush tank and all lines for at least 5 minutes using kerosine or fuel oil.
5. Finally, drain and again rinse the sprayer with water plus soap detergent and water alone.

To be safe, it is advisable to follow this suggestion: after cleaning the rig as outlined above, test it by applying rinse water to sensitive plants such as tomatoes or beans, (these plants are sensitive to phenoxy chlorinated compounds). If no injury is observed in a day or so, the equipment is probably safe to use.

Instead of household ammonia, activated charcoal can be used. Activated charcoal cleans very rapidly. If you use activated charcoal, put about 25 grams of it together with 25-50 grams of household detergent in 2 gallons of water and agitate thoroughly. Operate the sprayer with this mixture in it for about 2 minutes and it will be clean.

It is suggested to have a sprayer for herbicides only, and another for other chemicals like fungicides and insecticides.

15.15 Problems and conversion factors

A. Problems

1. A sprayer with 20 foot boom applies 4 gallons of spray per 300 feet. How much spray is being applied per acre?

Ans. 29.0 gal/A

2. Lawns are treated with 2,4-D to control dandelions at the rate of ½ lb/A acid equivalent and using 40 gal/A spray. 2,4-D product contains 4 lb acid equivalent per gallon. How many tablespoons or milliliters of the product will be needed to make 2 gallons of spray?

Ans. 1.6 tablespoons
Ans. 23.7 ml

3. A five acre lawn has been treated with 2,4-D at 1½ lb/A acid equivalent. A gallon of 2,4-D contains 4 lb acid equivalent and costs $5.75. How much did these herbicides cost to treat the lawn?

Ans. $10.78

4. In preparing lawn for seeding dalapon was used (dowpon) to control quack grass. A sprayer delivering 30 gallons per acre of spray is to be used to apply dalapon at 10 lb/A of acid equivalent. How many pounds of the product containing 74% acid equivalent must be mixed to prepare 55 gallon tank of spray?

Ans. 24.7 lb

5. Early in April two lawns were treated with granulated siduron to control crabgrass. Rate of application was 15 lb/A of active ingredient. How much 8% granulated siduron does one need to buy for 9,500 sq. ft. and for 3.7 acre lawns?

Ans. 41.2 lb for 9,500
Ans. 693.7 lb for 3.7 acres

6. To control aquatic weeds in a 1½ acre, 4 ft. deep pond, it was recommended that 2.5 ppm liquid 2,4-D or 30 lb/A acid equivalent granulated 2,4-D be used. Liquid 2,4-D has 4 lb/gallon acid equivalent and granulated is 10% acid equivalent. How much does the pond owner need to buy of liquid and granulated 2,4-D? *NOTE* a) one acre foot is an acre of water 1 foot deep; b) one acre foot of water weighs 2,722,500 lbs.

Ans. 10.1 gal.
Ans. 450 lb.

7. Weed control extension charts indicate that 2,4-D for broad-leaved weed control on lawn should be used at 1 lb/A acid equivalent applied as 40 gal/A spray. 2,4-D contains 4 lb/gallon acid equivalent. Prepare solution to treat 1500 sq. ft. lawn area and how much would one need of 2,4-D product to make 2 gallons of solution? Calculate in spoons and milliliters.

Ans. 33.1 ml & 47.3 ml
Ans. 2.2 sp & 3.1 sp

8. Prepare 10 liters each and 2 gallons each of: 100 ppm; 500 ppm; 2%; 5% solutions of 2,4-D. Our 2,4-D product has 4 lb/gallon acid equivalent. Answers in milliliters.

Ans.	Problem	10 liters	2 gallons
	100 ppm	2.1	1.7
	500 ppm	10.5	8.5
	2%	422	315
	5%	1005	785.5

B. Conversion factors

Liquid measure

1 gallon (U.S.) = 256 tablespoons; 231 cubic inches; 16 cups; 4 quarts; 3,785 ml; 128 fl. oz.
1 liter = 1,000 milliliters; 1.0567 liquid quarts (U.S.)
1 fluid ounce = 29.57 milliliters; 2 tablespoons
1 pint = 2 cups; 32 tablespoons; 96 teaspoons
1 tablespoon = 3 teaspoons; 14.79 milliliters
1 gallon of water = 8.355 pounds; 1 cubic foot of water = 62.43 lb; 7.48 gallons

Weight

1 gram (gm) = 1,000 milligrams
1 pound = 16 ounces; 453.59 grams
1 acre foot of water = 2,722,500 lb

Linear measure

12 inches = 1 foot
36 inches = 1 yard; 3 feet
1 rod = 16.5 feet
1 mile = 5,280 feet; 1,760 yards; 160 rods; 1.6094 kilometers (km)
1 inch = 2.54 centimeters (cm)
1 meter = 39.37 inches; 10 decimeters (dm)
1 micron (μ) = 1/1000 millimeter (mm)

Area

1 acre = 43,560 square feet; 160 square rods; 4,840 square yards; 208.7 ft. square
1 hectare = 2.471 acres

Summary

1. Preventive (sanitary) means in lawn weed control are of prime importance. The following points should be remembered:

   a) Seedbed should be clean of weed seeds, good topsoil and properly prepared seedbed.
   b) Highest quality seed of well adapted grass species.
   c) Good management (fertility, mowing, irrigation, pest control) practices.
   d) Vigilance: keep eyes open and watch your lawn weed situation all the time.

2. At the very beginning of weed infestations hand weeding can be a most practical method to eradicate them. Patches of perennial weedy grasses like tall fescue, nimblewill, quack grass, bents are best removed by digging. Weed patches close to tree trunks or between shrubs are often economical to remove by hand.

3. Herbicides are available for killing most of the weeds that infest lawns. The label on the containers specify the use of herbicides. Always read the label before using a herbicide.

4. In annual grassy weed control herbicides like benefin, bensulide, DCPA, terbutol, siduron and oxadiazon can be successfully used for preemergence treatment. Most of these materials for preemergence annual weedy grass control should be applied only on well-established lawns.

   Arsonates (DSMA, MAMA, MSMA) provide practical annual weed grass postemergence control.

5. Small patches or individual plants of perennial weedy grasses are easy to eradicate by cutting under the crowns and removing each plant or patch. Bare patches can be reseeded or sodded.

   In perennial weedy grass control herbicides can be used for spot treatments or to kill all vegetation when reconstruction (renovation) is applied. Dalapon, amitrole, or glyphosate can be used. In a few weeks after application, new grasses can be seeded. Soil heavily infested with nutsedge, quack grass or Bermuda grass often will need soil sterilization to get rid of these pests. Methyl bromide, metham, or Vorlex may be effectively used.

6. Broad-leaved weeds in established lawns can be controlled by 2,4-D, 2,4-DP, dicamba and mecoprop or their mixtures. Bromoxynil and dicamba can be used in new turf grass seedings for broad-leaved weed control.

7. The susceptibility of southern lawn grasses to various herbicides varies considerably. In St. Augustine and centipede turf grasses preemergence treatments of atrazine, benefin, bensulate, DCPA, terbutol effectively control annual weedy grasses. Postemergence applications of arsonates will control these annual weedy grasses in Bermuda and zoysia turf grass.

    2,4-D, mecoprop and dicamba can be used to control emerged broad-leaved weedy grasses in zoysia, Bermuda, and Bahia turf grasses. St. Augustine is susceptible to these treatments.

8. Complete plant kill for extended period on driveways, parking lots, patios can be done by amizine, ammate, atrazine, dalapon, and glyphosate.

9. In chemical renovation of deteriorated lawns dalapon plus amitrole, cacodylic acid, paraquat and glyphosate can be used. Within a few weeks the area can be reseeded.

10. Liquid herbicides on the lawn can be applied by compressed air knapsack sprayer, pump-type sprayer, bottle-type sprayer attached to the garden hose or gravity-flow "meter-mixer" sprayer. Spreader can be used for granulated herbicide application.

11. Clean your sprayer after each use. Have a sprayer for herbicides and another for fungicides and insecticides. To remove hormone type herbicides (e.g., 2,4-D) clean your sprayer thoroughly with detergent, household ammonia and activated charcoal.

CHAPTER 16
LAWN DISEASES

16.1 Infectious and Non-infectious Lawn Diseases

Broadly speaking, lawn diseases can be separated into (1) infectious (biotic) and (2) non-infectious (abiotic) diseases. Infectious or biotic diseases are caused by living pathogens. Many biotic pathogens may spread rapidly under conditions favorable for their reproduction and growth. Non-infectious (abiotic) diseases are caused by unfavorable environmental conditions such as: too wet or too dry soil, too much or too little fertilizer, extreme pH values, and many others. A pathogen then is any agent that generates suffering (*pathos* = suffering; *genesis* = origin; and genesis is from the Greek *gignomai* = to be born). Poor seedbed preparation and a subsoil which is ununiform may cause a spotty, unhealthy lawn. Under other extreme conditions, grass in areas that are too dry may die or be partly replaced by weeds. Deficiencies of iron and nitrogen may cause sickly, yellowing (chlorosis) of plants. These symptoms may easily be confused at times with infectious diseases of various kinds (melting out; fading out).

Proper seedbed preparation, a well adapted grass species, and good lawn management practices are effective and sometimes the only means in controlling certain physiological (abiotic) diseases. Preventative (sanitary) methods are of great importance in keeping a lawn free of certain pathogenic diseases. A properly managed lawn normally is more resistant to all kinds of diseases. Lawn grasses that are weakened due to insufficient moisture and plant nutrients are more susceptible. Too close mowing, overfertilization, and other intensive culture practices may increase the incidence of pathogenic diseases. Therefore, in golf courses where intensive management practices are a must, turf grass diseases may become more common and of greater importance than in average lawns.

Infectious lawn diseases are caused mostly by fungi (singular = fungus). Fungi are thallophytic plants that include mildews, molds, mushrooms, rusts, smuts, etc. They lack chlorophyll and reproduce mainly by asexual spores. Fungi usually occur as microscopical filamentous threads. The mass of threads is called mycelium. Many fungi reproduce by spores. Fungi which attack lawn grasses directly are true disease producing organisms. Sooty molds and mushrooms reportedly do not attack lawn grasses directly and are not considered parasites. The black molds are superficial, usually growing on various refuse from insects. Mushrooms usually develop upon decaying organic matter.

Bacteria, which are one-celled microscopic organisms cause very few diseases of turf grass. Fungi and bacteria may be parasitic or saprophytic. Saprophytic organisms live on dead plant material, decaying organic matter.

There are at least 8 viruses that infect turf grasses. Viruses are infectious agents too small to be seen by the compound microscope. They are large, high molecular weight protein bodies that can multiply and act like living organisms when in live tissues. They can be crystallized and stored many years and still retain their infectivity.

Conclusion

Identification of many diseases is often very difficult because the effects from a primary organism is often masked by those from a secondary invader. Also, effects from various environmental influences will mask or further complicate disease symptoms. In order to apply effective fungicides or other means of control, proper identification of the disease and the organism is essential.

16.2 Damping-off, Seed Rot

Seed may rot in the soil when subjected to conditions (high moisture and warm temperatures) favorable for increased activity of certain soil fungi (*Pythium* and *Phytophthora*). Small grass seedlings may be stunted, watersoaked, turn yellow to brown, and later may wilt and collapse. Later, affected turf areas usually are invaded by weeds. This disease is particularly troublesome on heavy, moist soils and during warm weather conditions. Bluegrasses, ryegrasses, fescue grasses, and bent grasses may all be affected.

Seed rot and damping-off diseases are usually caused by species of *Pythium* and *Phytophthora* under moist conditions and by *Rhizoctonia* and *Curvularia* under dryer conditions. Species of other genera also may be involved.

Control. A good grass seed and a fertile, well-prepared, seedbed are of first importance. Seed treatment with Thiram, Captan, and other proper fungicides before seeding is suggested. After seeding, overwatering should be avoided. A spray of Thiram, Captan, Dexon, Terrazole, or Zineb after seeding may be helpful in reducing disease occurrence. In extreme cases, seedbed sterilization with Methyl Bromide or Metham is suggested.

16.3 *Helminthosporium* Leaf Spot and Crown Rot

These are among the most prevalent and destructive of diseases of turf grasses. A variety of symptoms may be produced. The fungus produces a leaf spot symptom during the early spring and late fall during the cooler weather conditions. Leaf lesions usually are elongate, yellow-brown, and surrounded by brown margin. Common Kentucky bluegrass is susceptible to leaf spot while Merion Kentucky bluegrass is rather resistant. On common Kentucky bluegrass, the crown areas may be attacked resulting in the crown rot phase that produces melting-out, going-out, or drying out of the grass. During the summer, at higher temperatures, the leaf blight and crown rot phases of the disease occur. The turf appears to fade out in the summer leaving dead grass patches up to one foot or more in diameter. The leaves shrivel and stems, crowns, and rhizomes turn brown and rot. Weeds usually invade the dead grass areas. Common Kentucky bluegrass, bent grass, Bermuda grass, fescue grass are susceptible to diseases caused by species of *Helminthosporium*. Leaf spot and crown rot produced on various grasses have similar symptoms although they may be produced by different species of *Helminthosporium*. The so-called *spring dead spot* is generally considered as a non-infectious turf disease that involves *Helminthosporium* to some extent. Some reports indicate a toxin produced by a fungus may cause dying of the grass.

Control. Damage can be reduced by using lawn seed mixtures of several grasses. Kentucky bluegrass should be mowed higher than 1.7 inches. Lawns should be well fertilized but nitrogen applications, especially in the spring, should be only moderate. Clippings should be removed, especially on lawns with liberal fertilization. Broad-spectrum turf fungicides like Actidione-Thiram, Daconil, Dyrene, and Ortho lawn or turf fungicide can be used to control leaf spot and crown rot. Other fungicides are Tersan 1991, Chipco 26019, Duosan, and Fore.

16.4 *Rhizoctonia* Brown Patch

This disease appears as brown, roughly circular, areas that vary from 1-2 inches to several feet in diameter. The margins of the infected area may be smoke colored. Sometimes, only leaves are affected but if weather conditions are favorable, the disease can spread to crowns and kill the grass. The dead grass usually remains erect. Grass killed by Pythium blight usually lies flat. Brown patch occurs and spreads in hot, humid, summer weather when night temperatures are above 70°F and when grasses are wet for long periods. Damage occurs mostly on very tender turf.

Brown patch is most serious on bent grass, Bermuda grass, Kentucky bluegrass, centipede grass, fescue grass, ryegrass, St. Augustine grass, and zoysia grass. This is a very important disease in the warm, humid regions of the country. Excessive applications of nitrogen increase grass susceptibility to this disease.

Brown patch is caused by a soil-borne fungus, *Rhizoctonia solani*. This organism is present in most soils. High temperatures, prolonged humidity, dew, and dense growth of susceptible grasses are favorable conditions for disease development.

Control. Avoid overwatering and overfertilization; water early in the day and maintain good air drainage. Increased phosphorous and potassium and decreased nitrogen fertilization help to check the disease.

Chemicals used to control this disease are: Ortho lawn and turf fungicide, Benomyl (Tersan 1991), Bayleton, Daconil, Chipco 26019, and Actidione-thiram.

16.5 *Ophiobolus* Patch

This disease is widespread on grasses. On turf grasses it is more common in the western United States on Bermuda grass, Kentucky bluegrass and fescue grass. It is caused by the fungus *Ophiobolus graminis*. *Ophiobolus* patch first appears as small reddish-brown spots, which later turn brown to gray, and become circular, 2-24 inches or larger in diameter. Weeds invade affected areas.

Control. Balanced fertilization and low pH can be considered as means of control. Sulfur may be used to lower the pH and may also have limited fungistatic effects. Several grasses show resistance.

16.6 Rusts

Rust may occur from late spring throughout most of the season *depending on* the rust species involved, the geographical location and other factors such as temperature, moisture, fertility, and general culture techniques. Merion Kentucky bluegrass, ryegrass, and Meyer zoysia grass are particularly susceptible. Bermuda grass and St. Augustine grass also are affected. Leaf rust is caused by the fungus *Puccinia graminis* and other species of *Puccinia*. The yellow, orange, or rust circular or elongated pustules are produced on leaves and stems. Spores are easily dislodged by rubbing the leaf surface. The pustules are scattered over the upper surface of the leaves. Later in the season, dark brown pustules appear on the lower surface of the leaves. These pustules produce the black spores (teliospores) which overwinter.

Control. Merion Kentucky bluegrass is susceptible and therefore it is advisable as a preventive means to use mixtures of Merion Kentucky bluegrass with common Kentucky bluegrass and red fescue. Good management practices are helpful. Grass clippings should always be removed from the area.

Several fungicides may be used in controlling rust on lawn grasses. Usually, repeated applications are needed to keep rust under control. Actidione-Thiram Zineb, or Plantvax give satisfactory control in some instances. Daconil also has been recommended. Slightly injured Merion Kentucky bluegrass usually regains normal growth. Bayleton, Tersan LSR and Duosan have also been successfully used.

16.7 Dollar Spot (Small Brown Patch)

Dollar spot or small brown spot occurs on many species but particularly on bent grasses. In the southern region, Bahia grass, Bermuda grass, centipede grass, St. Augustine grass, and zoysia grass can be affected. The disease is most common in northern humid regions but has become quite destructive on Bermuda grass in the South also. The disease is caused by the fungus *Sclerotinia homoeocarpa* and occurs most frequently in the cool, damp, weather in spring or fall. Dollar spot is characterized by small tan to yellow spots in turf grass. Tan to white leaf lesions have distinct brown borders. The diseased areas become brown to straw-colored and form circular dead areas 1.5 to 2 inches in diameter. In some cases, the circles are much larger, reaching 4 to 6 inches in diameter and resemble Fusarium blight. At first, spots of diseased grass are dark and later bleach to nearly white. If the fungus grows actively, a white cobwebby mycelium can be seen when dew is on the grass.

Control. In controlling the disease, it is important to maintain adequate moisture and nutrient conditions and to prevent thatch build-up. Reportedly, dollar spot is more severe under low nitrogen fertility and when soil moisture reaches ¾ field capacity. Certain grass varieties show resistance.

Cadmium-containing fungicides (Caddy) and Dyrene are successful in controlling dollar spot in some areas of the country. In other areas, Benomyl, Thiram, and Daconil are best. Turf usually recovers quickly if treated with fungicides in the early stages of disease attack. Research shows that certain biotypes of the fungus are resistant to certain of the fungicides (Caddy, Benomyl) in some geographical areas and the material used must be selected for its activity against the particular biotype. Bayleton and Fungo have also shown excellent control qualities.

16.8 Snow Molds

Damage occurs during cold and wet periods from late fall to early spring. Symptoms usually are found near the edge of melting snow. Irregularly-shaped, dead, bleached areas, one to several feet in diameter, are produced. A gray-white, fluffy, fungal growth usually covers the infected area. It is most severe when snow covers grass for long periods.

Snow molds are evident as Fusarium patch (caused by *Fusarium nivale*) and as Typhula blight (caused by *Thphula* spp.). All lawn grasses are susceptible. Bent grasses are more severely attacked than coarser grasses. Fusarium patch, also known as pink snow mold, can occur during the growing season when the humidity is high and daily temperatures fall below 65°F.

Control. Avoid late fertilization of turf especially with nitrogen. Lawns should be cut in the fall to prevent a mat of the grass from developing. Maintain good water drainage and prevent heavy snow accumulations. Ortho lawn and turf fungicide or Benomyl can be used. The best time to apply them is before the first lasting snow. Certain grass varieties are resistant to the disease.

16.9 *Pythium* (Cottony) Blight

Pythium blight includes seedling damping-off, grease spot, and the cottony blight phase on mature grass. The disease is caused by species of *Pythium*. This is the most destructive lawn disease and severe outbreaks can destroy a lawn within a day or two. The cottony blight phase occurs mainly on ryegrasses in the South while grease spot may occur on most lawn grasses in many parts of the country.

Pythium diseases occur in humid regions during wet, warm weather conditions and in low, wet locations. Diseased areas vary in size from 2 to 6 inches which may coalesce. Infected leaves turn dark, become matted and have a slimy appearance. Infected grass lies close to the ground. Grass affected by brown patch disease remains upright. New grass usually does not grow back in the diseased area.

Control. Preventive means in controlling these disease phases are: good surface and subsurface drainage and avoid overwatering especially during warm periods. Cool and dry weather conditions check disease development and it is helpful to seed areas under these conditions best with sufficient moisture to permit seed germination.

Dexon, Koban (Terrazole) Ridomil and Tersan SP fungicides can be used to control the diseases.

16.10 *Fusarium* Blight

Fusarium blight is caused by the fungus *Fusarium roseum*. The disease occurs commonly on bent grass, Bermuda grass, bluegrass, fescue grass, ryegrass and zoysia grass.

Symptoms of Fusarium blight resemble those of dollar spot. Both diseases produce leaf lesions with white centers and brown margins. The number of lesions on a leaf vary but each lesion extends across the width of the leaf. Dollar spot and Fusarium blight result in circular, light tan areas of sod. Areas affected by Fusarium blight greatly increase in size and coalesce. Areas affected with dollar spot don't get much larger than 4 to 5 inches. Fusarium blight usually appears during the warm dry summer period. Sunny and warmest parts of the lawn usually are the most affected.

Control. Because drought conditions favor the disease, watering and keeping the lawn cool will help. Bayleton, Benomyl and Fore fungicide applications may be helpful in controlling this disease. Chipco 26019 as well as Fungo are also commonly used.

16.11 Gray Leaf Spot

This disease, caused by *Pyricularia grisea*, especially attacks St. Augustine grass under intensive management conditions. It results in round, oblong leaf spots that are brown to gray with purplish margins. Severely affected leaf blades turn brown and wither and a diseased lawn may appear scorched. The fungus also attacks centipede grass. It usually occurs during warm, rainy periods in the summer.

Thiram fungicide may be used as a control.

16.12 Powdery Mildew

Leaves and stems are covered with a white, powdery growth. Heavily infected leaves or stems turn yellow and may die. Disease severity is greater in heavily shaded and protected areas, especially in the fall and spring when nights are cool.

Powdery mildew is caused by the fungus *Erysiphe graminis* which is confined to the leaf surface. In the fall, brownish-black dots (fruiting bodies) may appear in the mildew growth.

Merion Kentucky bluegrass is highly susceptible while common Kentucky bluegrass is relatively resistant.

Control. Lawn grasses should be kept vigorous by good management practices and any decrease of shade will be helpful.

Karathane, Benomyl, Actidione-Thiram, Actidione TGF and Fungo fungicides also may be used.

16.13 Leaf Smuts

Stripe smut (caused by *Ustilago striiformis*) and flag smut (caused by *Urocystis agropyri*) are widely distributed and are destructive to lawn and other fine turf grasses. The spores infest the soil. Germinating spores produce infection threads which invade grass seedlings. Infected plants usually die during hot, dry, weather. Black stripes which rupture and expose masses of spores are produced on the leaves. Infected leaves curl and tear along the black stripes, resulting in shredded leaves. Smuts are more prevalent during cool weather in the spring and fall. Diseased plants occur singly or in spots from a few inches to a foot or more in diameter.

Infected plants are palegreen to slightly yellowed and stunted. Under close mowing, both smuts produce identical symptoms. Bent grasses, bluegrasses, and ryegrasses are usually susceptible. Merion Kentucky bluegrass is more susceptible than common Kentucky bluegrass.

Control. Grass varieties differ in resistance to leaf smuts therefore the use of resistant varieties is suggested. Apply Benomyl (Tersan 1991), a systemic fungicide, before winter dormancy occurs or in the spring as soon as growth begins. Bayleton, Chipco 26019 and Terrachlor are also used in control of leaf smut.

16.14 Slime Molds

Slime molds are usually evident during wet weather either as a dusty, bluish-white, gray-yellowish, or even a black slimy mass upon grass blades. The crusty masses are easily rubbed from the leaves. Slime molds (*Mucilago spongiosa, Physarum cinereum,* etc.) are non-parasitic microorganisms. They feed on decayed organic matter and in humid weather they move on to leaf blade surfaces as a slimy mass then produce the crusty or dusty fructifications.

Control. Slime molds eventually disappear if left alone. Any good fungicide will control them effectively. In some instances they may be swept off with a broom or hosed off with water.

16.15 Mushrooms and Fairy Rings

Many kinds of mushrooms, "toadstools" and puffballs grow on lawns or other turf areas. They usually develop from buried organic matter like logs, tree stumps, or manure piles. They develop especially during prolonged humid weather.

Control. These fungi are difficult to control until all the organic matter upon which they are growing is used up. These fungi may be controlled by soil fumigation or by drenching with fungicides. Holes should be punched in the soil 6 to 8 inches apart and 6 to 8 inches deep to receive the fungicide solution.

Fairy rings are evident as circular rings of dark green grass often surrounding a ring of thin light colored or dead grass. The ring may not be complete but appear as an arc or horseshoe. The rings vary in size from a few inches, to several feet, and upwards of several miles. In wet weather or after watering, mushrooms ("toadstools") may appear in the ring of dark green grass.

A fairy ring may be caused by fungi such as *Marasmius oreades, Psalliota campestris, Lepiota morgani,* or others. The fungus is usually several inches below the surface and forms a layer of mycelial threads that break down organic matter at the outer edge of the ring, resulting in greater nitrogen availability, therefore grass at the outer edge grows faster and it is darker in color.

Control. Fairy rings may not occur in lawns that have been treated with fungicides to control other diseases. Fungicides should be applied in the manner mentioned for mushrooms previously. Soil fumigation (Methyl Bromide) is expensive but the only really effective method to eradicate the disease. If the affected area is not too large, the soil may be removed and replaced with new soil.

16.16 Nematodes

Turf infected with nematodes may appear off color and stunted. Injured turf may thin out, wilt, and die in irregularly shaped areas. Affected grass usually does not respond to water or fertilization. Roots may be pruned, knotty, swollen, and be darkened. Damage is most apparent during times of stress as during dry periods.

Nematodes are microscopic round-worms (eel worms). They live in soil, penetrate the roots and feed on cell contents by use of a protrusible stylet (spear). Some nematodes are harmless and some may be beneficial to man.

Control. Good lawn management practices are highly important. A nematologist should be contacted if nematodes are suspected of being in the turf. They can provide accurate identification of the pest and the appropriate chemical for its control.

Summary

Disease and occurrence	Symptoms	Control fungicide[a]
I. Leaf spot, crown rot (melting-out-*Helminthosporium,* spp.). Occurs mostly during cool, moist weather. Merion K. bluegrass is resistant.	Reddish-brown to purplish-black spots on leaves and stems. Leaves will shrivel. Stems, crowns, rhizomes, roots discolor and rot. Turf is thinned in irregular shaped spots.	Actidione-thiram, dyrene, Daconil 2787, Captan, Zineb, Terrachlor, Tersan 1991, Chipco 26019, Duosan, Fore.
II. Brown patch-*Rhizoctonia solani.* Occurs during warm, humid weather. Encouraged by nitrogen fertilization.	Grass is killed in circular spots which may enlarge to several feet in diameter. Affected grass does not flatten. Grass may be thinned markedly.	Actidione-thiram, Bayleton, Chipco 26019, Daconil 2787, Duosan, Fore, Fungo, Tersan LSR, Tersan 1991.
III. Rust-*Puccinia graminis.* Occurs in late summer. Severe on Merion K. bluegrass.	Yellow-orange or red-brown powdery pustules on leaves and stems. Rust colored mass will rub on hands or clothing.	Actidione-thiram, Zineb, Bayleton, Duosan, Tersan LSR.
IV. Dollar spot-*Sclerotinia homeocarpa.* Occurs during mild, humid weather.	Grass is killed in small spots 2-3 inches in diameter. Grass in spots is straw colored. Patches may be found near the edges of affected grass.	Cadmium containing fungicides (Caddy), Thiram, Dyrene, Daconil, Bayleton, Fungo, Tersan 1991.
V. Pythium (cottony) blight-*Pythium* spp. Occurs during warm, humid weather in poorly drained areas.	Grass is killed in spots or streaks. A blackened, greasy appearance of the grass is first symptom. During humid weather a cottony growth may appear on the grass. Affected grass lies flat on the ground.	Dexon, Koban, Ridomil, Tersan SP.
VI. Snow molds (Fusarium patch-*Fusarium nivale* & Typhula blight-*Typhula* spp.) Most severe when snow covers grass for long periods.	Dead, bleached areas near edge of melting snow, from one to several feet in diameter. Gray-white fungal growth covers infected area.	Calochlor.
VII. Fusarium blight-*Fusarium roseum.* Usually appears during warm, dry periods.	Symptoms resemble those of dollar spot but infected area may increase in size until spots coalesce.	Bayleton, Fore, Chipco 26019, Fungo.

Summary, Continued

Disease and occurrence	Symptoms	Control fungicide[a]
VIII. Powdery mildew - *Erysiphe graminis*. Shaded from wind protected areas when nights are cool.	Leaves and stems are covered with a white, powdery growth. Heavily infected leaves or stems turn yellow and die.	Karathane, Actidione-thiram, Actidione TGF, Fungo, Tersan 1991, Thiram
IX. Leaf smuts - *Ustilago* sp. & *Urocystis* sp. During the cool weather in fall or spring.	Black stripes which rupture and expose masses of spores are produced on leaves. Leaves curl, tear, resulting in shredded appearance.	Bayleton, Chipco 26019, Terrachlor.
X. Slime molds, *Mucilago* sp., *Physarum* sp. Occurs during warm, humid weather.	Grass covered with white or yellowish slime mass. Later this slime becomes a gray to black sooty mass.	Any good garden or turf fungicide will control.
XI. Fairy rings, mushrooms, *Marasmius* spp. *Psalliota* spp., *Lepiota* spp. Following extended rainy periods.	Grass appears stimulated in a circular area. Later grass declines in this area. A circle of mushrooms usually develops around the edge of the area.	Soil fumigation.
XII. Nematodes. Damage is most apparent during dry weather.	Plants turn yellowish and lose vigor. Symptoms more apparent during drought. Stubby roots, galls, excessive branching, root surface necrosis.	a)

a) For specific local recommendations consult your local agent or Experiment Station in your state.
   Apply as label indicates.
   Where trade names are used for identification, no product endorsement is implied nor is discrimination intended.

CHAPTER 17
LAWN INSECTS

17.1 Introduction

Turf grass is subject to injury by a relatively small number of insect species. Generally insects do much more damage to vegetable or field crops than lawn grass. Also various insects are more troublesome in the southern warm region than in the north.

Turf insects can be classified into two main groups, based on their feeding habits (50):

    A. Root feeders
    B. Leaf feeders

Also belonging to the second group are insects which live by sucking juice from the grass.

17.2 Root feeders

A. Various grubs

Grubs are larvae of several species of beetles. They infest the soil and attack grass roots.

Grubs usually hatch from eggs laid in the ground by the female beetles. Most of the grubs spend a year or more in the ground consuming a lot of roots. Usually parent beetles differ in appearance, distribution, and habits from their larvae. Grubs have many enemies: moles, skunks, and many birds feed on the grubs. The main grubs which feed on lawn grass are discussed below.

May (June) *beetles, (Phyllophaga* spp.). There are many kinds of May beetles in the United States. In the northern part of the country they usually appear in May or June. Larvae of May beetles are whitish fleshy grubs, sometimes called white grubs. They usually lie in a curled position in the soil. Some of these grubs remain in the soil for 2-3 years and thus feed on the grass roots for a few seasons.

Japanese beetle (Popillia japonica). Adult insects may feed on many different plants. They are active for 5-6 weeks and are most common in the Eastern states.

Asiatic garden beetle (Maladera castanea) and *oriental beetle (Anomala orientalis)* are common along the Atlantic seaboard. Asiatic garden beetle insects fly usually at night and feed on various foliage. Grubs of the oriental beetle prefer unshaded lawns and short grass.

European chafer (Amphimallon majalis) and *masked chafer (Cyclocephala borealis* and *C. immaculata)* live in the soil during the day and emerge at night. Chafers are rather common throughout the country. *Rose chafers (Macrodactylus subspinosus)* are rather destructive to roses. Grubs of these chafers are less harmful to lawns than the previous ones.

176

Green June beetle (Cotinis nitida) is found mostly in the southern part of the United States. These grubs usually feed on decaying vegetable matter and may damage seedlings of newly sown lawns, especially in dry seasons.

B. Billbugs (*Sphenophorus* spp.)

Several species of billbugs damage lawns. Grubs of billbugs feed on the roots of the grass. They are more common in southern regions of the United States. This pest is spreading north and causing damage to zoysia turf. In the southwestern part of the country one species attacks Bermuda grass when another species infests zoysias.

C. Crickets *(Gryllidae)*

Mole crickets feed on the roots of the grass. Their burrowings uproot seedlings and one mole cricket can injure several yards of lawn in a single night. Crickets are rather prevalent in the southern part of the United States from the Atlantic Coast to Texas.

D. Wireworms *(Elateridae)*

Larvae of click beetle called wireworms bore into the underground part of the stems and feed on the roots of the grasses.

E. Ants *(Formicidae)*

Ants as well as wild bees may damage lawn by digging up the soil and making holes and forming hills and mounds.

17.3 Leaf feeders

A. Webworms

Several species of webworms (*Pachyzancla* spp., *Acrolophus* spp.) infest lawns. The adults are small whitish or gray moths (or millers). The female lays eggs in the lawn. The worms usually work at night and live in protective silken webs that they form around their bodies. They feed on the grass leaves. Some species feed on the grass crowns and even roots. The worms usually prefer new lawns. They attack almost all lawn grasses. At heavy infestations large areas of grass may be damaged.

B. Armyworms

Armyworms are larvae of moths *(Noctuidae)*. Their feeding causes circular bare areas in lawns. When these worms are numerous, they may devour the lawn grass down to the ground.

C. Cutworms

Cutworms are also larvae of night-flying moths *(Noctuidae)*. These worms feed on the leaves and cut off the grass near the soil. Bermuda grass, bent grass or ryegrass may be attacked by them.

D. Chinch Bugs

Chinch bugs (*Blissus* spp.) do damage when young bugs or nymphs. Yellowish spots appear in the infested lawn. The injury resembles that caused by drought. In the eastern part of the United States up to

Florida, nymphs hatch in the spring and infest lawns until late fall. The adults hibernate during the winter. In the deep south they are also active during the winter. Various species of plants are attacked by different species of chinch bugs.

E. Scale insects

Scale insects can feed by sucking the juice in the crowns, roots or above ground parts. The grass may be injured up to its death. Several kinds of scales damage the lawns more in the southern part of the country. Bermuda grass, St. Augustine grass, as well as centipede, may be attacked by several insects. One of these scale insects is the so-called ground pearl *(Margarodes meridionalis)*. The female secretes a white sack in which lays about one hundred eggs. Hatched nymphs feed on the grass rootlets. The nymphs cover themselves with hard globular shells which look like pearls about 3-4mm in diameter. Ground pearls may cause severe damage in the south to Bermuda and centipede grasses. The attacked grass may turn brown and die.

No satisfactory methods are as yet developed to control scale insects.

F. Leafhoppers

Leafhoppers *(Cicadellidae)* may infest lawns and do damage to the grasses. They suck the sap from the grasses and may cause extensive damage, especially in newly seeded lawns.

G. Mites

Several species of mites may infest lawns and do damage to the grasses. They are more prevalent and do more damage in the southern region.

17.4 Insect control

At the present time we have developed practical methods to control lawn insects with insecticides. Some insecticides are rather universal and kill most lawn insects when others are good only for specific problems. Insecticides are sold under various trade names and in various formulations like granules, dusts, liquids, wettable powders or emulsifiable concentrates.

Against insects that feed on or near the surface, such as chinch bugs and webworms, cutworms, insecticides should be applied after rain or after watering with a hose. It should not be watered for at least a couple of days after treating. For those pests that feed or work below the surface, such as grubs and ants, the insecticide should be soaked into the top few inches of soil. Full effectiveness of treatment is usually reached after several months. Generally, a treatment for underground feeders should last 2 to 5 years.

Insecticides may be applied at any time of the year except when the ground is frozen.

Insecticides should be applied as the label indicates. Most insecticides are poisonous and all precautions indicated on the label should be applied strictly.

For the latest developments in lawn pest control contact your county agent or state Agricultural Experiment Station.

Summary

Turf insects can be classified into two major groups based on their feeding habits: a) root feeders and b) leaf feeders. To the second group belong lawn insects which live by sucking juice from grass.

Root feeders

Here belong larvae of May beetles, Japanese beetles, Asiatic garden beetles, Green June beetles, and chafers. These larvae usually are whitish or grayish with brownish heads. They usually lie in a curled or "c" position in the soil. Adults are beetles. Larvae feed on grass roots below the surface, causing irregular patches of dead grass. In severe cases turf can be rolled back like a carpet.

Mole crickets and grubs of several species of billbugs feed on the roots of the grass. These insects are more common in the southern regions. Wireworms (larvae of click beetles) bore into the underground part of the stems and feed on the roots of the grass.

Leaf feeders

Sod webworms are brown, spotted caterpillars. They live in silken tubes just below the surface. Adults are small, pale moths, often snouted. At night the caterpillars eat grass off at ground level. Sod webworms are found most often in new lawns.

Armyworms as well as cutworms are larvae of moths which feed on the leaves of the grass and may cut off the grass down to the ground.

Chinch bugs as well as scale insects are sucking insects. Young chinch bugs or nymphs suck plant sap from the grass. Injury resembles that caused by drought. Scale insects also feed on the grass by sucking the juice in the crowns, roots or above ground parts. Scale insects are more common in the southern region of the United States.

Leafhoppers and several species of mites infest lawns and do damage to the grasses. Mites are more prevalent in the southern region.

Insect control

There are well developed practical methods to control insects with chemicals. The most common insecticides are: carbaryl, malathion, diazinon, and ethion. They should be used as the label indicates and the indicated precautions applied.

Table 17.1 Chemical Control of Insects (40)*

Insect	Insecticide[1]	Remarks
Annual white grubs	Diazinon	Apply as spray or granule and water-in thoroughly. Damage usually occurs in late August to September.
Ataenius grubs	Trichlorfon (Dylox, Proxol)	Damage occurs in June, July and September.
Wasps and ants	Diazinon	Water-in thoroughly after application.
Sod webworms	Carbaryl (Sevin), Diazinon, Chlorpyrifos (Dursban), Trichlorfon (Dylox, Proxol), Aspon	Damage occurs between late July and August. Do not water for 72 hours after treatment.
Millipedes and sowbugs	Sevin, Diazinon	Spray around home where insects are visible.
Armyworms and cutworms	Sevin, Dursban, Dylox, or Proxol	Apply as granules or spray. (5-10 gal. H_2O/1,000 sq. ft.)
Chinch bugs	Dursban, Aspon, Diazinon, Dylox, Proxol	Spray infested areas.
Aphids	Malathion	Spray turf thoroughly.
Chiggers	Diazinon	Spray turf thoroughly.
Slugs	Mesurol	Apply only where slugs are numerous. For use only in flower gardens and strawberry beds.

* Follow label recommendations carefully. Use the proper application rate for a given group of insects. Where trade names are used for identification, no product endorsement is implied nor is discrimination intended.

For specific local recommendations consult your local agent or Experiment Station in your state.

CHAPTER 18
SPECIFICATIONS FOR LAWN CONSTRUCTION

In establishing a home lawn or other turf grass areas a specialist's (contractor's) services are often used. Of course, before looking for a contractor or asking for bids to do the job, an owner should know exactly what he wants. It is advisable to prepare detailed specifications and get a contract signed for the specified job. An outline to prepare specifications for home lawn construction is presented below.

18.1 Outline*

I. *Area*

Description of each area (soil texture, pH, organic matter, fertility levels) with approximate size. Add drawings.

II. *Date of Planting*

(1) Spring (summer) planting. Not later than _____

(2) Fall planting. Not prior to _____ nor later than _____

III. *Materials*

(1) Lime. Shall be a standard commercial product delivered in bags or bulk and applied at rates specified. (Indicate kind (dolomite, calcite), and amount per 1000 sq. ft., acre, and total quantity for each area).

(2) Fertilizers. Shall be standard quality, delivered in original bags.
Analyses and rates as specified (per 1000 sq. ft., acre, and total quantity for each area).

(3) Seed. Shall be commercial grades and shall meet requirements of state seed laws.
For each area indicate species, percent, amount of mixture for 1000 sq. ft. and amounts needed of each species for 1000 sq. ft., acre, and total quantity. In preparing specifications for large areas it is advisable to obtain seeds delivered to the site in original containers and correctly labeled. Mixtures should be prepared with the consent of the owner or his respective representative.

(4) Sod. Indicate area, species (type), size, thickness and quantity.

(5) Stolons, sprigs. Indicate area, species, quality (how old), and quantity.

(6) Topsoil, gravel, sand, peat, manure, etc. Indicate area, type, quantity per 1000 sq. ft., acre, and total quantity.

(7) Mulch. Indicate area, material, quality, quantity per 1000 sq. ft., acre, total quantity.

---

* Adapted from a guide prepared for the Pennsylvania Turf grass Council by H. B. Musser, Pennsylvania State University, December 1958.

IV. *Methods*

Concisely indicate all steps in establishing a lawn, e.g., grading, seedbed preparation, applying lime, basic fertilizers, firming of seedbed (roller), application of starter fertilizers, seeding, sodding, sprigging, mulching, watering.

V. *Repair and Maintenance*

Indicate contractor's obligations concerning repair and maintenance.

(1) It is practical to guarantee and to do repairs only until the first lawn mowing.

(2) Maintenance: mowing height, mowing frequency, fertilization, watering (indicate source of water), pest control.

VI. *Payments*

A. Establishment:
   (a) Lime
   (b) Fertilizers
   (c) Seeds, sod, etc.
   (d) Other materials
   (e) Labor

B. Maintenance:
   (a) Fertilizer
   (b) Mowing
   (c) Watering
   (d) Pest control

Date _____

Contractor _____

Owner _____

18.2 *Problem I*

I.   Following the guide (See 18.1, Outline of a contract) handed out in class, prepare specifications for the establishment of turf grass on a 12,000 sq. ft. lawn of which ⅔ is partially shaded.

Rough grading has been completed. Assume that all work will be done using hand operated equipment and tools.

Prepare a list of all materials needed and calculate their cost. Estimate the man-hours necessary for each phase of the job (raking, rolling, seeding, etc.), and calculate cost.

Calculate total expenses for the establishment of the lawn.

II.   Description of area:

Soil texture — sandy loam, well drained
pH — 5.3
N, P and K — low

18.3 *Problem II*

I.   Prepare specifications for the establishment of turf grass at the site of a proposed public building A. (See plan on next page.)

Follow guide handed out in class

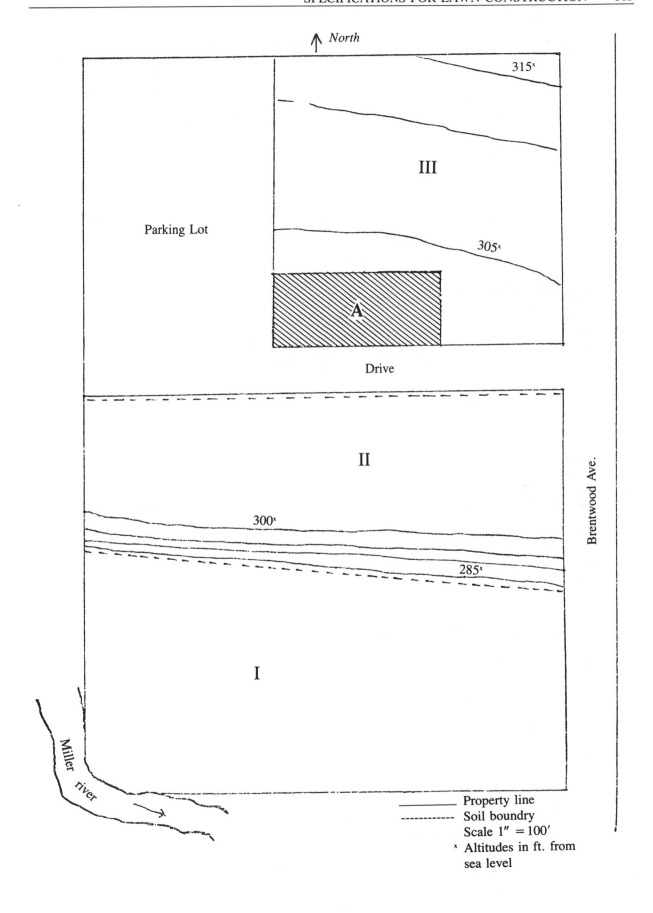

↑ *North*

315ˣ

III

Parking Lot

305ˣ

A

Drive

II

300ˣ

285ˣ

I

Brentwood Ave.

Miller river

—————— Property line
- - - - - - - Soil boundry
Scale 1″ = 100′
ˣ Altitudes in ft. from
  sea level

Include: (1) Extent of area including acreage to the nearest tenth of an acre
(2) Date of planting
(3) Materials
(4) Methods
(5) Labor in man-hours

II.   Prepare specifications for the maintenance of the turf areas for one year from date of establishment.

III.   Description of areas:

(1) Poorly drained (wet) area. Silty clay loam. Organic matter content 4.0%, pH 5.9, K — low, P — low.

(2) Well drained sandy loam. Organic matter content 2.8%, pH 5.7, P and K medium.

(3) Well drained gravely loam. Sloping area. Organic matter content 2.1%, pH 5.4, P and K — low.

IV.   Special Instructions

There are plans to construct a softball field and swimming pool in Area I. An area 200 x 200 feet should be put into suitable condition for softball field use. Also indicate swimming pool and its surroundings.

18.5 Calculating land areas

1. *Rectangle, square*

The most common shape of a lot is that of a rectangle or square. A rectangle is a four-sided figure with opposite sides parallel in which adjacent sides make angles of 90 degrees with each other. A square is a rectangle with all sides equal.

To compute the area of a rectangle, multiply the length by the width, as follows:

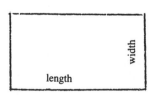

Figure 1.

Assume in Figure 1, a length of 150 ft and width of 90 ft.

Area = 150 X 90 = 13,500 sq ft

Area in acres = $\dfrac{13,500}{43,560}$ = 3.1 acres

2. *Four-sided figure with two sides parallel*

The area is found by multiplying the average length of the parallel sides (p + p), by the perpendicular or shortest distance between them (h).

$$Area = \frac{p_1 + p_2}{2} \times h$$

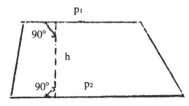

Assuming the p_1 measures 300 ft, p_2 measures 360 ft, and h 200 ft,

$$Area = \frac{300 + 360}{2} \times 200 = 66,000 \text{ sq ft}$$

$$Area \text{ in acres} = \frac{66,000}{43,560} = 1.52 \text{ acres}$$

Figure 2.

3. *Right triangle*

The area of a right triangle is $\frac{base \times altitude}{2}$

Assume in Figure 3, a base is 400 ft and an altitude of 550 ft.

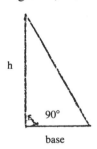

$$Area = \frac{400 \times 550}{2} = 110,000 \text{ sq ft}$$

$$Area \text{ in acres} = \frac{110,000}{43,560} = 2.52 \text{ acres}$$

Figure 3.

4. *Triangle*

The area of a triangle is $\frac{base \times altitude}{2}$

If base = 500 ft and h = 360 ft, then

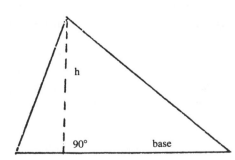

$$Area = \frac{500 \times 360}{2} = 90,000 \text{ sq ft}$$

$$or = \frac{90,000}{43,560} = 2.07 \text{ acres}$$

Figure 4.

5. Four-sided area; none parallel

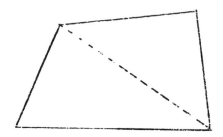

This kind of a figure should be divided into two triangles by a diagonal, and then the area of each triangle computed. The area sum of both triangles will be the area of the figure.

Figure 5.

6. Any number of sides

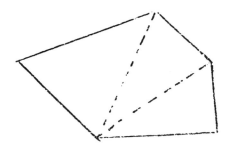

Any plot bounded by more than four sides may be divided into a series of triangles by diagonal lines and the area of each triangle computed as before. The sum of the triangular areas is the area of the figure.

Figure 6.

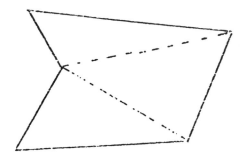

Figure 7.

7. Curved boundary

If the field contains one or more curved boundaries, each such boundary must be treated as follows: Lay off a straight line (construction line) connecting the extremeties of the two sides of the field which intersect the curved sides. In our case this is AB. Measure AB line and divide into equal parts which most nearly makes the length of each part 50 ft. Next, measure the perpendicular distance from this line to the curved boundary at the end of its parts. These distances are called "offsets".

The area of the portion of the field between the construction line and the curved boundary is computed by adding together all of the offsets and multiplying this sum by the uniform spacing between them.

Assume that AB, the construction line, in Figure 8 measures 500 ft. This permits a uniform distance of 50 ft to be laid off between offsets, thus dividing the line AB into 10 equal parts. Beginning at A the offsets are measured in order to be as follows: 0, 50, 70, 90, 100, 90, 70, 65, 70, 75, 0 feet. The sum of the offset distances is 680.

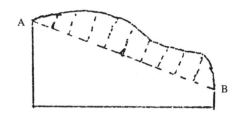

Area = 680 X 50 = 34,000 sq ft

or $\dfrac{34,000}{43,560}$ = .78 acres

Figure 8.

    The area of the balance of the field is then computed as that of any other straight-sided figure as already explained. These areas are then added together to give the total area of the field.

    The line AB should be laid off so that no part of the curved boundary falls inside it; otherwise the enclosed area must be subtracted.

REFERENCES

1. Beard, J. B. 1973. Turf grass; science and culture. Prentice-Hall, Englewood Cliffs, NJ, 658 p.

2. Brenchley, W. E. and K. Warington. 1933. The weed seed population of arable soil. II. Jour. Ecol., 21:103-127.

3. Bruno, V. F. and L. W. Rasmussen. 1958. The effects of fresh water storage on the germination of certain weed seeds. III. Weeds, 6:42-48.

4. Buckman, H. O. and N. C. Brady. 1969. The nature and properties of soils. The Macmillan Co., London. 653 p.

5. Couch, H. B. 1962. Diseases of turf grasses. Reinhold Publ. Co., New York.

6. Daniel, W. H. and E. C. Roberts. 1966. Turf grass management in the U.S. Advances in Agronomy 17:259-326.

7. Darlington, H. T. and G. P. Steinbauer. 1960. The eighty year period for Dr. Beal's seed viability experiment. Amer. Jour. Bot. 48:321-325.

8. Dawson, R. B. 1954. Practical lawn craft. Crosby Lockwood & Son, Ltd., London. 320 p.

9. Donahue, R. L. 1965. Soils. Prentice Hall, Englewood Cliffs, NJ. 363 p.

10. Evans, M. W., J. M. Watkins. 1939. The growth of Kentucky bluegrass and Canada bluegrass in late spring and in the autumn as affected by the length of day. Jour. Amer. Soc. Agron. 31:767-774.

11. Fermanian, T. W. 1981. Turf grass selections for Illinois. Coop. Ext. Service, Dept. of Horticulture, Univ. of Ill., Urbana IL.

12. Foth, H. D. 1978. Fundamentals of soil science. John Wiley & Sons, NY. 436 p.

13. Goss, R. L., K. G. Morrison and A. G. Law. 1962. Homelawns. Ext. Service Bul. 482, Washington State Univ.

14. Grau, F. V. 1963. Watering lawns. Handbook on lawns. Brooklyn Botanical Garden. Plant and Gardens 12 (2):4-10.

15. Hall, J. R. 1971. Alternatives to brown Bermuda grass. The Agronomist 8(11):5-6, Univ. of Maryland, College Park, MD.

16. Hanson, A. H. and F. V. Juska, ed., 1969. Turf grass Science. American Soc. of Agron., Madison, Wisc., 715 p.

17. Harmon, G. W. and F. D. Keim. 1934. The percentage and viability of weed seeds recovered in the feces of farm animals and their longevity when buried in manure. J. Amer. Soc. Agron., 26:762-767.

18. Herbicide Handbook. 1979. Fourth ed. Weed Science Society of America. Monograph. Champaign, Illinois. 479 p.

19. Hitchcock, A. S. 1950. Manual of the grasses of the United States. USDA. Government Printing Office, Washington, DC. 1051 p.

20. Horn, A. S., A. Slinkard, R. Higgins, R. Portman and L. Erickson. 1966. Idaho lawns. Idaho Agr. Ext. Service Bul. 464, Univ. of Idaho, Moscow, Idaho.

21. Juska, F. V., A. A. Hanson, and A. W. Hovin. 1969. Evaluation of tall fescue, *Festuca arundinacea* Schreb., for turf in the transition zone of the United States. Agron. Jour. 61:625-628.

22. Keen, R. A. and L. R. Quinlan. 1969. Lawns in Kansas. Circ. 327. Agr. Exp. Sta., Kansas State University, Manhattan, Kansas. 31 p.

23. Ledeboer, F. B. 1972. Cool-season grasses for South Carolina Piedmont lawns. Clemson University, Clemson, South Carolina. 20 p.

24. Levitt, J. 1956. The hardiness of plants. Academic Press., New York.

25. Madison, J. H. 1966. Optimum rates of seeding turf grasses. Agron. Jour. 58:441-443.

26. Madison, J. H. 1971. Principles of turf grass culture. Van Nostrand Reinhold Co. 420 p.

27. Madison, J. H. 1971. Practical turf grass management. Van Nostrand Reinhold Co. 466 p.

28. Muenscher, W. C. 1980. Weeds, 2nd ed., Cornell University Press. 586 p.

29. Musil, Albina F. 1963. Identification of crop and weed seeds. Agr. Handbook 219, USDA, Washington, DC.

30. Musser, H. B. 1962. Turf management. McGraw-Hill Book Co., New York. 356 p.

31. National Plant Food Institute. 1962. Our land and its care. Washington, DC. 73 p.

32. Pavlychenko, T. K. and J. B. Harrington. 1934. Competitive efficiency of weeds and cereal crops. Canada Jour. Res. 10:77-94.

33. Rader, L. F., Jr., L. M. White, and C. W. Whittaker. 1943. The salt index — a measure of the effect of fertilizers on the concentration of the soil solution. Soil Sci. 55:201-218.

34. Rahn, E. M., R. D. Sweet, Jonas Vengris and Stuart Dunn. 1968. Life history studies as related to weed control in the Northeast. 5-Barnyard grass. Agr. Exp. Sta. Bul. 368, Univ. of Delaware, Newark, Delaware. 46 p.

35. Schery, R. W. 1961. The lawn book. The Macmillan Co., New York, NY. 207 p.

36. Schery, R. W. 1967. Weed turf with fertilizer. Weeds, Trees and Turf. 6(11):20-21.

37. Skogley, C. R. and R. H. Hurley. 1972. Grasses for lawns. Bul. 178. Coop. Ext. Service, Univ. of Rhode Island, Kingston, RI.

38. Spurway, C. H. 1941. Soil reaction (pH) preferences of plants. Michigan Agr. Exp. Sta. Special Bul. 306, 36 p.

39. Stevens, O. A. 1932. The numbers and weights of seeds produced by weeds. Amer. Jour. Bot. 19:784-794.

40. Street, J. R., A. J. Turgeon, M. C. Shurtleft, and R. Rondall. 1980. Turf grass Pest Control. Coop. Ext. Service, College of Agr., Univ. of Illinois, Urbana-Champaign, ILL.

41. Stuckey, I. H. 1941. Seasonal growth of grass roots. American Jour. Bot. 28:486:491.

42. Taylor, J. C. 1969. Lawns. Publication 448. Ontario Dept. of Agr. & Food. 43 p.

43. Troughton, A. 1957. The underground organs of herbage grasses. Bul. 44. Commonwealth Bur. of Pastures and Field Crops. Com. Agr. Bur. Farnham Royal, Bucks, England. 163 p.

44. Truog, E. 1946. Soil reaction influence on availability of plant nutrients. Proc. Soil Sci., Soc. of America 1:305:308.

45. Tumbeson, M. E. and Kommedahl. 1960. Reproductive potential of yellow nut grass. Proc. 17th North Central Weed Control Conference, Milwaukee, Wisc.

46. U.S. Dept. of Agriculture. Climate and Man. Yearbook of Agriculture 1941. U.S. Government Printing Office, Washington, DC. 1248 p.

47. U.S. Dept. of Agr. 1952. Manual for testing agr. and vegetable seeds. Agr. Handbook 30, USDA, Washington, DC. 440 p.

48. U.S. Dept. of Agr. 1969. For transition area lawns Kentucky 31. Agr. Research, June 1969.

49. U.S. Dept. of Agr. 1970. Selected weeds of the United States. Agr. Handbook 366. USDA, Washington, DC. 463 p.

50. Vance, A. M. and B. A. App. 1971. Lawn insects. Home and Garden Bul. 53. USDA, Washington, DC. 23 p.

51. Vengris, Jonas. 1973. Lawns. Thomson Publications. Indianapolis, Indiana, 2 edition, 247 p.

52. Watson, J. R. 1967. Watering practices as a function of clipping height and frequency. Weeds, Trees and Turf. June issue.

53. Wise, Louis H. 1961. The lawn book. W. B. Thompson, State College, Miss.

54. Weihing, J. L., M. C. Shurtleff and R. E. Partyka. 1970. Lawn diseases in the Midwest. North Central Regional Ext. Publication No. 12, Univ. of Nebraska. 19 p.

55. Youngner, V. B. 1959. Growth of U-3 Bermuda grass under various day and night temperatures and light intensities. Agron. Jour. 51:557-559.

56. Youngner, V. B. 1961. Growth and flowering of zoysia species in response to temperatures, photoperiods, and light intensities. Crop. Sci. 1:91-93.

57. Youngner, V. B. and S. E. Spaulding. 1963. Influence of several environmental factors on flowering of Bermuda grass. Agron. Abst. Denver, Colorado 1963:120.

INDEX

NOTES

NOTES

NOTES